THE SPIRITUAL TEACHINGS OF BERNARD OF CLAIRVAUX
by
John R. Sommerfeldt

THE CISTERCIAN FATHERS SERIES: NUMBER ONE HUNDRED TWENTY-FIVE

The Spiritual Teachings of Bernard of Clairvaux

An Intellectual History of the
Early Cistercian Order

by

John R. Sommerfeldt

Cistercian Publications
Kalamazoo, Michigan
1991

©Copyright Cistercian Publications Inc., 1991

The work of Cistercian Publications is made possible in part by support from Western Michigan University to The Institute of Cistercian Studies.

Available in Britain and Europe from
Mowbray/Cassell, London

Available elsewhere from
Cistercian Publications (Order fulfilment)
St. Joseph's Abbey, Spencer, MA 01562

Printed in the United States of America.

PATRICIA

TABLE OF CONTENTS

TABLE OF ABBREVIATIONS ix
INTRODUCTION xiii
Notes: Introduction xviii

ANTHROPOLOGY
    I. The View of the Human 3
    II. The Soul.....................................7
    III. The Body....................................13
    IV. The Unity of the Human Being 15
        Notes: The View of the Human 18
    V. The Effects of the Fall 21
    VI. The Restoration of the Soul 27
    VII. The Role of the Body in Human Restoration.......31
        Notes: Fall and Restoration.......................39

EDUCATION
    I. The Path to Perfection 45
        Notes: Path 52
    II. Humility: The Perfection of the Intellect 53
        Notes: Humility 64
        A. Meditation................................66
            Notes: Meditation............................78
        B. Self-control 80
            Notes: Self-control 88
    III. Love: The Perfection of the Will 89
        A. Empathy: The Link Between Humility and Love ..89
            Notes: Empathy..............................94
        B. The Meaning of Love........................95
            Notes: The Meaning of Love 102
        C. The Objects of Love 103
            Love of Self 103
            Love for Others 104
            Friendship 107
            Love of God 111
            Notes: Objects 115
        D. The Nature of Love........................116
        E. The Fruits of Love 117
        F. The Way of Love 119
        Notes: Nature, Fruits, and Way 121

IV. The Life of Love 122
   A. Conversion: The Turning of the Will 122
      Notes: Conversion 132
   B. Self-discipline: The Recovery of Self-possession . 134
      Notes: Self-discipline 143
   C. The Gift of Love 145
      Notes: The Gift of Love 151
   D. Obedience: The Response to Guidance 152
      Notes: Obedience 158
   E. Silence 159
   F. Continence 161
      Notes: Silence and Continence 164
   G. Simplicity 165
      Notes: Simplicity 172
   H. Loving Service 173
      Notes: Loving Service 182
   J. Prudence, Discretion, and Temperance 183
      Notes: Prudence, Discretion, and Temperance 194
   K. Prayer 196
      Notes: Prayer 204
   L. The Happiness of Perfection 205
      Notes: Perfection 211

CONTEMPLATION
   I. The Bridegroom and the Bride 215
   II. The Contemplative Experience 217
   III. Was Bernard a Contemplative? 221
   IV. What Contemplation Is Not 223
Notes: Contemplation 228
   V. The Possibility of Contemplation 230
   VI. Readiness for Contemplation 234
      Notes: Possibility and Readiness 237
   VII. The Gift of Contemplation 238
   VIII. The Effects of Contemplation 241
   IX. The Overflow 248
      Notes: Gift and Effects 250

SELECTED BIBLIOGRAPHY 251

TABLE OF ABBREVIATIONS

General Abbreviations
ASOC   *Analecta Sacri Ordinis Cisterciensis; Analecta Cisterciensia.* Rome, 1945–.
CF   *Cistercian Fathers* series. Spencer, Massachusetts; Washington, D.C.; Kalamazoo, Michigan, 1969–.
Cîteaux   *Cîteaux in de Nederlanden; Cîteaux: Commentarii cistercienses.* Westmalle, Belgium; Nuits-Saint-Georges, France, 1950–.
CS   *Cistercian Studies* series. Spencer, Massachusetts; Washington, D.C.; Kalamazoo, Michigan, 1969–.
CSEL   *Corpus scriptorum ecclesiasticorum latinorum* series. Vienna, 1866–.
CSt   *Cistercian Studies* (periodical). Chimay, Belgium, 1961–.
James   Bruno Scott James (trans.), *The Letters of St. Bernard of Clairvaux.* London: Burns Oates, [1953].
Luddy   *St. Bernard's Sermons for the Seasons & Principal Festivals of the Year.* Trans. A Priest of Mount Melleray [Ailbe J. Luddy]. Reprint, Westminster, Maryland: The Carroll Press, 3 vols., 1950.
PL   J.-P. Migne (ed.), *Patrologia latina.* Paris, 221 vols., 1844–1864.
RB   *Regula monachorum sancti Benedicti.*

The Works of Bernard of Clairvaux
SBOp   Jean Leclercq *et al.* (edd.), *Sancti Bernardi opera.* Rome: Editiones Cistercienses, 8 vols. in 9, 1957–1977.
Adv   *Sermo in adventu Domini*
And   *Sermo in natali sancti Andreae*
Apo   *Apologia ad Guillelmum abbatem*
Asc   *Sermo in ascensione Domini*
Asspt   *Sermo in assumptione B.V.M.*
Circ   *Sermo in circumcisione Domini*
Conv   *Sermo ad clericos de conversione*
Csi   *De consideratione*
Ded   *Sermo in dedicatione ecclesiae*
Dil   *De diligendo Deo*
Div   *Sermo de diversis*

Ep	*Epistola*
Epi	*Sermo in epiphania Domini*
Gra	*De gratia et libero arbitrio*
IV HM	*Sermo in feria IV hebdomadae sanctae*
Hum	*De gradibus humilitatis et superbiae*
Mal	*Sermo in transitu sancti Malachiae episcopi*
Mart	*Sermo in festivitate sancti Martini episcopi*
Miss	*Homilia super 'Missus est' in laudibus Virginis Matris*
Mor	*Epistola de moribus et officiis episcoporum*
Nat	*Sermo in nativitate Domini*
Nat B.V.M.	*Sermo in nativitate B.V.M.*
I Nov	*Sermo in dominica I novembris*
OS	*Sermo in festivitate omnium sanctorum*
Palm	*Sermo in ramis palmarum*
Par	*Parabola*
Pasc	*Sermo in die paschae*
Pent	*Sermo in die pentecostes*
p Epi	*Sermo in dominica I post octavem Epiphaniae*
Pre	*De precepto et dispensatione*
PP	*Sermo in festo ss. Apostolorum Petri et Pauli*
Pur	*Sermo in purificatione B.V.M.*
QH	*Sermo super psalmum 'Qui habitat'*
Quad	*Sermo in quadragesima*
Res	*Sermo in resurrectione*
SC	*Sermo super Cantica canticorum*
S Mal	*Sermo de sancto Malachia*
Sent	*Sententia*
Sept	*Sermo in septuagesima*
Tpl	*Ad milites Templi de laude novae militiae*
V Mal	*Vita sancti Malachiae*
V Nat	*Sermo in vigilia nativitatis Domini*

Biblical Abbreviations

Ac	*Acts*
Am	*Amos*
Ba	*Baruch*
1 Ch	*1 Chronicles*
1 Co	*1 Corinthians*
2 Co	*2 Corinthians*
Col	*Colossians*
Dn	*Daniel*

Eph	*Ephesians*
Ex	*Exodus*
Ezk	*Ezekiel*
Ga	*Galatians*
Gn	*Genesis*
Heb	*Hebrews*
Ho	*Hosea*
Is	*Isaiah*
Jb	*Job*
Jl	*Joel*
Jm	*James*
Jn	*John*
1 Jn	*1 John*
Jr	*Jeremiah*
1 K	*1 Kings*
2 K	*2 Kings*
Lk	*Luke*
Lm	*Lamentations*
Lv	*Leviticus*
2 M	*2 Maccabees*
Mi	*Micah*
Mk	*Mark*
Ml	*Malachi*
Mt	*Matthew*
Na	*Nahum*
Nb	*Numbers*
1 P	*1 Peter*
2 P	*2 Peter*
Ph	*Phillipians*
Pr	*Proverbs*
Ps	*Psalm*
Qo	*Ecclesiastes; Qoheleth*
Rm	*Romans*
Rv	*Revelation*
Sg	*Song of Songs*
Si	*Ecclesiasticus; Sirach*
Tb	*Tobit*
1 Th	*1 Thessalonians*
1 Tm	*1 Timothy*
2 Tm	*2 Timothy*
Ws	*Wisdom*

INTRODUCTION

THE MIDDLE AGES SEEM more controversial than other periods of history. And no doubt this is due to their negative assessment by the *philosophes* of the Enlightenment whose manifold legacies include a pejorative connotation to the very word medieval. Among the many controversies surrounding the medieval period is its chronological extent. No scholar—at least none I know—would exclude the twelfth century from the middle ages, and a great many would assert that the twelfth century was somehow quintessentially medieval.

In 1927, Charles Homer Haskins called the attention of the scholarly world to *The Renaissance of the Twelfth Century*. In the preface to this work, Haskins admitted his title was shocking and, indeed, would '. . . appear to many to contain a flagrant contradiction.' Haskins' relatively positive assessment of the twelfth century, his acknowledgement that the middle ages were 'less dark and less static' than they had been previously judged, made a deep impression on American scholarship. That impression was not limited to Americans. This is shown well by the *Festschrift* published to celebrate the fiftieth anniversary of Haskins' book. In this collection, *Renaissance and Renewal in the Twelfth Century*,[1] not only American scholars but also professors teaching in France, Germany, Great Britain, and Italy are well represented.

Only one of the contributors to this volume is not associated with a university. Chrysogonus Waddell is a Cistercian monk of Gethsemani Abbey. The inclusion of his work on twelfth-century liturgy is symbolic of a significant shift in our understanding of, and scholarship on, the middle ages. Haskins' work had considered twelfth-century theology and spirituality only little and then peripherally. We, half a century later, are beginning to realize the centrality of these concerns to the self-understanding of twelfth-century folk and to our understanding of these folk and their culture.

Yet even Haskins began his description of the 'fresh and vigorous life' of the twelfth century with reference to another Cistercian monk, Bernard of Clairvaux. Bernard was surely the most influential spiritual writer of the twelfth century, but he was also the leader of Christendom in the first half of that century in so many aspects of the life of the time that it would be difficult to find a parallel figure in any similar period.

Bernard was the preceptor of popes and the conscience of kings. In 1130, Bernard decided, in effect, who was to be pope; he launched a crusade; his contribution to the thought of his time and his influence on the development of that thought were immense. All this leads one to ask: how is it that a monk could play such a role? How could a man dedicated to withdrawal from the world have so much influence on it?

My contention is that Bernard could lead Europe to a new crusade, decide—or heavily influence—who its leaders were to be and how they were to act, and mightily affect what its inhabitants were to hold dear, because his life embodied so many of the ideals of his age, some of which had not yet crystallized until his coming. The ideals of early twelfth-century Europe largely centered around spiritual values. Thus it was possible for one person, who as a contemplative monk embodied those ideals most perfectly, to give expression to the dominant values of his world, including that world's view of itself. Because of his genius, Bernard was able, not merely to reflect his world's values, but to articulate them by eloquent expression.

I intend this work not simply to make a contribution to the history of spirituality, but to offer some small assistance to those who seek to understand the twelfth century and its culture and society. But I hope too to make a contribution to a more generic understanding of medieval culture and society.

I am intrigued by the fact that the leadership of the early twelfth century should have been so largely charismatic, so largely prophetic. Bernard was not a pope or a prince—though he probably could have been the former. Bernard had little or no official standing in the hierarchies of power of his time. He was a simple abbot, living whenever possible in the simplicity of a deliberately remote monastery. He was a contemplative; yet he mightily influenced the world of action.

The thirteenth century, the period which immediately followed Bernard's and was surely much influenced by it, was far different. The giants of the thirteenth century were legion. And one would have to name many of them to equal the influence of Bernard on his age. The intellectual leadership of the thirteenth century was largely vested in scholars, masters of dialectic applied to questions of law and metaphysics; and the rationale of the thirteenth century was expressed, not in contemplative commentaries on Scripture, but in great syntheses, the *summae*. The leadership of the thirteenth century was diverse; no one man held a position in the thirteenth century comparable to Bernard's in the twelfth. And none of the leaders of the thirteenth century were monks, let alone Cistercians.

I believe that the basis for this change can be illuminated by a study of the intellectual history of the Cistercian Order in the twelfth and early thirteenth centuries. And this is the reason I propose to make this volume the first in a series which will investigate the shifts in the spirituality of Cistercian writers which led, in part, to the demotion of their Order from a central to a peripheral position in the culture of these centuries. I wish to discover why the Cistercian Order gave birth to the most important leader of the early twelfth century, only to be reduced to intellectual and institutional imitation in the thirteenth. And, perhaps, by so doing I may offer some assistance to those who seek to understand the changes in medieval culture during those centuries.

This work begins with this volume. If indeed the leadership of Bernard can be explained by his spiritual standing in the society of his time, then a statement—or restatement—of his spirituality must begin this series. The second volume, on Bernard's analysis of his society and culture, would flow from the first. Bernard's description of the path to perfection was simply the Christian life as the men of the twelfth century knew it. Indeed, they knew it largely through the teaching of Bernard and the other contemplatives of the time.

I hope to follow with studies of the other early Cistercian contemplatives: Guerric of Igny, William of Saint Thierry, and Aelred of Rievaulx. Perhaps I may have time to continue with studies of the thought of the subsequent generations of Cistercian writers, who, I believe, changed markedly the thrust of the spirituality of early Cîteaux. If possible, I shall conclude with a study of Cistercian scholasticism in the thirteenth century. This plan is ambitious. Perhaps my initial efforts will stimulate others to carry on with a task which I believe is worthwhile and instructive.

The present volume may strike the reader as a seemingly endless series of quotations from Bernard of Clairvaux. I should be pleased with such a response, for it is my intention here simply to lay out Bernard's doctrine on the spiritual life. And that can be best accomplished by listening to Bernard, not by reading a commentary by one who understands Bernard far less well than he understood himself, by one who will never be able to express himself as eloquently as the master rhetor who sometimes dwelt at Clairvaux.

Of course, this is not the first attempt to present a faithful account of Bernard's teaching on the spiritual life. And this fact highlights the fundamental problem faced—or which ought to be faced—by every historian: the selection of the data to be arranged. However much one may wish to be faithful to Bernard, the presentation of quotations from a corpus of writing as voluminous and varied as Bernard's must necessarily be selective. The danger is obvious: the historian may select, albeit unconsciously, only those quotations which suit a personal concept of Bernard's thought—or, worse yet, the historian's own perception of reality. I know that, had I written this volume thirty-five years ago, when I first began to study Bernard with some diligence, I should have written a different book, emphasizing—and perhaps distorting—different aspects of Bernard's thought. All I can claim for this book is that it is an honest attempt to convey Bernard's spirituality faithfully, in his own words and with as little interference between him and the reader as I have been able to manage. I know that failure to grasp the totality of Bernard's thought is a possibility. I welcome correction.

And I also welcome the assistance that I have received in the process of trying to understand Bernard's thought. As I wrote above the phrase 'preceptor of popes and conscience of kings' I wondered whether I should have surrounded the phrase with quotation marks, for surely such a happy alliteration came originally from a pen other than my own. But I do not remember whose it was. I owe a deep debt of gratitude to many scholars whose work I have made my own. In a partial attempt to acknowledge this, I have included in the Selected Bibliography not only those works quoted or cited in this volume, but also a few works which I do remember having influenced me greatly and which I believe may be of use to the reader. Among the works listed in the bibliography are a few of the overwhelming number of outstandingly excellent and marvelously insightful studies on Bernard by Jean Leclercq. To him this volume would have been dedicated were there not one still more important to this work, one whom I hold still dearer: my wife Patricia.

The bibliography also acknowledges my debt to the translators on whom I have heavily depended. Translation is a difficult task, and translating Bernard is a well-nigh impossible task. And so I trust those translators will not take it amiss if I have sometimes altered their fine work.[2] My own attempts at translation were immeasurably assisted by two fine latinists, Professor Elizabeth Giedeman of Western Michigan University and Professor Francis Swietek of the University of Dallas. I had originally intended to include the Latin texts of the quotations I have used in the notes. I have decided against that, lest the apparatus be cumbersome. Scholars who wish to check the translations will have the Latin text at their disposal. I should be grateful if they would correct me where I have erred.

I am not a monk. And I am well aware that a study of monastic spirituality must necessarily be aided beyond measure by a life lived in a monastic setting. And so I am deeply indebted to the Cistercian monks who have time and time again invited me to their houses in North America and Europe so that I might experience first-hand that of which I write. My greatest stimulus to reading and re-reading, to formulating and re-formulating my thoughts on early Cistercian spirituality, has been the opportunity to present lectures and seminars at numerous Cistercian abbeys.

Teaching is the best way to learn. And my students have been my best teachers. Legions of students at Western Michigan University, Michigan State University, and the University of Dallas have helped me clarify my views of Bernard's spirituality through their insights expressed in discussions, seminar papers, and theses. One cannot name a legion, but one can remember them.

I *can* name two ladies who not only translated my poor penmanship into typescript, but who corrected many of my errors and infelicities on the way. I am deeply grateful to Jeri Guadagnoli and Trudy Smith, grand ladies and important contributors to this volume. I am also grateful to my son John, who patiently and diligently coped with the many problems attendant on my ignorance of his specialty, computers, and their—to me—confusing languages. Professor E. Rozanne Elder's invaluable editorial supervision merits my special gratitude.

J. R. S.

The University of Dallas

1. Edd. Robert L. Benson and Giles Constable (Cambridge, Massachusetts: Harvard University Press, 1982).
2. Each of my quotations of, or references to, Bernard's works will be followed by a citation of the translation I have used or consulted.

ANTHROPOLOGY

I. THE VIEW OF THE HUMAN

OVER THE PAST SEVERAL YEARS, I have become more and more convinced that the key to understanding the spirituality of Bernard of Clairvaux, the spirituality of the twelfth century, indeed, the spirituality of any person or age, is anthropology. If the spiritual journey is a pilgrimage toward perfection, then that perfection is necessarily contingent on the nature which is to be perfected. The completion—the self-fulfillment, the happiness—of human beings necessarily depends on what human beings are. I am strengthened in my conviction that anthropology is central to spirituality by the support of the master of Cistercian and Bernardine studies, Jean Leclercq. Speaking of monastic life today, Leclercq writes: '... The basic problem is not one of *theology* but of monastic *anthropology*.'[1]

Bernard's anthropological link with the fathers—most notably with Augustine of Hippo—is obvious in his occasional use of Augustine's tripartite division of the soul into reason, memory, and will.[2] For example, Bernard writes in his *Sermon 11 on the Song of Songs*: 'Not to speak of the body, I discern in the soul three [faculties], the reason, the will, the memory, and these three may be said to be the soul herself.'[3]

Now and again, Bernard seems to reflect Augustine's hostility to the body as well.[4] For example, in his *Sermon 3 on the Ascension*, Bernard writes:

> The Lord of the Apostles revealed himself in such a manner that it could be no longer said of them that they saw 'the invisible things of God, being understood by the things that are made' [Rm 1:20], for they saw him face to face who made all things both visible and invisible. But inasmuch as the disciples were carnal, whereas God is a spirit, and spirit and flesh have little in common, he used the medium of a body to temper his brightness to their eyes, so that through a living veil of flesh they might see the Word in the flesh, the Sun of justice in a cloud, the Light of the world in an earthen vessel, the Candle in a lantern.[5]

Now one may read the phrase 'spirit and flesh have little in common' as a Neoplatonic or Augustinian denegration of the body,[6] but I think the context allows a much more positive reading. It is, after all, through the Incarnation of the Word that the Apostles came to see and know that Word. Bernard explains:

> But the reason why the Lord showed himself in the flesh to his disciples was this: to withdraw their thoughts and affections gradually from earthly things, attaching them at first to his own sacred flesh (by which, as they perceived, he spoke and wrought so many wonders), so that from there he might lift them up to a purely spiritual love of himself; for 'God is a spirit, and they who adore him must adore him in spirit and in truth' [Jn 4:24].[7]

I find an impressive affirmation of the body in Bernard's insistence that God himself used the body—indeed, his own body—to bring the Apostles to know him. Yet I admit that this affirmation retains an ambivalence toward the body, in that 'earthly things' are to be transcended in that process of coming to know the spiritual.

In his treatise *De consideratione*, written to direct his spiritual son and father in ecclesiastical authority, Pope Eugenius III, Bernard has some more harsh-sounding words to say—apparently about the body. He urges Eugenius:

> Therefore, take off these garments which you have inherited [from Adam and Eve] and which have been cursed from the beginning. Tear off the covering of leaves which hides your shame but does not heal your wound. Destroy the pretense of this fleeting honor and the luster of this specious glory, so that you can nakedly consider the naked [Christ], for you came forth naked from your mother's womb [Jb 1:21].[8]

Yet reflection on this quotation yields, I think, an interpretation in which the body is less the object of opprobrium than is the will. Bernard urges Eugenius to remove 'the covering of leaves which hides your shame'. That shame is the result of a self-defeating choice, not an ugly nature. Eugenius should consider his own 'nakedness', a nakedness which symbolizes his nature unfettered by sin or by the apparent glory of his office.

To be sure, the consequence of Adam's sin affects the body. Bernard writes, in the same place:

> If you scatter all these things and blow them away from the face of your consideration like the morning clouds which quickly pass and rapidly disappear [Ho 6:4, 13:3], you will catch sight of a naked man who is poor,

wretched, miserable [Rv 3:17]—a man grieving because he is man, ashamed because he is naked, weeping because he was born, complaining because he exists. A man born for labor, not for honor. A man born of woman and, because of this, with guilt; living for a brief time and, consequently, with fear; filled with sorrow [Jb 14:1]. Truly man's misfortunes are many, for they are of both body and soul. For what calamity is missing in man, born in sin with a frail body and barren mind? Man is truly filled with misfortunes in whom an infirm body and a foolish heart are compounded with the transmission of sin and condemnation to death.[9]

This is a grim depiction of the human condition. But I think it is important that Bernard does not reserve the effects of sin only for the body, the fleshly, the corporeal, the earthly. Bernard's apparent anthropological negativism is surely at least mitigated by his purpose. He is urging a pope not to be misled by the trappings and adulation which surround him:

There is a useful connection between thinking of yourself as Supreme Pontiff and paying equal attention to the vile dust which you not only were, but are.[10]

Bernard, as always, suits his language and expression to his audience. He must be read, here as elsewhere, as a rhetor, not as a philosopher.[11]

Indeed, if one reads on in the same place, one discovers a much more positive evaluation of the human condition, an evaluation which rejoices in human nature as a union of body and soul, a union imitative of both nature and the Author of nature:

Your thoughts should imitate nature, and what is more worthy, should imitate the Author of nature, in joining what is highest with what is lowest. Did not nature in the person of man join the breath of life with vile dust [Gn 2:7]? Did not the Author of nature, in his own person, mix together the dust of the earth and the Word?[12]

The union of body and spirit is an analogue of the hypostatic union.

A whole series of texts could be cited to demonstrate Bernard's positive attitude toward human beings and their bodies.[13] Perhaps one quotation may suffice for all. It is from Bernard's *Sermon 14 on the Psalm 'He Who Dwells'*:

> Think of what quality he [God] made you. For even with regard to your body he made you a noble creature; and still more so with regard to your soul, inasmuch as you are the extraordinary image of the Creator [Gn 1:26], sharing his rationality, capable of eternal happiness. In both body and soul man is the most admirable of all creatures, the body and soul being united by the incomprehensible ingenuity and unsearchable wisdom [Rm 11:33] of the Creator.[14]

Augustine too had failed to see '. . . how the soul, a spiritual substance, unites with the substance of the body to produce a third substance—man.'[15] But Bernard's view of the results of that union is surely much more positive than Augustine's.

II. THE SOUL

Bernard's teaching on the body cannot be separated from the rest of his anthropology. And as is so often—perhaps always—the case with Bernard, his anthropology is expressed in many formulations, some of which seem to contradict others. Yet I think that the formulation in his *Sermon 4 for the Feast of All Saints* is a fit summary of his teaching on the soul. There he writes:

> It is clear that the nature of souls is threefold. For this reason the wise men of the world [1 Co 1:20] have taught that the human soul is rational, irascible, and concupiscible. We are instructed about the triple power of the soul also by our own nature and by daily experience. It is clear, moreover, that, as regards our rational element, it is a matter of knowledge or ignorance, depending on whether we possess [its object] or are deprived of it. With regard to the concupisible element, there is desire or disgust, and, regarding what is called the irascible element, the question is of both joy and anger.[16]

Here Augustine's tripartite division of the soul is indeed retained, but that division is fundamentally altered. Instead of intellect, will, and memory, we find intellect, will, and feelings, the last of which includes one's ability to perceive and emote—functions closely associated with the body.

The functions of the three faculties of the soul are what identify them:

> Choice is an act of judgement. But even as it belongs to judgement to distinguish between what is lawful and what not, so it belongs to counsel to examine what is expedient and what not and to pleasure to experience what is pleasant and what not.[17]

The faculties are not independent entities. Bernard uses the analogue of the Trinity to express their unity: '...And these three may be identified with the soul itself.'[18]

The soul gives life and sensation to the body:

> There are two kinds of living beings, those which have sensation and those which do not. The sensate rank above the insensate, and above them both is life, by which one lives and senses. Life and living do not rank equally, much less life and lifelessness. Life is the liv-

ing soul, but it does not derive its life from any other source than itself; strictly speaking, we describe this as life rather than living. When it is infused into the body it gives life, so that the body, through the presence of life, becomes not life but living. From this it is clear that, even for a living body, to be is not the same as to live, since it can be but not be alive.[19]

The soul also gives direction to the body: 'Indeed, the soul has three functions in the body: to give life, to give sensation, to give direction.'[20] That direction is, in part, the function of all three faculties of the soul: the intellect, the will, and the feelings.

The rational soul, the intellect, is 'located' midway between God and the material body which it directs. This 'location' is really a description of function:

> There are two locations of the rational soul: the inferior, which it directs, and the superior, in which it rests. The inferior which it directs is the body; the superior, in which it rests, God.[21]

This rational faculty is a gift of God, made in his image:

> Our Elisha [Christ] has been lifted up bodily, but he has sent his servant. This boy is pure reason, made in the image of God [Gn 1:27].[22]

The intellect has as its primary function knowledge, knowing the truth, knowing what truly is: 'I am endowed with reason; I am capable of [knowing] the truth.'[23] This power comes from God in creation and, hence, is natural to humans—to all humans whether pagan or Christian:

> But see now, in trying to show that they who do not know Christ are sufficiently informed by natural law [see Rm 1:19ff.; 2:14-15], seen in the perfection of man's mind and body, to be obliged to love God for his own sake, we have lost sight of our subject. To state briefly what has been said, we repeat: is there an infidel who does not know that he has received the necessities for bodily life —by which he exists, sees, and breathes— from him who gives food to all flesh [Ps 135:25], who makes the sun rise on the good and the bad, and his rain fall on the just and the unjust [Mt 5:45]? Who, again, can be wicked enough to think the author of his human dignity, which shines in his soul, is any other than

he who says in *Genesis*: 'Let us make man to our image
and likeness' [Gn 1:26]?[24]

By their own God-given power of reason human beings may discover in nature the author of nature. Bernard reads Paul to support this view:

Hence even the [pagan] philosophers, as the Apostle
bears witness, 'understood the invisible things of God
from the things that are made' [Rm 1:20].[25]

Bernard has great confidence in the powers of the intellect. The light of reason is capable of illuminating the darkness of our post-Adamic existence:

We have been born, every one of us, in this darksome
day, if day it may be called and not rather night. However, I shall call it day on account of the light of reason
which, as a glimmering spark, has been left to relieve
its gloom by God's unconquerable mercy.[26]

The intellect knows what is—what is in nature, what is in God—but it also can discern the good[27] and make moral judgements. Bernard expresses this in the second of his *Parables*:

Then Prudence said: 'It is Reason, my armor-bearer,
who is the one to go ahead of us. He is familiar with
the route and is already known to Justice, since they
are kinsmen.' So Reason led the way, and the rest followed.[28]

Reason can know the proper order of things, and this is justice. Following that right order leads to the proper ordering of the will which is love:

Reason and natural justice urge the infidel to surrender
his whole being to him from whom he received it and
to love him with all his might.[29]

The will, like the intellect, is a natural human endowment: 'We have received from God as a part of our natural condition how to will, how to fear, and how to love.'[30] The will is by nature good, for it was made by God and, in its freedom of choice, is made in the very image of God:

From the first moment of its existence, it [the will] possesses in itself a twofold goodness: the one, general,
by the mere fact of creation, which means that anything
created by a good God cannot be other than good—
'for God saw everything that he had made, and, behold,

they were good' [Gn 1:31]; the other, special, arising from its freedom of choice, by which it was made in the image of him who created it [see Gn 1:26].[31]
The distinctive, natural characteristic of the will is that it is free from constraint;[32] thus human beings have free choice (*liberum arbitrium*):

> For voluntary consent is a self-determining habit of the soul. Its action is neither forced nor extorted. It stems from the will and not from necessity, denying or giving itself on no issue except by way of the will. But if it were compelled in spite of itself, then there would be violent, not voluntary consent. Where the will is absent, so is consent; for only voluntary motion may be called consent. Hence, where there is consent, there also is the will, but where the will is, there is freedom. And this is what I understand by the term 'free choice'.[33]

As Bernard McGinn has written: 'The freedom that the will possesses is inalienable, it cannot be lost as long as the will is still a will.'[34]

The action of the intellect must precede that of the will, for without knowledge there can be no choice. But the will is not necessarily governed by the intellect; the will may reject the correct judgements of the intellect or it would not be free. However, in another sense, the will precedes the intellect, for it chooses that to which the intellect turns its attention:

> Will is a rational movement, governing both sense-perception and appetite. In whatever direction it turns, it has reason as its mate—one might even say, as its follower. Not that it is moved invariably by reason—indeed it does many things through reason against reason, or, in other words, through the medium of reason, as it were, yet contrary to its counsel and judgement. But it is never moved without reason....Reason is given to the will for instruction, not destruction....If, I say, the will were incapable of reaching out to these [wrong or right] because of some prohibition of the reason, it would no longer be will. For the presence of necessity means the absence of will.[35]

Free choice, the freedom of the will from necessity, cannot be lost:

> Such consent, on account of the imperishable freedom of the will and the inevitable judgement of the reason

always and everywhere accompanying it, is, I think, well
called free choice, having free disposal of itself because
of the will and the power to judge of itself because of
the reason.[36]

Bernard sees choice as uniquely human—he considers the will the most important faculty in determining one's happiness.[37] Free choice is the source of one's progress and punishment:

True necessity knows no law and hence justifies dispensations. Free will, however, which alone can deserve punishment, is also our only means of progress.[38]

Bernard's *Parable of the Three Daughters of the King* personifies free choice and makes her custodian of the process which will perfect man: 'Thus establishing good order in all the houses, Free Choice was constituted steward, in charge of the whole city.'[39] The perfection of the will itself is love; and that perfection is of a natural passion.[40] Grace perfects nature, but does not destroy it.[41]

The irascible soul is also a natural and essential component of man. Bernard's rhetorical 'imprecision' also allows us to speak of the 'negative appetite'[42] or the 'feelings'.[43] Because the functions of the irascible soul—perception, feelings, emotion—are so closely bound to the operation and function of the body, I shall reserve my discussion of it to the section on the interaction of the soul and body.[44] Let it suffice for the moment to indicate that Bernard most often differentiates the irascible soul from the intellect and will in terms of the functions of perception:

In the material world, life is not identical with perception, nor perception with appetite nor appetite with consent. This should become more evident from the definitions of each. For life in any body is an internal and natural movement, having existence only within the confines of that body. Whereas perception is a vital movement in the body, alert and outward; and natural appetite, a force in living being, is intent on getting the senses moving.[45]

The irascible soul will find its perfection in feeling, the feeling of perfect calm, divine peace, and supreme joy which will infuse all the soul in the Beatific Vision:

Accordingly, God will fill our rational element with the light of wisdom, so that it will not be lacking any [1 Co 1:7] knowledge. He will fill our concupiscible element from the fountain of justice, so that we may

> desire it completely and be completely filled with it. . . .
> As regards what is called our irascible element, when
> God will fill it there will be perfect calm within us, and
> it will be filled with the divine peace which will result
> in supreme joy and gladness.⁴⁶

The blessed soul, then, has all her faculties filled and fulfilled. The intellect will be filled with wisdom and knowledge. The will will be ordered in justice toward that which fulfills it:

> When God has filled our concupiscible element with
> justice, the soul will reject whatever she should reject
> and yearn for whatever she should yearn. She will have
> an appetite for that which is more appealing to the appe-
> tite than anything else.⁴⁷

The soul will have her feelings perfected—not denied, not sublimated, not left behind as 'carnal'—in 'supreme joy and gladness'. And these three fulfillments will interact in the blessed soul as they interact in her life on earth:

> It can be seen that beatitude, as far as the soul is con-
> cerned, is a matter of bringing to complete fulfillment
> these three things: when knowledge is not puffed up
> [1 Co 8:1] because of the presence of justice and will
> is not saddened because of the presence of joy, . . . when
> justice is not excessive due to the presence of knowl-
> edge and is not burdensome because of joy, and when
> joy is not inappropriate, thanks to knowledge, nor im-
> pure, thanks to justice.⁴⁸

So much for the soul, in this life and the next, but what of the body?

III. THE BODY

In Bernard's *Sermon 4 for the Feast of All Saints*, he tells of the happy fate of the body, not left behind in the Beatific Vision. In that Vision the body becomes immortal and impassible:

But all these graces are for the soul, and as yet our exterior man has received nothing. Therefore, in order 'that glory may dwell in our earth' [Ps 84:10], that is, in our body also, and, as the same prophet sings in another psalm, that 'the whole earth may be filled with the majesty of the Lord' [Ps 71:19], four gifts are required for the body, which, as you know, is compounded of four elements. . . . Therefore, let this earth of our body be given immortality, so that it need no longer be afraid of being reduced to dust. For the body 'rising again from the dead, dies now no more; death shall no longer have dominion over it' [Rm 6:9]. But what avails this gift of immortality if our bodies are destined to live forever in the miseries and woes of this passible existence in which, namely, our corruptible flesh is exposed to incessant affliction—if instead of dying once and for all they are destined to die eternally. Consequently, they require also the endowment of absolute impassibility to safeguard them from all kinds of suffering, which have their cause, as we are told, in some disorder of the bodily humors.[49]

The body will, then, live forever and be immune from suffering. To these gifts will be added lightness or agility:

But the body wants another gift, even the gift of lightness—proper to that portion of itself which consists of air—so that it may not burden us with its weight. We must, therefore, believe that the glorified bodies of the blessed shall be so light and agile as to be able, if desired, to follow everywhere the rapid movements of thought, without the least delay or difficulty.[50]

It is significant, I think, that this gift is a grace which perfects the body's nature and does not destroy it—a theme on which Bernard frequently insists.[51]

Beyond immortality, impassibility, and agility, Bernard asks,

Is there anything more required for the perfect beatitude of the body? One thing only, beauty. This quality

too we shall possess in the highest degree. And I think
we may justly attribute it to that one of our bodily elements which is of the nature of fire.[52]

For Bernard, the soul *and* the body will be completely filled, fulfilled, and perfected in the Beatific Vision:

In this way, then, shall God fill our souls by infusing
in them perfect knowledge, perfect justice, and perfect
joy. In this way also shall 'the whole earth be filled with
his majesty' [Ps 81:19] when this earth of our body is
rendered incorruptible, impassible, agile, and 'made like
to the body of his glory' [Ph 3:20-21].[53]

The perfectibility of the body is equal to that of the soul; the body is no mere accessory to the soul. In the time of human completion and fulfillment, it is surely no burden nor prison. Both body and soul are necessary for one's complete happiness, for the human person is one. The human being is an entity, not a soul incidentally inhabiting a body.

IV. THE UNITY OF THE HUMAN BEING

Human unity consists in the fact that, for Bernard, following a long philosophical tradition, a person is a rational animal, in whom both the adjective and the noun are essential components. Bernard writes to Pope Eugenius:

> Although the investigation of the first division [who you are] belongs more to a philosopher than to an apostle, nevertheless, there is in the definition of man, whom they call a rational animal, the notion that he is mortal. And this you may look into more carefully, if you please. For there is nothing inherent in such an investigation which might stand in the way of your calling or oppose your dignity. On the contrary, it can benefit your salvation. Now, these two, rationality and mortality, are to be considered at the same time, for it is in this way that it is beneficial. The fact that you are mortal should humble the rational in you; likewise, reason should comfort your mortality. Neither of these should be neglected by the circumspect man.[54]

Bernard knows well the source of his definition in the ancient philosophers,[55] and he considers the union of rationality and animality positively wondrous because the components of persons are so dissimilar.[56]

Despite having two such diverse components, the human being is one: 'There is a natural unity whereby soul and flesh give birth to one man.'[57] Bernard insists on this unity in diversity: 'You may not, however, . . . except most absurdly, predicate either flesh of the soul, or soul of flesh, even though . . . soul and flesh are one man.'[58]

This unity is marvelous. The result is a glorious human nature:

> In the first work of our creation, 'God formed man of the earth's dust and breathed into his face the spirit of life' [Gn 2:7]. Oh, what an artist, what a compounder of things diverse, at whose command the earth's dust and the spirit of life are thus intimately welded together! The dust indeed had already received existence when 'in the beginning God created heaven and earth' [Gn 1:1]. But the spirit had a creation proper to itself; it was not produced in common with other things.

Neither was it in the [earthly] mass but was breathed
into it in a singular and excellent manner. Acknowledge,
O man, your dignity; acknowledge the glory of the human condition.[59]

The material nature of humans is a fitting part of that glory: 'You have a body like other creatures, since it is only fitting that, as you are set over all the material world, you should resemble it at least in part.'[60]

In the unity that is the human being, the relationship between soul and body is one of mutual interdependence: 'Souls need bodies and bodily senses by which they reciprocally acquire knowledge and power.'[61] Thus, the soul provides the body not only with life but also with sensation:

For who does not know how much the soul benefits
the body? What would the body be without the soul
but a lifeless trunk. To the soul it owes its beauty, to
the soul it owes its increase and development, to the
soul it owes its clarity of vision and the sound of its voice;
simply put, it owes to the soul all its various powers
of sensation.[62]

So close is this dependence and interaction that Bernard speaks of the sensing organs almost as if they belonged to the soul:

...The soul sees with the eyes, hears with the ears,
smells with the nose, tastes with the mouth, [and]
touches with the rest of the body....[63]

Conversely, the body provides the soul with the means through which it perceives.[64]

Moreover, the body provides that which the soul cannot: place.

But if we take a corporeal thing as having a single place,
the measure of incorporeal things will be in time and
not in place. For neither can the soul be in a corporeal
place, nor is the body itself, it seems quite likely, the
place of the soul.[65]

Bernard does not mean that the soul is not connected to the body, but that it is not located in any part of the body.[66] My point is, however, that Bernard recognizes location as an essential contribution of the body to the entity which is a human being: 'We see that place is necessary and useful.'[67] The location in place which the body provides is essential to one's accomplishment of good—better put, to God's accomplishment of good in humans:

> If, then, God works these three things in us —namely thinking, willing, and accomplishing the good—the first he does without us, the second with us, and the third through us. By suggesting the good thought, he goes one first step ahead of us; by also bringing about the change of our ill will, he joins it to himself by its consent; and by supplying consent with faculty and ability, the operator within makes his appearance outwardly through the external work that we perform.[68]

The human being is good by nature; through him, with him, and in him God can accomplish the good.

Why, then, does Bernard complain, with the authors of *The Book of Wisdom* and the *Letter to the Romans*, that the establishment of the kingdom of God on earth is hindered by the body?

> It is a process which is still unfinished because of this perishable body which weighs down the soul [see Ws 9:15; Rm 7:24] and because of the needy condition of this earthly dwelling [see Ws 9:15; 2 Co 5:1; 2 P 1:13] which burdens the mind full of thoughts [see Ws 9:15].[69]

One reason that the body is a burden surely is that the price which humans must pay for physical location is the care and feeding of the body, the means by which they acquire that necessary location. The care of the body requires time, time which must be taken from spiritual concerns:

> No doubt, the first obstacle and heavy burden is the need of the unfortunate body—which demands at one time sleep, at another food, now clothing, and then something else—often hinders us from applying ourselves to spiritual matters.[70]

The body gives one definite advantages, but these are had at a price.

Yet, all things considered, Bernard believes that the price is well worth paying:

> The flesh is clearly a good and faithful comrade to a good spirit. If the spirit is burdened, the flesh helps; if it does not help, it relieves; it surely helps and is by no means a burden.[71]

The body is, in the end, so important to the soul that it constitutes no burden at all.

1. Jean Leclercq, 'Monastic Life Today', CSt 15 (1980) 141. An excellent study of Bernard's anthropology may be found in Michael Casey, *Athirst for God: Spiritual Desire in Bernard of Clairvaux's Sermons on the Song of Songs*, CS 77 (Kalamazoo: Cistercian Publications, 1988) pp. 131-89. See also Emero S. Stiegman, Jr., *The Language of Asceticism in St. Bernard of Clairvaux's* Sermones super cantica canticorum (Diss. Fordham, 1973) pp. 5-45, 108-152.
2. See, for example, *De Trinitate*, X, 11; PL 42:983.
3. SC 11, 5; SBOp 1:57; CF 4:73. See also Par 7 (SBOp 6/2:301; CSt 7:52), and Conv 6, 11 (SBOp 4:84-85; CF 25:44).
4. For Augustine, the body was the 'prison of the soul' (*Contra Academicos* 1, 3, 9 [PL 32:910]; and *Epistola 166*, 27 [CSEL 44:583]). Augustine sometimes defined man as 'a soul using a mortal and earthly body' (*De moribus ecclesiae* 1, 27, 52 [PL 32:1324-25]; and *In Ioannis evangelium* 19, 5, 15 [PL 35:1552-53]). As Bernard McGinn puts it: 'The systematic side of Augustine's thought, largely Neoplatonic, pushed him toward an equation of man with the soul...' ('Introduction' to *Three Treatises on Man: A Cistercian Anthropology*, CF 24 [Kalamazoo, Michigan: Cistercian Publications, 1977] p. 8). Clemens Baeumker had already affirmed this reading: for Plato, for Augustine, and for the entire platonic-augustinian tradition, 'the soul is the true human being' (*Der Platonismus im Mittelalter* [Munich: Verlag der K. B. Akademie der Wissenschaften, 1916] p. 22). Wilhelm Hiss takes the argument one step further. After listing the pejorative adjectives with which Bernard described the body, Hiss attempts to apply Baeumker's analysis to Bernard: Bernard's anthropology stands in the line not only of Plato and Augustine, but that of Tertullian and Gregory the Great as well. See *Die Anthropologie Bernhards von Clairvaux*, Quellen und Studien zur Geschichte der Philosophie, 7 (Berlin: Walter De Gruyter, 1964) p. 50 and n. 17 on that page. Hiss admits (on p. 49) that he is not sure whether the list refers to the natural body or the body after original sin.

    It should be noted that Augustine's '...sense of the historical materiality of man in the Bible...' made it impossible for him to ignore the body completely (McGinn, 'Introduction' to *Three Treatises*, p. 8).
5. Asc 3, 3; SBOp 5:132; Luddy 2:242.
6. This seems to be Hiss' approach. See *Die Anthropologie*, p. 49.
7. Asc 3, 3; SBOp 5:133; Luddy 2:243.
8. Csi 2, 9, 18; SBOp 3:425; CF 37:70.
9. Csi 2, 9, 18; SBOp 3:426; CF 37:70-71.
10. Csi 2, 9, 18; SBOp 3:426; CF 37:71.
11. As I see it, this is the great difficulty with Hiss' work. For example, Hiss devotes a good deal of space (see, especially, pp. 55 and 58) to determining whether or not Bernard saw the soul as the form of the body. None of his citations satisfactorily answers the question. And this, I contend, is because Bernard did not ask the question. In footnote 36 on p. 61, Hiss declares: 'Bernhards Urteil über die sichtbare, materielle Welt ist—seiner Eigenart entsprechend—natürlich existentiell. In diesem Urteil sind theologische und philosophische Aspekte miteinander verworben.' As a matter of fact, Bernard did not make this distinction between philosophical and

theological views of the world. Because of Hiss' attempts to deal with Bernard's cosmology in philosophical terms, he misunderstands Bernard's meaning of 'world' as nature (see p. 62) rather than as a disorder of the will. See below p. 241. Hiss persists, however, by extracting a 'philosophical', rather than 'theological' meaning from Bernard's teaching on the origin of sin (see p. 63). One wishes that Hiss had applied the same insight to these questions which he used in analyzing the question of the hierarchical relationship between the reason and the will: 'Die Neigung zu rhetorischen Überspitzungen ist nicht zu übersehen. Veilleicht erklärt sich aus dieser Tatsache die Unklarheit, ob der ratio oder der voluntas der höchste Rang zuzusprechen ist' [p. 139].

12. Csi 2, 9, 18; SBOp 3:426; CF 37:71.
13. Bernard's treatise on the necessity of loving God is a particularly rich source for this. See, for example, Dil 2, 2; SBOp 3:121; CF 13:95.
14. QH 14, 1; SBOp 4:468-69; CF 25:229.
15. McGinn, 'Introduction' to *Three Treaties*, p. 8.
16. OS 4, 5; SBOp 5:358; Luddy 3:377-78. Bernard employs the same division of the soul in Par 5, 1 (SBOp 6/2:282; CSt 20:28). In his excellent translation of this *Parable* in CSt 20 (1985) 28-31, Michael Casey renders *rationabilitas, concupiscibilitas, irascibilitas* as 'reason, positive appetite and negative appetite.' Casey gives his reasons for following McGinn in this on p. 23, n. 1. I have no quarrel, surely, with this translation, but I believe my reading of the text is made clearer by using the more literal translation.
17. Gra 4, 11; SBOp 3:173; CF 19:67.
18. SC 11, 5; SBOp 1:57; CF 4:73.
19. SC 81, 3; SBOp 2:285; CF 40:159.
20. Div 84, 1; SBOp 6/1:325.
21. Div 84, 1; SBOp 6/1:325.
22. Sent 3, 88; SBOp 6/2:131.
23. SC 77, 5; SBOp 2:264; CF 40:126.
24. Dil 2, 6; SBOp 3:123; CF 13:98.
25. OS 4, 4; SBOp 5:358; Luddy 3:377.
26. V Nat 3, 2; SBOp 4:212; Luddy 1:329-30.
27. Dil 2, 5; SBOp 3:123; CF 13:97.
28. Par 2, 4; SBOp 6/2:270; CSt 18:197.
29. Dil 5, 15; SBOp 3:131; CF 13:107-108.
30. Gra 6, 17; SBOp 3:178; CF 19:73.
31. Gra 6, 19; SBOp 3:180; CF 19:75.
32. See Gra 3, 7 (SBOp 3:171; CF 19:62); Par 1, 1 (SBOp 6/2:261; CSt 18:18).
33. Gra 1, 2; SBOp 3:167; CF 19:55-56. On this definition, see Bernard McGinn, 'Introduction' to Bernard of Clairvaux, *On Grace and Free Choice*, in *Treatises III*, CF 19 (Kalamazoo, Michigan: Cistercian Publications Inc., 1977) pp. 15-16.
34. McGinn, 'Introduction' to *On Grace and Free Choice*, p. 18.
35. Gra 2, 3-4; SBOp 3:168; CF 19:58. McGinn analyzes this statement: 'Bernard appears to be saying that some kind of reason must accompany any act of the will, but that good acts of the will will

be preceded by correct judgements.' See McGinn, 'Introduction' to *On Grace and Free Choice*, p. 17.
36. Gra 2, 4; SBOp 3:169; CF 19:59.
37. Gra 2, 5; SBOp 3:168-69; CF 19:59.
38. Pre 5, 11; SBOp 3:261; CF 1:113. See also Gra 2, 4; SBOp 3:168; CF 19:58-59.
39. Par 5, 3; SBOp 6/2:283; CSt 20:29.
40. Dil 8, 23; SBOp 3:138; CF 13:115.
41. See below, p. 90.
42. See Michael Casey's translation of a part of Div 74 (SBOp 6/1:312-13) in Cst 20 (1985) 26.
43. See above, p. 7. For an excellent study of the feelings, see Casey, *Athirst for God*, pp. 94-110.
44. See below, pp. 21-26.
45. Gra 2, 3; SBOp 3:167; CF 19:57. See also V Nat 3, 8; SBOp 4:217; Luddy 1:337-38.
46. OS 4, 5; SBOp 5:359; Luddy 3:378.
47. OS 4, 5; SBOp 5:359; Luddy 3:378.
48. OS 4, 5; SBOp 5:359; Luddy 3:378-79.
49. OS 4, 6; SBOp 5:359-60; Luddy 3:379-80.
50. OS 4, 6; SBOp 5:360; Luddy 3:380.
51. See above, p. 11 and below, p. 90.
52. OS 4, 6; SBOp 5:360; Luddy 3:380.
53. OS 4, 6; SBOp 5:360; Luddy 3:380.
54. Csi 2, 4, 7; SBOp 3:415; CF 37:54.
55. Ded 5, 7; SBOp 5:393; Luddy 2:425.
56. Ded 5, 7; SBOp 5:393; Luddy 2:425.
57. Csi 5, 8, 18; SBOp 3:482; CF 37:163. Much the same language—surely the same idea—occurs in Div 80, 1; SBOp 6/1:320.
58. Csi 5, 9, 21; SBOp 3:484; CF 37:165. See also Nat 5, 4; SBOp 4:268; Luddy 1:414.
59. Nat 2, 1; SBOp 4:251-52; Luddy 1:390-91.
60. Nat 2, 1; SBOp 4:252; Luddy 1:391.
61. SC 4, 5; SBOp 1:20; CF 4:24. See also SC 5, 5; SBOp 1:23; CF 4:28.
62. Nat 2, 2; SBOp 4:252; Luddy 1:391-92. See also SC 30, 9; SBOp 1:215; CF 7:119-20.
63. Csi 5, 5, 12; SBOp 3:476; CF 37:154.
64. See Div 2, 8 (SBOp 6/1:85); SC 5, 8 (SBOp 1:24-25; CF 4:29-30).
65. Div 86, 1; SBOp 6/1:328.
66. Div 86, 1; SBOp 6/1:328. Sometimes Bernard suggests that the soul 'inhabits' the head more than other parts of the body, since more of the senses are located there. But this hardly means that he assigns a *locus* to it. See QH 1, 4; SBOp 4:389; CF 25:123-24.
67. Div 106, 2; SBOp 6/1:378.
68. Gra 14, 46; SBOp 3:199; CF 19:105.
69. Gra 4, 12; SBOp 3:175; CF 19:68. See also Asc 6, 2 (SBOp 5:151); Tpl 11, 24 (SBOp 3:234; CF 19:159); and Tpl 11, 28 (SBOp 3:236; CF 19:162).
70. Sept 1, 5; SBOp 4:348; Luddy 2:60-61. See also Par 7; SBOp 6/2:301; CSt 22:52.
71. Dil 11, 31; SBOp 3:145; CF 13:122. See also SC 5, 1; SBOp 1:21-22; CF 4:25.

V. THE EFFECTS OF THE FALL

The body constitutes no burden at all to a *good* soul. This statement contains the germ of Bernard's teaching on the trials and tribulations of human beings and their bodies. Human pains, limitations, even mortality, are the products not of bodies but of souls—more specifically, of that part of the soul we know as the human will.

Humans are made in the image and likeness of God, Bernard believes. Bernard speaks of the location of God's image and likeness in the will:[1]

> I believe that in these three freedoms [freedom of choice, freedom of counsel, and freedom of pleasure] there is contained the image and likeness of the Creator in which we were made [see Gn 1:26]. I believe that in freedom of choice lies the image, and in the other two is contained a certain twofold likeness.[2]

Freedom of counsel and freedom of pleasure, each of which have two degrees, are lost through original sin—with disastrous consequences:

> The higher freedom of counsel consists in not being able to sin, the lower in being able not to sin. Again, the higher freedom of pleasure lies in not being able to be disturbed, the lower in being able not to be disturbed. Thus, man received in his very nature, along with freedom of choice, the lower degree of each of these freedoms. And, when he sinned, he fell from both. In losing completely his freedom of counsel, he fell from being able not to sin to not being able not to sin. Likewise, from being able not to be disturbed, he fell to not being able not to be disturbed, with the total loss of his freedom of pleasure. There only remained, for his punishment, the freedom of choice through which he had lost the others; that he could not lose. Enslaved by his own will to sin [see Rm 6:17f.], he deservedly forfeited freedom of counsel. Through his sin he became a debtor of death [see Rm 5:12], so how could he hold onto his freedom of pleasure? Three freedoms he had received. By abusing the one called freedom of choice, he deprived himself of the others.[3]

By participating in the sin of Adam,[4] humans have lost their freedom of counsel and pleasure; humans have lost their likeness to

God. But they remain the images of God; without freedom of choice they would cease to be human.[5]

The primary effect of sin, then, is a will misdirected, a will directed toward that which will not fulfill human nature and bring happiness:

> The wicked walk round in circles [Ps 11:9], naturally wanting whatever will satisfy their desires, yet rejecting that which will lead them to their true end, which is not in consumption but in consummation.[6]

This misdirection of the positive appetite or will is what Bernard calls lust:

> Meanwhile, in the house of Hope, Lady Lust has entered the positive appetite and appropriated everything, re-directing desire from the highest things to the lowest. She gave Continence over to be trampled underfoot and mocked by carnal desire, Constancy by the lust of the eyes, and Humility by worldly ambition.[7]

If the will is the primary *locus* of sin, and of the effects of sin, Bernard teaches that sin also has its effect on the other faculties of the soul, intellect and feelings:

> It is difficult—indeed, impossible—for a man, by his own power of free choice... to turn wholly to the will of God and not rather to his own will and keep the gifts [God has given him] for himself as his own, as is written: 'All seek what is their own' [Ph 2:21] and 'Man's feelings and thoughts are inclined to evil' [Gn 8:21].[8]

All three powers of the soul, then, are corrupted by sin:

> The soul subsists by a threefold power. It is rational, concupisible, and irascible. Health of the intellect consists in knowledge of the truth; its corruption is pride....Vain glory corrupts the positive appetite and envy the negative appetite.[9]

Bernard tells the same story allegorically in his *Parable of the King's Son*:

> ...The ancient villain drew near to him. Full of wicked wiles, he handed him the little apple of disobedience. And then, having won his consent, he turned against the poor boy. He threw him down to earth and to the level of earthly desires. To prevent his getting up, he bound his feet (that is, the affections of his mind) with

the stout chains of worldly concupiscence, and did the
same to the activity of his hands and to the eyes of his
mind. He set him in the ship of false security, and, with
the powerful aid of the strong wind of flattery, he con-
veyed him to the distant Land of Unlikeness.[10]

The 'eyes of his mind' are misdirected by the will. This misdirection of the intellect toward the false or inappropriate is what Bernard calls 'curiosity':

It also happens when a man, not appreciating the gift
of reason, starts mingling with the herds of dumb
animals to the extent that, ignoring his own interior glory
[see Ps 44:14], he models his conduct on the object
of his senses. Led on by curiosity, he becomes like any
other animal since he does not see he has received more
than they.[11]

Not only the intellect and feelings, but the body too suffers the
effects of the will's misdirection. The body feels this effect as misery,[12] but the body is the recipient, not the source of this misery.
To be sure, Bernard knows the body to be full of undisciplined
energy, but the energies of the soul he believes to be equally un-
restrained. In Bernard's *Parable 3*, he gives us an image of this
in a story of a king's young son, eager for battle:

His horse was restive—this was his own body, still bub-
bling with worldly energy, ostentatious and lustful. And
his soul within, whose banner it carried, was likewise....[13]

The body's energy must be properly directed, but it is not; and
this is because the will is not properly directed:

God is indeed the life of the soul, just as the soul is
the life of the body. By wilful sin the soul has willingly
given up life, though she is unwilling to give up the body.
She has freely rejected life since she does not wish to
live; therefore she is no longer able [after the Fall] to
give life where and when she pleases. She did not want
to be governed by God; therefore she is unable to govern her body. How can she command an inferior when
she ignores her own superior? If the Creator has found
his creature in revolt, the soul will find her footman a
rebel as well. Man has been guilty of transgressing divine law [Jm 2:11], so he finds another law in his mem-

bers resisting the rule of reason and imprisoning him
in the law of sin [Rm 7:23].[14]

The world, the flesh, and the Devil are indeed sources of temptation.[15] The problem lies, however, not with the world of nature, which is good because it is the creation of God. Bernard is filled with wonder at the glories of nature which encourage one in following Christ:

> When I look for an example among created things to illustrate this disburdening burden [of Truth], nothing occurs to me more apt than the wings of a bird. For they, in an extraordinary way, render the body both greater and yet more nimble. What a wonderful achievement of nature that a body should be rendered lighter by its very increase in size, so that the more it increases in bulk the more it decreases in weight. Here certainly we have a clear illustration of the sweet burden of Christ which carries those who carry it.[16]

As Jean Leclercq has written:

> He [Bernard] was truly inclined toward the book of nature, which he speaks of in the ninth of his miscellaneous Sermons. Here he found moral lessons and salutary comparisons. And these artificial themes, which could have furnished mere faded images, were expressed with a freshness, occasionally a fondness, which is an indication of his good humor and mental health.[17]

The 'world' which is the source of temptation is not the world of nature.

Nor is the 'flesh' the human body. That body is not only beautiful, it is also a reproach to the soul, by sin deformed in intellect and will:

> God indeed gave man an upright stance of body, perhaps in order that this corporeal uprightness, exterior and of little account, might prompt the inward man, made to the image of God, to cherish his spiritual uprightness, that the body of clay might rebuke the deformity of the mind. What is more unbecoming than to bear a warped mind in an upright body?[18]

The body, unlike the soul, has maintained the likeness to God lost by the soul in the Fall.[19] This body rightly glories in the beauties of the world—the world of nature:

It is wrong and shameful that this body shaped from
the dust of the earth should have its eyes raised on high,
scanning the heavens at its pleasure and thrilled by the
sight of sun and moon and stars, while, on the contrary,
the heavenly and spiritual creature lives with its eyes,
its inward vision, and its affections centered on the earth
beneath — the mind that should be feasting on dainties
is wallowing in the mire, rolling in the dung like a pig
[Lm 4:5].[20]

The body is an Eve to the soul's Adam. Intended as a helpmate to the soul, she has instead abused it:

Instead, however, I gave into softness and idleness and
lay down on the bed of pleasure in the bosom of my
Eve, that is, of my fleshly nature which was joined to
me, which God gave me as a helpmate to bring forth
good works as children....[21]

As Adam should love his Eve, so too should the soul love the body:

I do not wish to say that you should hate your own flesh
[Eph 5:28-29]. Love it as something given you as a helper [Gn 2:18] and a partner prepared to share in eternal
happiness.[22]

Good by its nature, the body is morally neutral:

Those other things listed above: life, sense perception,
and appetite, of themselves make one neither happy
nor unhappy. Were this not so, trees because of their
life, and animals because of the other two, would be
subject to sorrow or worthy of beatitude. But this is out
of the question. We have life in common with the trees,
and sense perception, appetite, and, again, life with the
animals. It is, then, what we call our will which distinguishes us from both of them.[23]

The evil which is accomplished in humans by humans is not by the body but in the body.

The obstacles to one's happiness are not physical but mental — or, better put, volitional. The 'world' which is a danger is not the natural world, but 'worldly' desires:

...What sign, I ask, of the humility of the [newborn]
God can you discover in a proud mortal? What trace
of his lowliness is visible in those who still pursue with

all the ardor of desire the honors and wealth of this world?[24]

The 'flesh' which is a threat is not the body but the will which misuses the body's natural (and good) energies:

> It [union with the Bridegroom in love] is not so with one who has not renounced her own will. She lies down by herself; she dwells by herself. Or rather, not by herself, for she lives licentiously in the company of prostitutes [Lk 15:11-32], I mean the lusts of the flesh, on which she squanders her goods and that share of the estate which she demanded to be set aside for her.[25]

The world, the flesh, and the Devil are indeed sources of temptation,[26] but the will is the faculty which chooses evil. The flesh may war against the spirit, but '. . . it is not a civil war, but a domestic conflict. . .' within the will.[27] ' "The body is a load upon the soul" indeed, but only after it has been "corrupted" ' [Ws 9:15].[28] An 'immoderate and inordinate passion for pleasure'[29] may be ruinous; however, it is not the passion that is evil, but the will which fails to order it properly. It is sensuality not sensation which impedes one's search for happiness.[30] But as vice is in the will, so too is virtue—the virtue of chastity, for example:

> [In the third degree of love] he loves chastely and does not find it hard to obey a chaste commandment, purifying his heart, as it is written, in the obedience of love [1 P 1:22]. He loves with justice and freely embraces the just commandment. This love is pleasing because it is free. It is chaste because it does not consist of spoken words but of deed and truth [1 Jn 3:18].[31]

Chastity is a condition not of the body but of the will. Again, the body is good in itself but morally neutral, neither virtuous nor vicious.

VI. THE RESTORATION OF THE SOUL

The restoration of humans which leads to their fulfillment, their happiness, then, is a restoration of the soul—and, indeed, of all the faculties of the soul:

> Everyone who is 'guided by the Spirit' [Ga 5:16, 25], realizes how greatly in the present life the three [faculties] are lacking in integrity and perfection. And what reason for this can there be, except that God is not yet 'all in all' [1 Co 15:28]? Hence it comes about that the reason very often falters in its judgements, the will is agitated by a fourfold perturbation,[32] and the memory confused by its endless forgetfulness.[33]

Despite its present disordered state, the human being is still noble, and should have hope for fulfillment. The only efficacious hope is hope in God:

> Man, noble though he may be, was unwillingly subjected to this triple form of futility, but hope, nevertheless, was left to him.... Put your hope in God. I shall praise him yet [Ps 41:6], when error will have gone from the reason, pain from the will, and every trace of fear from the memory. Then will come that state for which we hope, with its admirable serenity, its fullness of delight, its endless security.[34]

The source of this restoration is God's free gift of himself, which is grace:

> The God who is truth is the source of the first of these gifts; the God who is love, of the second; the God who is all-powerful, of the third. And so it will come to pass that God will be 'all in all' [1 Co 15:28], for the reason will receive unquenchable light, the will imperturbable peace, the memory an unfailing fountain from which it will draw everlastingly.[35]

Typically, Bernard tells this story of restoration in different ways, using a varying vocabulary:

> Therefore, although it is true that man is a kind of heaven, and has, unquestionably, a relation of similitude to the celestial spirits both in his substance and in his form—in his substance because it is spiritual, in his form because he is rational—nevertheless, these two

properties of his being are not now sufficient to lift him
so high that he may deserve to hear the welcome words:
'Because you are heaven, to heaven you shall go.' In
vain he prides himself on his power of free choice, with
which his soul is endowed, for he is 'a prisoner of that
law of sin in his members' [Rm 7:23]....But when grace
has been given, then, beyond a doubt, the cord of iniquity by which we are drawn—rather, which we draw
with us—is readily dissolved. For grace mediates between God and our souls, not as a wall of separtion,
but as a bridge of union, making good the rupture caused
by sin.[36]

Bernard repeats here his assertion that humans are not devastat-
ed by sin; they remain basically good. But God's grace is necessary to their restoration. God's greatest gift is of himself in Jesus.
Not only is he God, he is the model human being to whom other
human beings can conform and be conformed:

That very form came [see Ph 2:6], therefore, to which
free choice was to be conformed, because, in order that
it might regain its original form, it had to be reformed
from that out of which it had been formed.[37]

The re-formation of humans must begin with the will, since that
is the faculty through which they became de-formed. Through this
re-formation, the likeness—or image[38]—of God is restored:

And so, man will no longer be the slave of sin, since
he does not commit sin [see Jn 8:34 and Rm 6:6]. Further, set free from sin, he can now begin to recover his
freedom of counsel and vindicate his dignity, while setting up in himself a worthy likeness to the divine image, restoring completely in fact his former loveliness.
But let him take care to do this no less gently than
mightily, that is, not reluctantly or under compulsion
[see 2 Co 9:7]—for that is the beginning, not the fullness of wisdom—but with a prompt and ready will,
which makes the offering acceptable, since 'God loves
a cheerful giver' [2 Co 9:7]. In this way, in all he does,
he will be imitating wisdom, mightily resisting vices and
gently at rest within his conscience.[39]

The process of restoration requires one's response to God's grace,
but Bernard is no Pelagian or semi-Pelagian. The will responds

to God as a direct result of God's gift of himself in Christ by the Spirit:

> We cannot achieve these things, however, without the help of him by whose example we are spurred on to desire them. With it, and by it, we ourselves are conformed, and transformed into the same image from glory to glory, as by the Spirit of the Lord [see 2 Co 3:18]. But, if by the Spirit of the Lord, then hardly by free choice.[40]

Humans have retained free choice, but they have lost freedom of counsel and freedom of pleasure. These are restored by Christ, making human perfection possible:

> And this is where Christ comes in. In him man possesses the necessary 'power of God and wisdom of God' [1 Co 1:24], who, inasmuch as he is wisdom, pours back into man true wisdom, and so restores to him his free counsel. And, inasmuch as he is power, he restores his full power, and restores to him his free pleasure. As a result, being by the former perfectly good, he may now no longer know sin, and being by the latter completely happy, he may no longer feel its sting.... In this life, it is no small wisdom not to consent to sin, though one cannot be rid of it altogether. And it is no inconsiderable power manfully to despise adversity for the sake of truth, though one cannot yet, in total happiness, avoid feeling it at times.[41]

One's restoration is a process, a process of education which will lead to one's happiness, to one's perfect self-fulfillment:

> Here below, we must learn from our freedom of counsel not to abuse free choice, that one day we may be able to enjoy fully freedom of pleasure. Thus we are repairing the image of God in us, and the way is being paved, by grace, for the retrieving of that former honor which we forfeited by sin. Happy then will be the man who shall deserve to hear said of him: 'Who is he, and we shall praise him? For he has done wonderful things in his life. He had the power to transgress, and he did not transgress; he had the power to do evil, and he did not do it' [Si 31:9ff.].[42]

Bernard's confidence in the restorative power of grace is so great that he can speak of human perfection even in this life:

> [The perfected man] will not be afraid to speak the wisdom of God when he is in the company of perfect men [1 Co 2:6], comparing one spiritual truth with another [1 Co 2:13].[43]

The process of perfection begins with God's prevenient grace, moving the will to choose the good:

> ...I recognized myself as impelled to good by the prevenient operation [of God's grace]. I felt myself borne along by it and helped, with its help, to find perfection.[44]

Grace perfects human nature, enabling humans to order their natural and, therefore, good desires:

> This means only that grace sets in order what creation has given, so that virtues are nothing other than ordered affections.[45]

Bernard knows that these affections, once ordered, will lead one to seek, find, and cling to God:

> Virtue is that by which man seeks continuously and eagerly for his Maker, and, when he finds him, adheres to him with all his might.[46]

Humans are thus capable of perfection, '...capable of ascending from strength to strength right up to the summit'[47] of the mountain which is God. Bernard is sensitive to the wondrous potential of humans for good: '...Whoever desires the greatest good can succeed in reaching it....'[48] This awareness, Bernard reckons, is itself a virtue: 'What glory is there in having something you do not know you have?'[49] Bernard expresses his confidence allegorically in his *Story of the King's Son*:

> There are four stages on the boy's return to freedom. First, repentance, though not well grounded; second, flight, but rash and unthinking; third, the battle terrible and frightening; and fourth, victory in all its strength and wisdom. You will find that all who flee the world pass through these phases. At first they are weak and silly; then, with better times, they become precipitate and rash. When troubles come, they begin to be fearful and lose heart. And, finally, when they arrive at the kingdom of love, they are far-seeing, experienced, and made perfect.[50]

Human perfection, fulfillment, and happiness lie in freedom, freedom from evil, freedom to do good.

VII. THE ROLE OF THE BODY IN HUMAN RESTORATION

Since the body has not lost its natural goodness by sin,[51] it does not require the same reformatory process as the soul. But the body is necessary not only to one's being but to one's becoming, not only to one's nature,[52] but to the process of one's perfection. For Bernard, the Incarnation is the symbol, indeed the sacrament, of the role of matter in the salvific process:

> And nevertheless, with so much condescension has God lowered himself to the level of matter, with that much honor has matter been raised to the level of God that, by an ineffable and incomprehensible mystery, whatever God has done in it, matter may be said to have done. And whatever matter has suffered in him, God may be said to have suffered.[53]

One's fallen nature makes the body a burden, to be sure, but that is a burden caused by the disordered soul.[54] Even in her disordered state, the soul recognizes how important, how pleasant is her union with the body. This is shown by the pain she feels at the parting of the two in death:

> What is there, I ask, but labor and sorrow [Ps 9:28; 89:10] and vexation of spirit [Qo 1:14; 2:17] among all the things that are under the sun [Qo 9:3], since even that which in itself is most agreeable to the spirit—I mean the communication of life and sensibility to the flesh—can become for it an intolerable burden? For how pleasant to the spirit is its union with the flesh is shown by the pain she feels at parting, since she can scarcely be torn from the society of the body even then when corruption has rendered the body no longer a suitable subject for her vitalizing influence.[55]

Until the time of death, the body offers the soul the starting place for the spiritual growth which will make that death a happy one:

> In this way, man who is animal and carnal [1 Co 2:14], and knows how to love only himself, yet starts loving God for his own benefit, because he learns from frequent experience that he can do everything that is good for him in God [Ph 4:13] and that without God he can do nothing good [Jn 15:5].[56]

The soul's happy union with the body provides a means of restoring in the soul that which she—not the body[57]—has lost in the

Fall. The body, at home in God's world, must care for the soul which is in disharmony with the created world:
> O mortal flesh, noble is the guest you entertain, very noble, and on her welfare your own entirely depends. Honor your guest so distinguished. You are residing here in your native country [Mi 4:10], but the soul which has taken lodging with you is a pilgrim and an exile on the earth.... Do not consider the sufferings and inconveniences you may have to endure, provided your guest can be honorably lodged with you. Esteem it your greatest honor to be stripped of all honor in this life for the sake of the soul.[58]

If the body is a happy burden to the soul, the body must also bear happily the burden of the soul.

It is precisely the body's essential role in the process of human perfection that justifies Bernard's concern with the organization of external life, for the external is essential to the internal:
> I do not mean by this that external means can be overlooked, or that the man who does not employ them will quickly become spiritual. Spiritual things are certainly higher, but there is little hope of attaining them or receiving them without making use of external exercises. As it is written: 'It is not the spiritual that comes first but the physical, and then comes the spiritual' [1 Co 15:46]. Jacob was unfit to receive Rachel's longed-for embraces until he had knowledge of Leah [see Gn 29:23]. So too we read in one of the psalms: 'Strike up a song and play on the drum' [Ps 81:2]. This means: take up spiritual things, but first make use of physical things.[59]

The rational, irascible, and concupisible parts of the soul —the intellect, will, and feelings—must support each other and must also interact with the body in the process of perfection. This is most obvious in the irascible soul, for the sensation and feeling which are the irascible function are the result of an intimate association of the body with that part of the soul:
> And lest you [the body] should perhaps feel tempted to despise your guest [the soul], because she seems to you a stranger [1 Ch 29:15; Ps 38:13] and a pilgrim, consider diligently the many precious advantages which

you owe to her presence. For it is she that gives sight
to your eyes and hearing to your ears [Mt 11:5]. It is
from her your tongue borrows its power of speech, your
palate its discernment of taste, and all your members
their various motions. Whatever of life, whatever of
sense or feeling, whatever of beauty you possess in yourself, know that is is all the benefit of your guest.[60]

Sensations, perceptions, and their derivitive emotions are a potential source of spiritual progress. Speaking of the pilgrim at the Holy
Sepulcher, Bernard writes:

Still I think that those who are actually able to see even
with their bodily eyes the bodily resting place of the
Lord must experience the strongest emotions, from
which they will receive no little profit.[61]

The pleasure to be found 'in goods of the body' is useful in drawing one to the food, drink, clothing, and shelter which are essential to one's physical well-being.[62] Spiritual pleasures, which likewise
involve both body and soul, are similarly sources of spiritual
nourishment:

There are those who are always full of devotion...send-
ing up sighs at their meditations. Everything is pleasant and agreeable to them, and through the whole
[Easter] season 'Alleluia' is sung to them.[63]

The joy of laughter,[64] the sadness of grief,[65] and even the rush
of anger[66] are all good when properly controlled. These emotions,
the result of an intimate cooperation between body and irascible
soul, must be directed by the reason's knowledge and the will's
wise love:

I am not saying that we should be without affection and
that with an arid heart we move only our hands to work.
Among the many great and grievous evils that the Apostle ascribes to men I have read, this one is to be reck-
oned: to be without affection [Rm 1:31; 2 Tm 3:3].
But there is an affection which the flesh begets, and
one which reason controls, and one which wisdom seasons. The first is that which the Apostle says is not subject to the law of God, nor can be [Rm 8:7]. The
second, on the contrary, he shows to be in agreement
with the law of God because it is good [Rm 7:16]—
one cannot doubt that the insubordinate and the agree-

able differ from each other. The third, however, is far from either of them, because it tastes and experiences that the Lord is sweet [Ps 33:9]; it banishes the first and rewards the second. The first is pleasant, of course, but shameful; the second is emotionless but strong; the last is rich and delightful.[67]

Because Bernard believes one's will is the source of one's unhappy state,[68] it is also the key to one's process of restoration and perfection. The reorientation, the conversion of the will must begin in the body, for human beings are by nature physical. Conversely, the will must direct the natural affections of the flesh toward their proper end:

> Since we are flesh [Rm 7:14] and born of fleshly desire, our cupidity or love must begin with the flesh, and, when this is set in order, our love advances by fixed degrees, led on by grace, until it is consummated in the spirit [Ga 3:3]....[69]

However, this process does not render the body morally defective:

> Cupidity in turn is set in right order by the arrival of charity, which moves one to reject evil altogether and prefer what is better to what is good, desiring what is good only on account of what is better. When this state is fully achieved, the body and all its good things are loved only on account of the soul, the soul on account of God, and God on account of himself.[70]

The proper ordering of the body requires that it sometimes be denied what it desires; this restraint is, in the end, directed not so much toward the body as toward the will. The will achieves its proper orientation through the process of directing the body toward its appropriate ends:

> If, faithful to the sage's counsel, you turn away from sensual delights [Si 18:30] and content yourself with the Apostle's teaching on food and clothing [1 Tm 6:8], you will soon be able to guard your love against 'carnal desires which war against the soul' [1 P 2:11]. And I think you will not find it a burden to share with those of your nature that which you have withheld from the enemy of your soul. Then your love will be sober and just if you do not refuse your brother that which he needs out of that pleasure which you have denied your-

self. Thus carnal love becomes social when extended to others.[71]

The body provides the will the means by which it can grow in love. The will orients the body toward that which is most beneficial to the whole person. The interaction of the body and soul are essential to the progress toward perfection which will result in the happiness of the blessed.

At death, the body is not left behind, as we have seen.[72] In the Beatific Vision it, like the soul, is perfected, and that Vision is impossible without the body:

> In the first state [life on earth], therefore, the faithful soul eats her bread, but, alas, in the sweat of her brow [Gn 3:19]. While in the flesh she moves by faith [2 Co 5:7] which necessarily acts through love [Ga 5:6], for, if it does not act, it dies [Jm 2:20]. Moreover, according to our Savior, this work is food: 'My food is to do the will of my Father' [Jn 4:34]. Afterwards, having cast off her flesh, the soul no longer feeds on the bread of sorrow [Ps 126:2]. But, having eaten, she is allowed to drink more deeply of the wine of love—but not pure wine, for it is written of the bride in the *Song of Songs*: 'I drank my wine mixed with milk' [Sg 5:1]. The soul mixes the divine love with the tenderness of that natural affection by which she desires to have her body back, a glorified body. The soul, therefore, glows already with the warmth of love's wine, but not to the state of intoxication, for the milk moderates the strength of the wine. Intoxication disturbs the mind and makes it wholly forgetful of itself, but the soul, which still thinks of the resurrection of her own body, has not forgotten herself completely. For the rest, after finding the only thing needed [the body], what is there to prevent the soul from taking leave of herself and, passing entirely into God, ceasing all the more to be like herself as she becomes more and more like God? Then only the soul is allowed to drink wisdom's pure wine, of which it is said: 'How good is my cup; it inebriates me' [Ps 22:5]! Why wonder if the soul is inebriated by the riches of the Lord's dwelling [Ps 35:9] when, free from earthly cares, she can drink pure, fresh wine with Christ in his Father's house [Mt 26:29; Mk 14:25]?[73]

At death humans are incomplete. Since a person is an entity, not merely a soul inhabiting a body, the loss of that body renders the person incapable of complete happiness, of the perfect bliss of the Beatific Vision:

> It is not fitting that complete beatitude be granted before the one who will receive it is a complete man—no more than perfection can be bestowed on a still imperfect Church.[74]

Bernard believes that the soul deprived of a body by death becomes free from sin and suffering, but she is not perfectly united with God:

> This much is certain: that both these freedoms, from sin and suffering, are fully and perfectly present in those perfect souls who have been loosed from fleshly bonds, even as they are in God and his Christ, and the angels in heaven. For, though the souls of the just lack undoubtedly some measure of glory while they have not yet received their bodies, they experience no trace of sorrow.[75]

The soul may have become perfect, but for perfect happiness the perfection of the whole person is necessary; and the whole person is body and soul:

> But what about those souls which are already separated from their bodies? We believe they are completely engulfed in that immense ocean of eternal light and everlasting brightness. But if, which is not denied, they wish they had received their bodies back or, certainly, if they desire and hope to receive them, there is no doubt that they have not altogether turned from themselves, for it is clear they still cling to something of their own to which their desires return, though ever so slightly. Consequently, until death is swallowed up in victory [1 Co 15:54] and eternal light invades from all sides the limits of night and takes possession to the extent that heavenly glory shines in their bodies, souls cannot set themselves aside and pass into God. They are still attached to their bodies, if not by life and feeling, certainly by a natural affection, so that they do not wish nor are they able to realize consummation without them. The rapture of the soul which is her most perfect and highest state, cannot, therefore, take place before the resurrection of

the bodies, lest the spirit, if it could reach perfection
without the body, would no longer desire to be united
to the flesh. For indeed, the body is not deposed or
resumed without profit to the soul. To be brief: 'The
death of his saints is precious in the sight of the Lord'
[Ps 115:15]. If death is precious, what must life be—
especially that life?[76]

The body which the soul requires is a body that will partake
of the glory of the resurrected body of Christ:

...He himself—the Lord God of Sabaoth [Rm 9:29],
the Lord of hosts, and the King of glory [Ps 23:10]—
will come down to reform our bodies and make them
like to the body of his brightness.[77]

This, Bernard believes, is the meaning of the passage in Paul's
Letter to the Philippians which speaks of the glorification of the human body.[78] That glorification will free the body of all its mortal restraints:

...So, to the thought of judgement is added that of
the kingdom in which we reflect on what we shall be:
first on the condition of the body no longer subject to
suffering and death, then on its glorification when it will
assume a splendor and beauty which beggar description. As it is written: 'The just will be as resplendent
as the sun' [Mt 13:43].[79]

In the Beatific Vision the body will be freed from all carnal necessity:

Then each member of Christ [1 Co 6:15] can assuredly say of himself what Paul said of the Head: 'If we have
known Christ according to the flesh, we no longer know
him so' [2 Co 5:16]. Nobody there knows himself according to the flesh because 'Flesh and blood will not
possess the kingdom of God' [1 Co 15:50]. This does
not mean the substance of the flesh will not be present, but that all carnal necessity will disappear; the love
of the flesh will be absorbed by that of the spirit, and
our present, weak human affections will be changed into
divine.[80]

The union of the perfected soul and glorified body in the Beatific Vision is the highest form of human existence.[81] The intimate union of body and soul which is the human person finds its completion, its perfection, its fulfillment, in the Beatific Vision. This is perfect happiness for human beings.

Bernard's views of the person as an entity, a whole, yet composed of body and soul, of matter and spirit, are both essential to his definition of the human as a rational animal. Bernard betrays no hint of a semi-dualism which sees humans as souls which only incidentally, and unfortunately, inhabit bodies. The consequences of this radical anthropology are fundamental to understanding the society and culture of the age in which he played so prominent a role.

1. Augustine locates image and likeness in the intellect, according to McGinn, 'Introduction' to *On Grace and Free Choice*, pp. 32-33.
2. Gra 9, 28; SBOp 3:185; CF 19:84.
3. Gra 7, 21-22; SBOp 3:182; CF 19:79.
4. See, for example, Tpl 11, 24; SBOp 3:233; CF 19:158.
5. In SC 80-82 (SBOp 2:277-98; CF 40:145-79) and Nat 2, 3 (SBOp 4:253; Luddy 1:392), Bernard teaches that the image is lost, but not the likeness. Bernard is well aware of his apparent inconsistency (see SC 81, 11; SBOp 2:291; CF 40:168), strengthening my conviction that, though his terminology varies, his doctrine remains fundamentally consistent.
6. Dil 7, 19; SBOp 3:135; CF 13:112.
7. Par 5, 5; SBOp 6/2:284; CSt 20:29-30. See also Dil 8, 23; SBOp 3:138; CF 13:115.
8. Dil 2, 6; SBOp 3:124; CF 13:98.
9. Div 75; SBOp 6/1:312.
10. Par 1, 2; SBOp 6/2:261-62; CSt 18:18.
11. Dil 2, 4; SBOp 3:122; CF 13:96. See Michael Casey, 'Introduction' to 'The Last Two Parables by Bernard of Clairvaux', CSt 22 (1987) 41.
12. Par 5, 5; SBOp 6/2:284; CSt 20:30.
13. Par 3, 1; SBOp 6/2:274; CSt 18:285.
14. Tpl 11, 19; SBOp 3:230; CF 19:155.
15. See SC 1, 9; SBOp 1:7; CF 4:5-6.
16. Ep 72, 2; SBOp 7:176; James, pp. 104-105.
17. Jean Leclercq, *Bernard of Clairvaux and the Cistercian Spirit*, trans. Claire Lavoie, CS 16 (Kalamazoo, Michigan: Cistercian Publications, 1976) p. 18.
18. SC 24, 6; SBOp 1:157; CF 7:46.
19. Div 12, 1; SBOp 6/1:128.
20. SC 24, 6; SBOp 1:157-58; CF 7:46-47.
21. Par 7; SBOp 6/2:299; CSt 22:49.
22. QH 10, 3; SBOp 4:444; CF 25:226.
23. Gra 2, 4; SBOp 3:168-69; CF 19:59.
24. Res 4, 1; SBOp 5:110; Luddy 3:513. See also Div 52, 1 (SBOp 6/1:274-75); and SC 85, 4 (SBOp 2:310; CF 40:199).
25. SC 46, 4; SBOp 2:58; CF 7:243. See also Gra 12, 41; SBOp 3:195-96; CF 19:98.
26. SC 11, 6 (SBOp 1:58; CF 4:74); SC 85, 4 (SBOp 2:309; CF 40:199).
27. OS 5, 8; SBOp 5:366; Luddy 3:391. Bernard reiterates many of Paul's negative comments on the flesh in Adv 6, 2 (SBOp 4:192; Luddy 1:45), but the rest of the sermon indicates the real problem is with the will.
28. Mart 3; SBOp 5:401; Luddy 3:5. See also Dil 4, 13 (SBOp 3:129; CF 13:105-106); Dil 2, 4 (SBOp 3:122; CF 13:96); Pre 22, 59 (SBOp 3:292; CF 1:148-49); SC 21, 1 (SBOp 1:122; CF 7:4); and Sept 2, 2 (SBOp 4:351; Luddy 2:65).
29. Circ 2, 1; SBOp 4:274; Luddy 1:431. See also SC 85, 4; SBOp 2:310; CF 40:199.
30. SC 52, 4 (SBOp 2:86; CF 31:52-53); Csi 5, 1, 2 (SBOp 3:468; CF 37:141).

31. Dil 9, 26; SBOp 3:141; CF 13:118.
32. These are the four passions of love, joy, fear, and sadness. See Div 50, 2; SBOp 6/1:271.
33. SC 11, 5; SBOp 1:57; CF 4:73. On this Augustinian division of the soul, see above p. 3.
34. SC 11, 5-6; SBOp 1:57-58; CF 4:73-74.
35. SC 11, 6; SBOp 1:58; CF 4:74.
36. Mart 5; SBOp 5:401; Luddy 3:5-6.
37. Gra 10, 33; SBOp 3:189; CF 19:89.
38. See above, p. 39, n. 5.
39. Gra 10, 34; SBOp 3:190; CF 19:90.
40. Gra 10, 35; SBOp 3:190; CF 19:90.
41. Gra 8, 26; SBOp 3:184-85; CF 19:82-83.
42. Gra 8, 27; SBOp 3:185; CF 19:83.
43. Tpl 6, 12; SBOp 3:225; CF 19:147.
44. Gra 1, 1; SBOp 3:165; CF 19:53.
45. Gra 6, 17; SBOp 3:178; CF 19:72-73.
46. Dil 2, 2; SBOp 3:121; CF 13:95.
47. Gra 12, 41; SBOp 3:195; CF 19:99.
48. Dil 7, 19; SBOp 3:136; CF 13:112.
49. Dil 2, 3; SBOp 3:121; CF 13:95.
50. Par 1, 7; SBOp 6/2:266-67; CSt 18:23.
51. See above, p. 24.
52. See above, pp. 15-16.
53. V Nat 3, 8; SBOp 4:217; Luddy 1:338.
54. See above, p. 23.
55. Sept 2, 2; SBOp 4:351; Luddy 2:65.
56. Dil 8, 25; SBOp 3:140; CF 13:117.
57. See above, pp. 24-25.
58. Adv 6, 3; SBOp 4:192-93; Luddy 1:46-47.
59. Apo 8, 14; SBOp 3:94; CF 1:51.
60. Adv 6, 4; SBOp 4:193; Luddy 1:47.
61. Tpl 11, 29; SBOp 3:236; CF 19:162.
62. Gra 5, 14; SBOp 3:176; CF 19:70.
63. Res 4, 2; SBOp 5:111; Luddy 3:514. See also SC 4, 4 (SBOp 1:20; CF 4:23); and Mal 1 (SBOp 5:417; CF 10:97).
64. S Mal 4; SBOp 6/1:53; CF 10:110.
65. V Mal 31, 72 (SBOp 3:376; CF 10:90); Mal 5 (SBOp 5:420; CF 10:101).
66. S Mal 3; SBOp 6/1:52; CF 10:109.
67. SC 50, 4; SBOp 2:80; CF 31:32-33. See also Par 2, 1; SBOp 6/2:268; CSt 18:185.
68. See above, p. 22.
69. Dil 15, 39; SBOp 3:152; CF 13:130.
70. Dil 14, 38; SBOp 3:152; CF 13:130.
71. Dil 8, 23; SBOp 3:139; CF 13:116. See also Div 106, 2; SBOp 6/1:378.
72. See above, pp. 13-14. See also Casey, *Athirst for God*, pp. 234-37.
73. Dil 11, 32; SBOp 3:146; CF 13:123-24.
74. OS 3, 1; SBOp 5:350; Luddy 3:365.
75. Gra 4, 9; SBOp 3:172; CF 19:65.

76. Dil 11, 30; SBOp 3:144-45; CF 13:121-22. See also Div 78; SBOp 6/1:318. See Jean Leclercq's comments in *Bernard and the Cistercian Spirit*, p. 92. Thomas Aquinas seems to have a position similar to Bernard's; see *Summa contra Gentiles*, 4, 11.
77. Adv 6, 5; SBOp 4:194; Luddy 1:49.
78. Dil 5, 14; SBOp 3:131; CF 13:107.
79. Par 6; SBOp 6/2:291-92; CSt 21:105.
80. Dil 15, 40; SBOp 3:153; CF 13:131. See also Csi 5, 1, 1; SBOp 3:467-68; CF 37:140.
81. Div 2, 6; SBOp 6/1:83.

EDUCATION

I. THE PATH TO PERFECTION

THE DEMOCRATIZATION OF EDUCATION in the second half of the twentieth century, however commendable, has led to a blurring of the meaning of the word. When education is considered a right and is available to all, it can lead—and has led, at least in North America—to 'educational' programs which would have seemed strange to our ancestors. Instruction in television production, computer repair, or football technology, would not have been called 'education' by earlier generations. At least this instruction in technical competence would not have been lumped together with 'education' in the humanities and sciences. Bernard's contemporary, Hugh of St. Victor, distinguished between education in the liberal arts and training in what he called the mechanical arts.[1] And so I owe the reader an explanation of my use of the word.

I have deliberately avoided both 'training', which seems to me to imply mastery of a skill, and 'formation', the commonly-used expression for development in 'religious' life. I have done so because I do not believe either word adequately expresses Bernard's view of the process of growth and development of human beings on their path to perfection, to self-fulfillment, to happiness.

For Bernard, this process is not the development of a skill or skills, although there are skills which he would have people master in their growth toward completion. And—for me, at least—'formation' evokes an image of clay being kneaded and shaped according to the mind of the potter. The passivity of the subject of this formation does not, I believe, correspond to the notion of growth and self-development which informs Bernard's writing on the subject.

So I have chosen 'education'. By 'education' I mean the process of leading out (eduction)—for Bernard, a leading out of the kingdom of unlikeness, out of a sinful condition, into a freedom which is essential to one's completion, one's perfection:

> Those, therefore, who are possessed of true wisdom acknowledge a threefold operation, not indeed of free choice, but of divine grace in, or concerning, free choice. The first is creation, the second reformation, and the third consummation. Created first in Christ [see Eph 2:10] into freedom of will, by the second we are

reformed through Christ into a spirit of freedom [see 2 Co 3:17f.], lastly to reach fulfillment with Christ into an everlasting state.[2]

All the elements of eduction, of education in the sense I am using, are here. There is an outside agent, God, who is educator. He educates, educes, by a free gift, grace. The subject is not, however, passive; fulfillment is an active process of recovering freedom and applying that freedom toward the goal of maturity, a maturity which will lead to fulfillment:

> . . . The members should be perfected in no other way than with the head. This will happen when we all shall have attained 'to mature manhood, to the measure of the stature of the fullness of Christ' [Eph 4:13], when Christ, who is our life, appears, we shall appear with him in glory [see Col 3:4].[3]

Bernard's education is not simply training; it is not merely formation. Whatever word one chooses, Bernard's teaching on the process itself is clear.

Yet even that clarity may be obscured initially by the wealth of images, the multitude of metaphors Bernard employs. His teaching is rich; his means of conveying his teaching is equally rich. The steps in the spiritual life seem to vary from treatise to treatise. The *Steps of Humility* are both twelve and three. There are twelve steps of pride[4] corresponding to the twelve steps of humility in Benedict's *Rule for Monks*.[5] There are three steps of knowledge: knowing oneself, knowing one's neighbor, knowing God.[6] There are four steps of love in Bernard's *On the Necessity of Loving God*: loving oneself for one's own sake, loving God for one's own sake, loving God for God's sake, and loving oneself for God's sake.[7] Bernard has a sermon on the seven steps of obedience,[8] another on seven steps of confession.[9] The list could go on.[10]

Bernard's images of progress toward perfection are equally varied. In his *Sermon 7 on the Song of Songs*, the progression is through the stages of slave, wage-earner, student, son, and lover.[11] The stages are kisses—of feet, hand, and mouth of the Bridegroom— in the third through ninth sermons on the *Song of Songs*.[12] In Bernard's *Parable 1*,

> There are four stages to be noted on the boy's return to freedom. First, repentance, though not well grounded; second, flight, but rash and unthinking; third, the

battle terrible and frightening; and fourth, victory in all its strength and wisdom.[13]

There are still more.[14]

Through all this apparent diversity, there is, however, a pattern which, I believe,[15] underlies all Bernard's descriptions of human growth. This and the following sections will be organized according to this tripartite scheme which is perhaps best expressed in Bernard's *Steps of Humility and Pride*. In the first instance—in 2, 5—Bernard describes the steps as spiritual food: 'The first food, then, is humility, bitter but medicinal; the second is love, sweet and soothing; the third is contemplation, solid and strength-giving'.[16] A bit farther on, in 6, 19, Bernard gives the same list, but identifies it as steps to truth:

These are the three steps of truth. We climb to the first by the toil of humility, to the second by a deep feeling of compassion, and to the third by the ecstasy of contemplation. On the first step we experience the severity of truth, on the second its tenderness, on the third its purity. Reason brings us to the first as we judge ourselves; compassion brings us to the second when we have mercy on others; on the third the purity of truth sweeps us up to the sight of things invisible.[17]

This consistently tripartite division of the path to perfection is symbolic, not accidental. It corresponds to the triune nature of the God who initiates and fulfills one's quest for happiness:

It occurs to me here that it is possible to allot each of these three works to one of the persons of the undivided Trinity, that is, in so far as a man still sitting in darkness [Lk 1:79] can make a distinction in the work of the three persons who always work as one. There would seem to be something characteristic of the Son in the first stage, of the Holy Spirit in the second, of the Father in the third.[18]

The initial step of humility seems to Bernard to exhibit the exemplary work of the Incarnate Word:

What is the work of the Son? 'If I, your Lord and teacher, have washed your feet, how much more ought you also to wash one another's feet' [Jn 13:14]. The teacher of truth gave his disciples an example [Jn 13:15] of humility and opened to them the first stage of truth.[19]

Love is then inspired by the gift of the Holy Spirit:
> Then the work of the Holy Spirit: 'Love is spread abroad in our hearts by the Holy Spirit who is given to us' [Rm 5:5]. Love is a gift of the Holy Spirit [Ac 2:38]. By it those who, under the instruction of the Son, were led to the first step of truth through humility, now under the guidance of the Holy Spirit reach the second stage through compassion for their neighbor.[20]

The third step, truth, Bernard assigns to the Father; it is he who embraces humans in the glory of contemplation:
> Finally, listen to what is said of the Father: 'Blessed are you, Simon son of Jonah, for flesh and blood have not revealed it to you, but my Father who is in heaven' [Mt 16:18]. Again: 'The Father will make known the truth to the sons' [Is 38:19]; and 'I confess to you Father, for you have hidden these things from the wise and made them known to little ones' [Mt 11:25]. You see, by word and example the Son first teaches men humility; then the Holy Spirit pours out his love on those whom the Father receives finally into glory. The Son makes them disciples; the Spirit consoles them as friends; the Father bestows on them the glory of sons.[21]

Bernard does not wish his audience to be misled by this division into a quasi-Sabellian interpretation of the functions and activities of the persons of the Trinity:
> However, Truth is the proper title, not only of the Son alone, but of the Spirit and the Father too. So that it must be made quite clear, while giving full acknowledgment to the properties of the persons, that it is the one Truth who works at all these stages: in the first teaching as a master, in the second consoling as a friend and brother, in the third embracing as a father.[22]

The triune God, then, acts as teacher, friend, brother, and father. God is, in short, a lover who calls and carries the human person to the bliss of perfect union with himself:
> Those whom the Son beckoned to the first heaven by his humiliation, the Spirit brought to the second by love, and the Father raised to the third in contemplation. First they are humiliated in truth and say: 'In your truth you have humbled me' [Ps 118:75]. Then they rejoice in

the truth, singing: 'How good and pleasant it is, brothers dwelling in unity' [Ps 132:1], for we read that love rejoices in truth [1 Co 13:6]. Finally they are carried up to the hidden home of truth itself [2 Co 12:4], and there they say: 'My secret to myself, my secret to myself!' [Is 24:16].²³

In all this, it is clearly God who operates. Happiness, fulfillment, is the result of a salvific process, not of human initiative or accomplishment. The response is obvious, and Bernard has heard it: ' "What part do you play, then", asked a bystander, "or what reward or prize do you hope for, if it is all God's work?" '²⁴ The third stage, contemplation, is indeed all God's work, as Bernard sees it; and so I shall defer my discussion of contemplation to another section.²⁵ But humility and love require not only God's gift, but one's growing response. Contemplation is the conclusion of the educative process toward perfection; humility and love are the elements of that process. And to the co-operative stages we shall now turn.

In his *Apologia to Abbot William*, Bernard reaffirms the centrality of humility and love in human life and defines them by describing their opposites: '. . . Humility is lost when you put yourself on a pedestal, and love when you trample on others. . . .'²⁶ Humility and love provide the antidote to the diseases infecting the soul, '. . . misguided love of the world and excessive love of self [1 P 2:11]. . . .'²⁷ For Bernard, humility and love are divine precepts and cannot be called into question. Those who possess these virtues have acquired an enviable psychological stability, the security of a reasonable expectation of salvation:

> The sons of obedience [see 1 P 1:14] then have great security, that very peace promised to men of good will [see Lk 2:14]. For one cannot be damned unless one be impenitent, which is quite impossible for those who love God [see Lk 12:5]. No one can sin gravely except by pride, from which the fear of hell should suffice to restrain us.²⁹

This security is made possible by the gifts of God: the gift of human nature which includes the power of free choice (creating grace), and the gift of the power to choose the good (saving grace):

> For to will the good indicates an achievement, and to will the bad a defect, whereas simply to will denotes

the subject itself which does either the achieving or the failing. To this subject, however, creating grace gives existence. Saving grace makes it an achievement. But when it fails, it is to blame for its own failure. Free choice, accordingly, constitutes us willers; grace, willers of the good. Because of our willing faculty [a gift of creation], we are able to will; but, because of [saving] grace, to will the good.[30]

This is Bernard's answer to the question posed by the 'onlooker'.[31] One's happiness is indeed a gift which is 'all God's work'. But one must respond to that gift by not rejecting through free choice the gift of saving grace which enables, but does not force one to do the good.

The process of perfection is thus possible through God's generosity. God is also the goal, but the process of obtaining happiness in union with him is an arduous one:

Thanks to the help of him who called me, I have built a ladder to take me to it. This is my road to God's salvation [Ps 49:23]. Already I see God resting on the top of the ladder [Gn 28:12-13]; already I have the joy of hearing the voice of Truth. He calls to me, and I reply to him: 'Stretch out your right hand to the work of your hands' [Jb 14:15]. You have numbered my steps, O Lord [Jb 14:15], but I am a slow climber, a weary traveler, and I need a resting place. Woe is me if the darkness should overtake me [Jn 12:35], or if my flight should be in winter or on the Sabbath [Mt 24:20], seeing that now, in an acceptable time, on the day of salvation [2 Co 6:2], I can hardly grope my way to the light. Why am I so slow? O, if any is to me a son, a brother in the Lord, a comrade, one who shares my journey, let him pray for me! Let him pray to the Almighty that he may strengthen the weary foot and not let the foot of pride come nigh to me [Ps 35:12]. The weary foot is a poor help in climbing to the truth, but the other [foot] cannot even stand on the place it has gained: 'They are all cast out; they cannot stand' [Ps 35:13].[32]

A long and arduous ascent cannot be achieved by a single leap. The climb can only be accomplished by measured steps, by slow degrees, progressing only within the limits of human nature:

I am now able to see what I must seek for and receive
before I may hope to attain to a higher and holier state
[Mt 7:8]. I do not wish to be suddenly on the heights;
my desire is to advance by degrees. The impudence
of the sinner displeases God as much as the modesty
of the penitent gives him pleasure. You will please him
more readily if you live within the limits proper to you
and do not set your sights on things beyond you [Si
3:22]. It is a long and formidable leap from the foot [of
humility] to the mouth [of contemplation], a manner
of approach that is not commendable.[33]

But one should have confidence that day-by-day progress will be made in the realization of God's kingdom:

This kingdom is not yet wholly established among us.
But it comes closer by degrees each day, and daily, more
and more, it gradually extends its bounds. It does so
only in those whose interior self, with the help of God,
is renewed from day to day [see 2 Co 4:16].[34]

Confidence is indeed the motif which Bernard repeats throughout his song of human progress to perfection:

Even though we are children and have a long, a very
long and dangerous way to go, with such [angelic] protection what have we to fear?[35]

1. See, for example, Hugh of St. Victor, *Didascalion*, 2, 20. In the edition by Charles Henry Buttimer (Washington, D.C.: Catholic University Press, 1939) pp. 38-39.
2. Gra 14, 49; SBOp 3:201; CF 19:108-109.
3. Gra 14, 49; SBOp 3:201; CF 19:109.
4. See Hum 10, 28-21, 51; SBOp 3:38-55; CF 13:57-78.
5. RB 7. In the translation by David Parry, *Households of God: The Rule of St Benedict with Explanations for Monks and Laypeople Today*, CS 39 (Kalamazoo: Cistercian Publications, 1980) pp. 41-47.
6. Hum 3, 6; SBOp 3:20-21; CF 13:34.
7. Dil 8, 23-10, 29; SBOp 3:138-44; CF 13:115-21.
8. Div 41; SBOp 6/1:243-54; Luddy 3:461-80.
9. Div 40; SBOp 6/1:234-43; Luddy 3:444-60.
10. See, for example, George Bosworth Burch, 'Introduction' to *The Steps of Humility by Bernard, Abbot of Clairvaux* (Cambridge, Massachusetts: Harvard University Press, 1942) pp. 101-108.
11. SC 7, 2; SBOp 1:26-27; CF 4:38-39.
12. SC 3-9; SBOp 1:14-48; CF 4:16-60.
13. Par 1, 7; SBOp 6/2: 266; CSt 18:23.
14. See Leclercq, *Bernard of Clairvaux and the Cistercian Spirit*, p. 40.
15. Two classic works that were most influential in the formation of my understanding of Bernard's views on growth in the spiritual life are: Etienne Gilson, *The Mystical Theology of Saint Bernard*, trans. A.H.C. Downes (London, New York: Sheed and Ward, 1940); and Jean Leclercq, *Saint Bernard mystique* (n.p.: Desclée De Brouwer, 1948). My article, 'The Educational Theory of St. Bernard: The Role of Humility and Love', *Benedictine Review* 20 (1965) 25-32, contains, in preliminary form, some of the ideas in this section. See also Stiegman, pp. 171-98.
16. Hum 2, 5; SBOp 3:19; CF 13:33.
17. Hum 6, 19; SBOp 3:30-31; CF 13:47.
18. Hum 7, 20; SBOp 3:31; CF 13:47.
19. Hum 7, 20; SBOp 3:31; CF 13:47-48.
20. Hum 7, 20; SOBp 3:31; CF 13:48.
21. Hum 7, 20; SBOp 3:31; CF 13:48.
22. Hum 7, 20; SBOp 3:31; CF 13:48.
23. Hum 8, 23; SBOp 3:34-35; CF 13:52-53.
24. Gra 1, 1; SBOp 3:165; CF 19:53.
25. See below, pp. 213-249.
26. Apo 7, 13; SBOp 3:93; CF 1:50.
27. SC 1, 2; SBOp 1:3; CF 4:2.
28. Pre 1, 2; SBOp 3:255; CF 1:107.
29. Pre 12, 30; SBOp 3:274; CF 1:128.
30. Gra 6, 16; SBOp 3:177-78; CF 19:72. See Hum 14, 49; SBOp 3:201; CF 13:108-109.
31. See above, p. 47.
32. Hum 9, 24; SBOp 3:35; CF 13:53.
33. SC 3, 4; SBOp 1:16; CF 4:18-19.
34. Gra 4, 12; SBOp 3:175; CF 19:68.
35. QH 12, 8; SBOp 4:461-62; CF 25:219.

II. HUMILITY: THE PERFECTION OF THE INTELLECT

In Bernard's educational program, the first step on the path to perfection, to happiness, is humility. But humility does not mean for Bernard what it has so often meant in modern spirituality. Bernard's humility is not meekness; humility is not going about with hands piously folded and eyes meekly lowered. Bernard's humility is knowledge: 'To define humility: humility is a virtue by which a man has a low opinion of himself because he knows himself well.'[1] Humility then is an intellectual virtue; it is self-knowledge. Bernard is well aware that his is an ancient teaching: 'I am more concerned to know myself, as the Greek motto advises, that, with the Prophet, "I may know what is wanting in me."'[2]

If humility is self-knowledge, then it is clear that pride is self-deception:

> If the words of the Disciple do not impress you enough, perhaps you will take warning from the stern words of the Master: 'Hypocrite, first cast the beam from your own eye, and then you will see better to cast the mote from your brother's' [Mt 7:5]. The heavy, thick beam in the eye is pride of heart. It is big but not strong, swollen not solid. It blinds the eye of the mind and blots out the truth. While it is there you cannot see yourself as you really are, or even the ideal of what you could be, but what you would like to be—this you think you are or hope to be. For what else is pride but, as a saint [Augustine] has defined it, the love of one's own excellence. We may define humility as the opposite: contempt of one's own excellence.[3]

From this definition of pride one learns still more about Bernard's definition of humility. Humility is seeing oneself as one truly is; in humility one measures this self-knowledge against another knowledge, the knowledge of what one could be. Humility is a link between Bernard's anthropology and his educational theory. In humility one knows both the standard, what a human is, and the reality, what I am.

Since humility is a form of knowledge, the faculty which this virtue perfects is the intellect. Humility is an intellectual virtue. Humility is the right ordering of one's intellect, and humility is attained by reason:

> This is very important for you: you have need of strength, and not simply strength, but strength drawn from above [Lk 24:49]. For this strength, if it is perfect, will easily give the mind control of itself, and so it will be unconquered before all of its adversaries. It is a strength of mind which, in protecting reason, does not know how to retreat. Or, if you like, it is strength of mind standing steadfast with reason and for reason. Or again, it is a strength of mind which gathers up and directs everything toward reason.[4]

The rational activity of acquiring self-knowledge requires the gift of Reason; one's natural, rational power requires the perfection of grace:

> The Son of God, the Word and Wisdom of the Father, mercifully assumed to himself human reason, the first of our powers. He found it oppressed by the flesh [Ws 9:15], held captive by sin, blinded by ignorance, distracted by outward things. He raised it by his might, taught it by his wisdom, drew it to things interior. More wonderfully still, he delegated to it his own power of Judge. To judge is the proper act of Truth, and in this it is shared when, out of reverence for the Word to which it is joined, it became accuser, witness, and judge against itself. Humility had been born from the union of the Word with human reason.[5]

As we have seen,[6] Bernard assigns the perfection of the intellect in humility to the Second Person of the Trinity, to the Word, to Reason itself.

A rightly ordered intellect is able to see the right order of things, and this is justice. The humble are thus able to imitate the Son as judges. The humble are just, and do not appropriate to themselves that which belongs to another, to God:

> The just man, of course, refuses to appropriate to himself the glory of God; he refuses to accept it when it is offered by another. If he is just, he justly pursues what is just. He does not practice his justice before men [Mt 6:1], and, even though he is just, he does not hold his head high. This virtue consists especially in humility. It purifies his intention and obtains greater and more effective merit in arrogating less to self.[7]

Justice requires that one appreciate both the power of God and one's own weakness.

The humble know both: 'Humility has two feet: appreciation of divine power and consciousness of personal weakness.'[8] But the humble know more; they know that their lowliness is more than compensated for by the fatherly love of the Son:

> What wonder that the cry of the humble should reach to him [the Son] whose dwelling-place [Ex 2:23] is at that source of all kindliness, where his happiness is most intimate and his goodness consubstantial with the Father. And the timorous glance will see in his royal power nothing that is not fatherly. Therefore the Lord says: 'Because the poor are despoiled, because the needy groan, I will now arise' [Ps 11:6]. The bride knows this because she is a well-loved member of his household. She knows that her Bridegroom's favors will not be limited by the poverty of her merits, for she puts her trust solely in her lowliness.[9]

It is in light of Bernard's confidence in God's love that we can best read his many seemingly negative assessments of the human condition. In humility, one does indeed know oneself as 'nothing':

> We can think of him [the Prophet] as saying: When as yet I did not fully know the truth, I thought myself something, whereas I was nothing [Ga 6:3]. But when I had come to know Christ, to imitate his humility, I saw the truth and exalted it in me by my confession. But 'I myself was humbled exceedingly' [Ps 115:10]; in my own eyes I fell very low.[10]

One is properly humble in '...acknowledging one's own defects';[11] the humble do indeed have '...contempt for their own excellence'.[12] But this realistic and honest self-assessment leads to a reliance on the loving kindness which the humble know awaits them:

> When men know themselves in the light of truth and so think less of themselves, it will certainly follow that what they loved before will now become bitter to them. They are brought face to face with themselves and blush at what they see. Their present state is no pleasure to them. They aspire to something better and, at the same time, realize how little they can rely on themselves to

achieve it. It hurts them, and they find some relief in judging themselves severely. Love of truth makes them hunger and thirst after justice [Mt 5:6] and conceive a deep contempt for themselves....They fly from justice to mercy.[13]

That mercy is necessary. To discover this truth, Bernard urges honest self-appraisal:

> I wish, therefore, that before everything else a man should know himself, because not only usefulness but right order demands this. Right order, since what we are is our first concern. And usefulness because this knowledge gives humility rather than self-importance; it provides a basis on which to build. For, unless there is a durable foundation of humility [1 Co 3:12], the spiritual edifice has no hope of standing [Mk 3:25]. And there is nothing more effective, more adapted to the acquiring of humility than to find out the truth about oneself. There must be no dissimulation, no attempt at self-deception, but a facing up to one's real self without flinching and turning aside.[14]

The truth that results from this honest self-evaluation is a hard truth but a necessary one:

> When a man thus takes stock of himself in the clear light of truth, he will discover that he lives in a region in which likeness to God has been forfeited, and, groaning from the depths of a misery to which he can no longer remain blind, will he not cry out to the Lord as the Prophet did: 'In your truth you have humbled me' [Ps 118:75]? How can he escape being genuinely humbled on acquiring this true self-knowledge, on seeing the burden of sin that he carries [2 Tm 3:6], the oppressive weight of his mortal body, the complexities of earthly cares, the corrupting influence of sensual desires; on seeing his blindness, his worldliness, his weakness, his embroilment in repeated errors; on seeing himself exposed to a thousand dangers, trembling amid a thousand fears, confused by a thousand difficulties, defenseless before a thousand suspicions, worried by a thousand needs; one to whom vice is welcome, virtue repugnant? Can this man afford haughty eyes, a proud lift of the

head [Si 23:5]? With the thorns of his misery pricking him, will he not rather be changed for the better [Ps 31:4]?[15]

Change for the better, growth in the spiritual life is the happy result of realistically confronting one's unhappy condition.

But self-knowledge comprises more—much more. Knowledge of our weakness and God's loving mercy must be complemented and completed by knowledge of our '. . . dignity and also the other good qualities that are in us, in us but not of us.'[16] Our creation has bestowed on us great dignity; true humility demands that we see and acknowledge that dignity:

> Therefore, dignity without knowledge is unprofitable; without virtue it can become an obstacle. The following reasoning explains both these facts. What glory is there in having something you do not know you have? Then, to know what you have but to be ignorant of the fact that you do not have it of yourself, this is for glory here, but not before God [Rm 4:2]. The Apostle says to him who glorifies himself: 'What have you that you have not received? And, if you have received it, how can you boast of it as if you had not received it [1 Co 4:7]?' He does not say simply: 'How can you boast of it,' but adds: 'as if you had not received it', to show that the guilt lies not in boasting of something but in treating it as if it were not a gift received. This is rightly called vainglory, for it lacks a solid base of truth. Saint Paul marks the difference between true and vain glory: 'He who boasts, let him boast in the Lord' [1 Co 1:31; 2 Co 10:17], that is, in the truth, for the Lord is truth [Jn 14:6].[17]

Realistic, honest appraisal of oneself leads to knowledge of one's weakness and one's strength.

In humility, one knows one's strength and the source of that strength, which is God: 'There are two facts you should know—first, what you are; secondly, that you are not that by your own power—lest you fail to boast at all or do so in vain.'[18] The true boast is one which glories in the gifts God gives and then glorifies the giver:

> On receiving such a grace, then, you must kiss his hand, that is, you must give glory to his name, not to your-

self [Ps 113:9]. First of all you must glorify him because he has forgiven your sins, secondly because he has adorned you with virtues.[19]

When honored for one's virtue, one should remember the source all the more:

> When promised pendants of gold, she [the bride] acquiesced with humility; the more she is honored the more she humbles herself in all things. She does not boast of her merits or forget her humility when she hears her praises multiplied....[20]

Indeed, the properly humble response to the praise and to the virtues praised should not be dissimulation but gratitude:

> I know that there are some who are, as it were, wisely ignorant of the gifts they have received from the Lord, for fear they may become puffed up with pride and fall into the snare of the Devil if they pay any attention to them [see 1 Tm 3:6]. But, for myself, I think it a good thing to know what I have received from the Lord, 'so that I may know what I lack' [Ps 38:5]. And, with the Apostle, I think it my duty 'to recognize what God has bestowed on us' [1 Co 2:12], so that I may know for what to pray and sigh. A man who has received a gift and yet does not know what sort of gift it is stands in the twofold danger of being both ungrateful for what he has received and careless in guarding it. How can a man return thanks for a gift if he does not know he has received it?[21]

The humble know they are sinners, and they know they are forgiven: '...The humble man accuses himself, knowing that God will not judge him a second time [Na 1:9], and that if we judge ourselves we shall indeed escape judgment.'[22] The humble know themselves as at once inferior, equal, and indeed superior to others—in some, if not all respects.[23] The truly humble know that both overconfidence in one's power and despair at one's weakness are the results of ignorance, of pride; they know that 'Christ has wondrously cured those laboring under differing and even opposite infirmities with a single medicine, his cross....'[24]

The redemptive act, symbolized and effected by the cross, is the source of one's growth in humility. True humility demands that one recognize the source of that humility: 'But, God, you know my stupidity [Ps 68:5], unless, perhaps, it is wisdom for me to recognize it—and even this is your gift.'[25] Knowledge of the ready availability of that gift gives confidence to one beginning the hard process, the long pilgrimage toward humility:

> Supposing, then, that you go on to the object: 'I see the way—humility; I long for the goal to which it leads—truth. But what if the way is so difficult that I can never reach the goal?' The answer comes promptly: 'I am the life', that is, 'I am the food, the viaticum, to sustain you on your journey.'[26]

And the end of the journey makes its hardships worthwhile. For the reward of the traveler, the peak attained by the climber, is truth:

> If a man wants to know the full truth about himself, he will have to get rid of the beam of pride which blocks out the light from his eye [Mt 7:5], and then set up in his heart a ladder of humility so that he can search into himself. When he has climbed its twelve rungs he will then stand on the first step of truth. When he has seen the truth about himself, or better, when he has seen himself in truth, he will be able to say: 'I believed, therefore I have spoken; but I have been exceedingly humbled' [Ps 115:10]. Such a man has come to a deep heart [Ps 63:7], and truth is exalted....[27]

And in the process, Bernard thinks, one is exalted as well:

> This [humility] is the virtue that belongs to those who have set their heart on the climb and have gone from virtue to virtue, from step to step, until they reached the highest peak of humility and gazed on truth from the watch-tower of Zion [Ps 83:6].[28]

The truth thus attained is more precious than any other:

> Although you know every mystery—the width of the earth, the height of the heavens, the depth of the sea—if you do not know yourself you are like a building without foundation; you raise not a structure but ruins [see Lk 6:49]. Whatever you construct outside yourself will be but a pile of dust blown by the wind.[29]

For humility is the starting point in the process of perfection: 'Indeed, humility is the true and firm foundation of the virtues.'[30] To accomplish the good, one must know the good:

> Your soul has received great profit if your will is unswerving and your reason enlightened, willing and

recognizing the good. By the first she receives life and, by the second, vision; for she was dead when she desired evil and blind when she did not recognize the good.[31]
One who knows the good, and acts on it, will receive the gift of life and lead the good life:

> My beloved, you must persevere in the lesson you have learned: raise yourself up by humility. That is the way; there is no other. He who seeks to make progress in some other way falls more quickly than he climbs. Humility alone exalts and leads to life.[32]

Bernard's models for the humble life are Christ and his Mother. Bernard prays that he may imitate Christ in humility, thus following Jesus' own admonition:

> Of all his virtues, and he possessed them all, Christ specially commends one to us, humility. 'Learn from me, for I am gentle and humble in heart' [Mt 11:29]. How glad I too should be, Lord Jesus, if I could, in my infirmity, in the shrinking of my sinew [see Gn 32:25; 2 Co 12:9], that your virtue, your humility, might be made perfect in me.[33]

Bernard sees the humility of Jesus in every event in his life. The Incarnation was the Son's initial great act of humility:

> 'He emptied himself, taking the form of a servant' [Ph 2:7], and so gave us the pattern of humility. He emptied himself, he humbled himself, not under constraint of an assessment of himself but inspired by love for us.[34]

Jesus' humble birth should also inspire imitation: 'Why, my brother, or by what necessity has the Lord of majesty so humbled himself, so emptied himself, so shortened [see Rm 9:28] himself, unless to induce us to do likewise?'[35] Jesus' hidden early years are likewise an example:

> Until when, O noble king, O king of heaven, will you allow yourself to be known as and be called the son of a carpenter?. . . Did Christ, keeping silence so long, hiding himself for so many years, fear vainglory?. . . He feared, yes, but not for himself but for us. . . .He warned us; he taught us. He kept his mouth closed, but he taught us by his action. . . .[36]

Bernard sees Jesus' passion as an overwhelmingly impressive act of humility:

He had ceased to be 'beautiful above the sons of men' [Ps 44:3], to become the reproach of the world, and, as a leper, the vilest of mortals, truly a man of sorrows, struck and humiliated by God so that he had no longer form or comeliness. O vilest of men and, at the same time, most exalted! O man humbled and yet so preeminent! There is none so great as he, and none more despised. He is covered with spittle, wearied with insults, condemned to a shameful death, and numbered among the wicked. What merit does not belong to such immeasurable humility?[37]

Bernard wonders at Jesus' passion and at the pride of those '... who carry Christ's cross without following him, who share in his sufferings with no thought of imitating his humility.'[38] Bernard admonishes his audience:

... Because he is gentle and humble in heart, let us learn from him, lest he who is great, even God, should have been made a little man, lest he should have died for no purpose [Ga 2:21] and have been crucified in vain. Let us learn his humility, imitate his gentleness, embrace his love, share his sufferings [1 P 4:13], be washed in his blood [Rv 1:5].[39]

Unless humans heed this admonition, their ascent to perfection will be an impossible climb:

'Who dares climb the mountain of the Lord; who will stand in his holy place [Ps 23:3]?' Only he who has learned from the Lord Jesus Christ how to be gentle and humble in heart.[40]

For Bernard, the most profound response to the model of Christ's humility was that of Mary, his mother:

... He wanted her to be humble as well, someone of whom he could himself be born gentle and humble in heart, because he intended to give all mankind the necessary and most beneficial example of these virtues. So now he gave the blessing of childbirth to the virgin in whom he had first inspired the vow of virginity and from whom he had first demanded humility.[41]

Mary's response was exemplary:

So that she might conceive and give birth to the Holy of Holies [Dn 9:24] she was made holy in her body by the gift of virginity, and she accepted that gift of humility to become holy in spirit too.[42]

Mary's response evokes Bernard's prayerful admiration:

> O, if you only knew how pleasing your humility is to the Most High and what greatness has been prepared for you close to him, then you would not consider yourself too unworthy of this greeting [the angelic salutation] and this homage.[43]

One's happiness, like Mary's, begins in a life humbly led.

Bernard seems never to tire of this teaching. Writing to Pope Eugenius, he declares: 'A good estate is humility, on which every spiritual building is constructed and grows into a holy temple in the Lord' [Eph 2:21].[44] The motif is sounded throughout Bernard's sermons on the liturgical year. Christmas finds him urging: 'Be diligent in acquiring humility, which is the foundation and guardian of the virtues...',[45] and '...The virtue of humility is the sole way to repair the harm done to love.'[46] The Ascension finds Bernard recognizing and rejoicing in the humility his audience has attained: 'I seem to see signs of your calling, your justification in the humble lives you lead.'[47] This humility is truly pleasing to God, one learns on the first Sunday in November, for 'Nothing can give him pleasure, in angels or in men, but humility alone....'[48]

Humility is a theme which runs throughout Bernard's sermons on the *Song of Songs*; in *Sermon 37*, for example, he reminds his audience that '...no one is saved without self-knowledge, since it is the source of that humility on which salvation depends, and of the fear of the Lord that is as much the beginning of salvation as of wisdom [Ps 110:10; Si 1:16].[49] In *Sermon 57*, Bernard maintains that humility is the condition of one's union with God:

> So sagacious is she [the bride], so experienced, so keenly vigilant, that she spied him [the Bridegroom] coming a long way off. She heeded him leaping as he sped along, bounding over the proud [Sg 2:8], that, through humility, he might draw near to her who is humble.[50]

Bernard's letters echo the theme; for example, his letter to Thomas, the provost of Beverley:

> ...Thus a man is justified so that he begins to know himself even as he is known. [In humility] he begins to experience something of his future blessedness, as

it has lain hidden from all eternity in God who foreordained it, to appear all the more plainly when he confers it.[51]

Naturally Bernard sings his refrain loudly, clearly, and repeatedly in his *Steps of Humility* where 'The way is humility, the goal is truth. The first is the labor, the second the reward.'[52] For '... truth is hidden from the proud and made known to the humble.'[53] At the top of Jacob's ladder, above the highest step of humility, stands God whose place '... shows us that the knowledge of truth is to be found only at the summit of humility.'[54] At that summit, Truth will refresh with love those who have scaled the ladder:[55] 'When Christ came he brought grace; when truth is known it brings love....'[56]

In his penultimate sermon on the *Song of Songs*, Bernard's appreciation of humility assumes a rapturous quality:

> There is nothing clearer than the transparent goodness which is the light of truth shining in the mind. There is nothing more glorious than the mind which sees itself in the truth.[57]

In humility the intellect can ultimately transcend its natural capabilities and become fecund in its union with the Word:

> Humility, my brothers, is a great virtue, great and sublime. It can attain to what it cannot learn. It is counted worthy to possess what it has not the power to possess. It is worthy to conceive by the Word and from the Word what it cannot itself explain in words.[58]

Bernard's message is clear: knowing of the reward, who would not seek the treasure of humility? The question that comes in response is equally clear: how?

1. Hum 1, 2; SBOp 3:17; CF 13:30.
2. SC 23, 9; SBOp 1:144; CF 7:33.
3. Hum 4, 14; SBOp 3:26-27; CF 13:42. See Div 47; SBOp 6/1: 267.
4. SC 85, 4; SBOp 2:310; CF 40:200.
5. Hum 7, 21; SBOp 3:32; CF 13:48-49.
6. See above, p. 45.
7. QH 14, 10; SBOp 4:475; CF 25:238.
8. Ep 393, 3; SBOp 8:367; James, p. 296.
9. SC 42, 10; SBOp 2:39-40; CF 7:218.
10. Hum 4, 15; SBOp 3:28; CF 13:44.
11. Apo 1, 3; SBOp 3:83; CF 1:36.
12. Mor 5, 19; SBOp 7:115.
13. Hum 5, 18; SBOp 3:29; CF 13:45-46.
14. SC 36, 5; SBOp 2:7; CF 7:177-78.
15. SC 36, 5; SBOp 2:7; CF 7:178.
16. Dil 2, 3; SBOp 3:121; CF 13:95.
17. Dil 2, 3; SBOp 3:121-22; CF 13:95-96.
18. Dil 2, 4; SBOp 3:122; CF 13:96.
19. SC 3, 4; SBOp 1:16; CF 4:19. See also SC 4, 3; SBOp 1:19; CF 4:22-23.
20. SC 42, 9; SBOp 2:39; CF 7:217.
21. Ep 372; SBOp 8:333; James, p. 485.
22. Tpl 8, 14; SBOp 3:227; CF 19:150.
23. SC 23, 6; SBOp 1:142; CF 7:30.
24. Par 6; SBOp 6/2:293; CSt 21:106.
25. SC 20, 1; SBOp 1:114; CF 4:148.
26. Hum 1, 1; SBOp 3:17; CF 13:29-30.
27. Hum 4, 15; SBOp 3:27-28; CF 13:43.
28. Hum 1, 2; SBOp 3:17; CF 13:30. See also SC 36, 6 (SBOp 2:8; CF 7:179) and Div 9, 2 (SBOp 6/1:119).
29. Csi 2, 3, 6; SBOp 3:414; CF 37:53.
30. Csi 5, 14, 32; SBOp 3:493; CF 37:179.
31. SC 85, 2; SBOp 2:308; CF 40:197.
32. Asc 2, 6; SBOp 5:130; Luddy 2:237-38.
33. Hum 9, 25-26; SBOp 3:36; CF 13:54.
34. SC 42, 7; SBOp 2:37; CF 7:215.
35. Nat 1, 1; SBOp 4:244-45; Luddy 1:381.
36. Epi 1, 7; SBOp 4:299; Luddy 2:12-13.
37. IV HM 3; SBOp 5:58. Déchanet has found some seventy passages in Bernard's works devoted to the humiliations of Christ. See Jean-Marie Déchanet, 'Les fondements et les bases de la spiritualité bernardine', Cîteaux 4 (1953) 302.
38. Apo 1, 2; SBOp 3:82; CF 1:36.
39. Miss 3, 14; SBOp 4:45; CF 18:44.
40. Ep 393, 2; SBOp 8:366; James, p. 296.
41. Miss 2, 1; SBOp 4:22; CF 18:15-16.
42. Miss 2, 2; SBOp 4:22; CF 18:16.
43. Miss 3, 10; SBOp 4:42-43; CF 18:41.
44. Csi 2, 6, 13; SBOp 3:421; CF 37:63.
45. Nat 1, 1; SBOp 4:245; Luddy 1:382.
46. Nat 2, 6; SBOp 4:256; Luddy 1:396.
47. Asc 2, 5; SBOp 5:129; Luddy 2:237.

48. I Nov 2, 3; SBOp 5:309; Luddy 2:351.
49. SC 37, 1; SBOp 2:9; CF 7:181.
50. SC 57, 2; SBOp 2:120; CF 31:96.
51. Ep 107, 10; SBOp 7:274; James, p. 163.
52. Hum 1, 1; SBOp 3:16; CF 13:29.
53. Hum 1, 1; SBOp 3:17; CF 13:30.
54. Hum 2, 3; SBOp 3:18; CF 13:31.
55. Hum 2, 3; SBOp 3:18; CF 13:32.
56. Hum 2, 5; SBOp 3:20; CF 13:34.
57. SC 85, 10; SBOp 2:314; CF 40:206-207.
58. SC 85, 14; SBOp 2:316; CF 40:210.

A. Meditation

Bernard is convinced that perfection cannot be obtained by instantaneous sanctification. Education in virtue, the eduction of one's true capabilities is a process:

> No one attains perfection at a single bound. It is not by rapid flight but by laborious climbing that we reach the topmost rung of the ladder. Let us mount, therefore, with the two feet of meditation and prayer. The former will point the way; the latter will lead us along it. By meditation, then, we may discover the dangers which threaten us, and by prayer we may avoid them....[1]

The attainment of humility, of self-knowledge, clearly requires reflection on self. The perfection of the intellect clearly requires the use of that intellect. In short, consideration (an often-used equivalent of meditation) is not contemplation:[2]

> First of all, consider what it is I call consideration. For I do not want it to be understood as entirely synonymous with contemplation. The latter concerns more what is certainly known, while consideration pertains more to the investigation of what is unknown. Consequently, contemplation may be defined as the mind's true and sure intuition, the apprehension of truth without doubt. Consideration, on the other hand, can be defined as thought searching for truth, the mind's searching to discern truth. Nevertheless, both terms are often used interchangeably.[3]

The human mind seeks truth in meditation, '...consideration seeks...',[4] by means of the natural gift of reason, a gift humans share with the angels: 'You and the angels have one excellence in common: reason....'[5] But one's reflections in consideration or meditation also require God's inspiration:

> The word of God, winged with the Holy Spirit's fire, can cook the raw reflections of the sensual man, giving them a spiritual meaning that feeds the mind, inspiring him to say: 'My heart became hot within me, and as I meditated a fire burst forth' [Ps 38:4].[6]

For Bernard, it is this inspiration which distinguishes meditation from common-sense reflection and what he calls scientific investigation. He makes a clear distinction between what he calls practical consideration, through which we discover, on a day-to-day basis, what we should do; scientific consideration, which is the analytic process we employ in intellectual disciplines such as theology, philosophy, history, or natural science; and speculative consideration, which is meditation properly so called:[7]

> Do you wish these kinds of consideration to be distinguished by their proper names? If it be acceptable, let us call the first practical, the second scientific, the third speculative. The definitions will indicate the rationale behind these names. Consideration is practical when it uses the senses and sense objects in an orderly and unified manner to win God's favor. Consideration is scientific when it prudently and diligently scrutinizes and ponders everything to discover God. Consideration is speculative when it recollects itself and, insofar as it is aided by God, frees itself for the contemplation of God.[8]

True meditation requires both the rational, natural activity of the human mind and the gift of inspiration which fructifies that activity.

The effects of meditation are many and salutary for Bernard:

> Now, of primary importance is the fact that consideration purifies its source, that is, the mind. Notice also that it controls the emotions, guides actions, corrects excesses, improves behavior, confers dignity and order on life, and even imparts knowledge of divine and human affairs. It puts an end to confusion, closes gaps, gathers up what has been scattered, roots out secrets, hunts down truth, scrutinizes what seems to be true, and explores lies and deceit. Consideration anticipates adversity and, when adversity comes, it stands firm....[9]

Meditation is the process by which one discovers the right ordering of things--and human relationships--which, as we have seen, is justice:

> Now, concerning justice, one of the four virtues, is it not a fact that consideration guides the mind into conformity with this virtue? For the mind must first reflect on itself to deduce the norm of justice, which is not to do to another what one would not wish done to oneself nor deny another what one wishes for oneself [Mt 7:12]. In these two rules the entire nature of justice is made clear.[10]

But it is not only justice which one discovers by meditation; one also discovers that the right ordering of things is infused and informed by love:

> Whoever meditates on this [God's love] is, I believe, sufficiently aware why man ought to love God, that is, why God deserves to be loved. . . .Hence it is no wonder that he [man] loves him [God] less whom he knows less.[11]

Just as one learns to be just by discovering justice, one learns to love by meditation on God's love:

> What else is achieved by meditating on such great and so undeserved mercy, such gratuitous and so proved a love, such unexpected condescension, undaunted mildness, and astonishing kindness? What else, I insist, will all these carefully considered qualities achieve if they do not, in a wonderful way, captivate the mind of him who, completely freed from all unworthy love, considers them? Those qualities attract the mind deeply so that it despises in comparison whatever cannot be desired without despising them. Then the bride surely runs more eagerly in the odor of their perfumes [Sg 1:3]. She loves ardently, yet, even when she finds herself completely in love, she thinks she loves too little because she is loved so much.[12]

In '. . . readings, meditations, prayers, contemplations, precious fabrics will be unrolled. . . .'[13]

The subjects of meditation are oneself, that which is below and around oneself, and that which is above oneself. Bernard advises Pope Eugenius:

> Now to achieve the fruit of consideration, I think you should consider four things in this order: yourself, what is below you, around you, and above you.[14]

Truly to know oneself, one must know oneself in relationship to others, to the natural world, and to God.

> Consideration of, meditation on oneself should include . . . what you are, who you are, and what sort of man you are: what you are in nature, who you are in person, and what sort of man you are in character.[15]

One should examine too what one does and one's motivations in so acting. Bernard gives a negative example in the monk who

'...swallows all the praise others give him. He is quite complacent about his conduct, and he never examines his motives....'[16] He is thus confirmed in his own self-delusion.[17] Honest appraisal of one's motivations will reveal much that is disquieting:

> For if you sincerely examine your inward dispositions in the light of truth, and judge them unflatteringly for what they are, you will certainly be made humble by the baseness that this true knowledge reveals to you....[18]

One should 'Tear off the covering of leaves which hides your shame but does not heal your wound.'[19] This honesty will result in gracious forgiveness which will, in turn, restore right order in one:

> ...Only let us confess our inequities, and for the glory of his grace, he [God] will justify us freely. For he loves the soul who is constantly examining herself in his sight and judging herself with sincerity.[20]

And this justification will lead one to a state in which one '...will not reach out to other things in vain because one has neglected oneself.'[21]

Meditation on one's own condition is helped immeasurably by consideration of the world around oneself: 'Look over the earth, that you may know yourself. It speaks to you of yourself because "Dust you are, and to dust you shall return [Gn 3:19]." '[22] Consideration of that world reveals the glory of material creation:

> And consider first of all the creation of the universe and the disposition and ordering of all its various parts. What a display of power in the production of a world out of nothingness! What benignity in their manifold combination![23]

And the glory of the world is compounded by the addition of life to matter:

> Reflect on the multitude and magnitude of the things created by almighty power, how wisely they are distributed, with how much goodness they have been compounded, the highest being united to the lowest, with a love as amiable as it is admirable. For to the dust of earth has been added the vital force, as, for instance, in the trees, where its presence is manifested in the beauty of the foliage, in the brilliancy of the flowers, and in the sweetness and wholesomeness of the fruit.

> Not content with thus ennobling our common clay, the Creator has further endowed it with the principle of sentiency in the brute beasts, which are not only gifted with life but also possess a fivefold faculty of perception.[24]

The glory of nature is enhanced still further by the creation of humankind. One should consider that

> He [God] has not stopped even at this, but in order to honor the material element still more, he has associated with it the rational soul in the case of man, who, in addition to life and sensibility, is invested with the power of discriminating between what is helpful and what is harmful, between good and evil, between truth and falsity.[25]

If one is to remember that one is but dust, one should meditate on one's glorious nature, a nature which, among other things, includes the very power to meditate which Bernard urges one to employ to one's benefit.

Material, vegetable, animal, and human existence are all worthy of meditative attention. Their source must also be the object of one's considerations. Reflection on one's weakness should turn one to mediation on God, whose goodness will overcome that weakness:

> As for me, as long as I look at myself, my eye is filled with bitterness [Jb 17:2]. But if I look up and fix my eyes on the aid of the divine mercy, this happy vision of God soon tempers the bitter vision of myself, and I say to him: 'I am disturbed within, so I will call you to mind from the land of Jordan' [Ps 41:7]. This vision of God is not a little thing. It reveals him to us as listening compassionately to our prayers, as truly kind and merciful, as one who will not indulge his resentment [Jb 2:13]....[26]

Self-knowledge is thus a means to knowledge of God:

> ...His very nature is to be good, to show mercy always, and to spare. By this kind of experience and in this way, God makes himself known to us for our good. When a man first discovers that he is in difficulty, he will cry out to the Lord, who will hear him [Ps 90:15], and say: 'I will deliver you, and you shall glorify me' [Ps 49:15]. In this way your self-knowledge will be a step to the knowledge of God; he will become visible

to you according as his image is being restored within
you....[27]

If self-knowledge is a means to knowledge of God's nature, it is also true that reflection on that nature enhances one's knowledge of self. And that knowledge includes the fact that, through God's gifts, his likeness is being restored in one's soul--a soul marred by sin.[28] The restoration of the intellect consists in its ability to see the truth of things as they are. Meditation on God not only brings humility, the perfection of the intellect, it also benefits the will, perfecting it in love:

> A second kind [of meditation] is necessary: it consists in observing the judgments of God. While this meditation disturbs the onlooker by its fearful aspect, it drives out vices, establishes virtues, initiates into wisdom, preserves humility.... The third meditation is occupied, or, rather, takes leisure in, the remembrance of blessings, and, lest it abandon a person as ungrateful, it urges the rememberer toward love for his benefactor. Of such the Prophet speaks, saying to the Lord: 'They shall declare the memory of the abundance of your sweetness' [Ps 144:7].[29]

Since the will can choose only what the intellect knows, God's will is a very appropriate object of one's reflection because it is this will to which the meditator must learn to conform his own will:

> Scrutinizing God's majesty is then a fearful thing, but scrutinizing his will is as safe as it is dutiful. Why should I not tirelessly concentrate on searching into the mystery of his glorious will, which I know I must obey in all things?[30]

Meditation on the things above us, which Bernard urges on one experienced in the process of perfection,[31] should also include subjects other than God for reflection. This is especially useful to those still in the early stages of the process:

> Accordingly, she [the Church] dwells in the clefts of the rock through her perfect [members] who, by the purity of their conscience, dare to explore and penetrate the secrets of wisdom--and can achieve this by their keenness of mind. As for the crannies of the wall, those who of themselves are unable or will not presume to dig in the rock, let them dig in the wall, content to gaze mentally on the glory of the saints. If even this is not

possible to someone, let him place before himself Jesus
and him crucified [1 Co 2:2], that, without effort on
his part, he may dwell in those clefts of the rock at
whose hollowing he has not labored [Jn 4:38].[32]

If '... the majesty, the eternity, and the dignity...'[33] of God seem
to the beginner too exalted for meditation, that beginner may concentrate his or her consideration on '... the state and happiness
and glory of the heavenly city, in which either by activity or by
repose a great crowd of its citizens are engaged....'[34] Meditation
on the events of salvific history, on the life of Christ and its effect
on the life of the saints, is a source of great consolation:

'The angel of the Lord encamps around those who fear
him' [Ps 33:8]. If that is accepted, the meaning will be
that two things console the Church in the time and place
of its pilgrimage [Ps 118:54]: from the past, the memory of Christ's passion, and, for the future, the thought
and confidence of being welcomed among the saints
[Col 1:12]. In these glimpses of the past and future she
contemplates both events with an insatiable longing;
each aspect is entirely pleasing to her, each a refuge
from the distress of troubles and from sorrow [Pss 31:7;
106:39]. Her consolation is complete, since she knows
not only what to hope for but also the ground of her
confidence.[35]

The effects of salvific history on the lives of fellow pilgrims on
the path to perfection is likewise available to '... studious and devout minds... by thought and eager desire.'[36] One should strive

... to visit the patriarchs now, to salute the prophets
now, to mingle with the assembly of apostles now, to
slip into the choirs of martyrs now, even to run, with
all the swiftness of mind that devotion can inspire,
through the orders and dwellings of the blessed spirits,
from the smallest angel to the Cherubim and Seraphim.[37]

But Bernard maintains that experienced minds should not fear to
go beyond the things and saintly people of God to consideration
of God himself:

Happy the mind which frequently works at hollowing
a place for itself in this wall [of heavenly things], but
happier still the one which does so in the rock [of God
himself]! For it is all right to hollow even in the rock;

but for this the mind must have a keener edge, a more eager purpose, and merits of a higher order.[38]

Though Bernard assigns the highest place to meditation on God himself and a lower to meditation on Christ's life, the great bulk of the reflections he has shared with others are on the life of Christ—perhaps because of his perception of the spiritual maturity of his audience. He often combines the fruits of his reflections on Christ with admonitions to do likewise. For example, in *Sermon 11 on the Song of Songs*:

> Now with regard to the manner [of the redemption], which if you remember, we defined as God's self-emptying, I venture to offer three important points for your consideration. For that emptying was neither a simple gesture nor a limited one. But he emptied himself even to assuming human nature, even to accepting death, death on a cross [Ph 2:7f.]. Who is there who can adequately gauge the greatness of the humility, gentleness, self-surrender, revealed by the Lord of majesty in assuming human nature, in accepting the punishment of death, the shame of the cross?[39]

This is an admonition, perhaps even a challenge, to attempt that gauging. Bernard continues:

> For, more obvious than the light of day is the immense sacrifice he has made for you, O man. He who was Lord became a slave; he who was rich became a pauper; the Word was made flesh; and the Son of God did not disdain to become the son of man. So, may it please you to remember that, even if made out of nothing, you have not been redeemed out of nothing. In six days he created all things, and among them you. On the other hand, for a period of thirty whole years he worked your salvation in the midst of earth [Ps 73:12]. What endurance was his in his labors! To his bodily needs and the molestations of his enemies did he not add the mightier burden of the ignominy of the cross, and crown it all with the horror of his death?... Meditate on these things; turn them over continually in your minds.[40]

Bernard's *Sermons on the Song of Songs* are filled with reflections on the life of Christ and the salutary effects of such meditation. That meditation is essential to one's progress on the path to perfection:

> Concerning this work [of redemption], I wish to suggest for your consideration two important points that now occur to me.... The two are manner and fruit. The manner involved the self-emptying of God; the fruit was that we should be filled with him. Meditation on the former is the seed-bed of holy hope; meditation on the latter an incentive to the highest love. Both of them are essential for our progress because hope without love is the lot of the time-server and love without hope grows cold.[41]

In *Sermon 25*, he reminds his audience: 'Happy the man who, by attentive study of your [Christ's] life as a man among men [Ba 3:38], strives according to his strength to live like you.'[42] In *Sermon 43*, he indicates how helpful meditation on Christ's passion was to him as a young man:

> ...Preserve without fail the memory of all those bitter things he endured for you; persevere in meditating on him and you will be able in turn to say: 'My beloved is to me a little bunch of myrrh that lies between my breasts' [Sg 1:12]. As for me, dear brothers, from the earliest days of my conversion, conscious of my grave lack of merits, I made sure to gather for myself this little bunch of myrrh and place it between my breasts....[43]

In the same sermon, Bernard describes the abundant fruits of such meditation:

> I have said that wisdom is to be found in meditating on these truths. For me they are the source of perfect righteousness, of the fullness of knowledge [Is 33:6], of the most efficacious graces, of abundant merits. Sometimes I draw from them a drink that is wholesomely bitter, sometimes an unction that is sweet and consoling. When I am in difficulties they bear me up; when I am happy they regulate my conduct....[44]

In *Sermon 45*, Bernard commends his hearer for his progress through meditation on Christ's life. He has Christ say to him:

> You no longer occupy yourself with great affairs or marvels beyond your scope [Ps 130:1], but, like that guileless bird who builds her nest in the crevices of the rock [Sg 2:14], you are content to be unpretentious, to lin-

ger near my wounds, happy to contemplate with dove-like eyes the mysteries of my incarnation and passion.[45]
In *Sermon 61*, Bernard casts Christ in the role of a beneficent leader who inspires his followers through reflection on his battlescars:

> ...The kindly captain wants the faithful soldier to lift up face and eyes to his own wounds and, by his own example, to give him greater courage to endure.[46]

In *Sermon 62*, Bernard asks rhetorically: 'What greater cure is there for the wounds of conscience and for purifying the mind's acuity than to persevere in meditation on the wounds of Christ?'[47] Meditation on Christ is indeed the means to the humility which perfects the intellect.[48]

One of Bernard's most impressive affirmations of the efficacy of meditation on the life of Christ occurs in his sixth *Parable*, 'The Story of the Ethiopian Woman Whom the King's Son Took as His Wife':

> Christ's humanity was like a wall which yet allowed divinity to shine forth within that humanity. Therefore Christ is a window. Indeed, five windows may be pondered in him: his incarnation, his way of life, his teaching, his resurrection, and his ascension. It is through these five realities that the things spoken regarding contemplation are seen.[49]

Christ is the window through which one can see divinity, the light of which enables one truly to see oneself and the world around one. And Christ's life is most accessible through meditation on Scripture.

Although Bernard does speak of meditation on nature and reflective analysis of humans and their environment,[50] it is in Scripture that he discovers the matter for most of his meditations. Scripture is not only the vehicle through which one discovers the life of Christ, it is also the starting point for one's meditations on the vast range of other topics one finds a fruitful source of reflection.

Bernard's method is one of great antiquity. The meditative, prayerful reading of Scripture was particularly appealing to one who listened day-by-day, year-by-year to the reading of Benedict's *Rule*—a rule which makes *lectio* a cornerstone of the spiritual life.[51] Bernard describes the method with rich saporous imagery:

> As food is sweet to the palate, so does a psalm delight the heart. But the soul that is sincere and wise will not

> fail to chew the psalm with her teeth, as it were, of the mind. Because, if she swallows it in a lump without proper mastication, her palate will be cheated of the delicious flavor, sweeter even than honey that drips from the comb [Ps 18:11]. Let us with the Apostles offer a honey-comb at the table of the Lord in the heavenly banquet [Lk 24:42]. As honey flows from the comb, so should devotion flow from the words; otherwise, if one attempts to assimilate them without the condiment of the Spirit, 'the written letters bring death' [2 Co 3:6]. But if like Saint Paul you sing praises not only with the spirit but with the mind as well [1 Co 14:15], you too will experience the truth of Jesus' statement: 'The words I have spoken to you are spirit, and they are life' [Jn 6:64] — the truth too of the words of *Wisdom*: 'My spirit is sweet above honey' [Si 24:27].[52]

Reading involves much more for Bernard and his brethren than it does for us. It does indeed involve the activity of the mind, but the mind does not rapidly devour the text; it slowly and meditatively chews it.[53] Reading requires human effort,[54] but it also requires an openness to the Spirit, who will inform the text with rich meaning. Sometimes Bernard's imagery describing reading involves not only the sense of taste but hearing and smell as well:

> He [David] opened his mouth [Ps 118:131] and drew in his breath, and when he was filled full he not only breathed forth but also sang. Good Jesus! With what sweetness he suffused my nostrils and my ears when he breathed forth and sang of the oil of gladness with which God anointed him above his fellows [Ps 44:8]. . . . If only you would count me worthy of meeting such a prophet. . . . In that hour my mouth shall be filled with joy and my tongue with gladness [Ps 125:2], for I shall sense the fragrance of every Psalm — not merely of every Psalm, but of every verse, every breath more fragrant than any perfume [Sg 2:10]. What is more fragrant than the breath of John, who makes sweet for me the eternal generation and divinity of the Word? What shall I say about Paul's breathings, how they have filled the world with sweetness? Now the sweet savor of Christ is everywhere [2 Co 2:15].[55]

Through meditative reading of the words of Scripture, of David, Paul, and John, the Word himself is revealed.

Reflective reading of Scripture enables one to penetrate obscure passages and discover their meaning: 'As the deer penetrates the wood's dark avenue, so does the contemplative spirit penetrate the obscure meanings of things.'[56] Meditative reading enables one to transcend the literal meaning of the text and discover its allegorical senses:

> Such is the literal sense.... But, for me, following the counsel of the Lord, I shall search for the treasure of spirit and life hidden in the profound depths of these inspired utterances....[57]

The text is inspired, so too must be the reader:

> Let us now endeavor, under the guidance of the Spirit of truth, to extract the meaning which lies underneath the rind of the letter.[58]

With the guidance of the Spirit

> ...the texts of Scripture hitherto dark and impenetrable at last became bright with meaning for you. Then, in gratitude for this nurturing bread of heaven, you must charm the ears [of God] with a voice of praise, a festal song [Ps 41:5].[59]

Prayerful reflection on Scripture gives one insights into the deeper meanings of the text. But it is also part of a program of meditation on, of consideration of, oneself and one's relation to God, other people, and the world. And all of this takes time.

1. And 1, 10; SBOp 5:433; Luddy 3:50.
2. For the interchangability of the terms 'meditation' ('consideration') and 'contemplation', see Csi 2, 2, 5 (SBOp 3:414; CF 37:52), and Leclercq, *Saint Bernard mystique*, p. 108. For Bernard's meaning of 'contemplation', see below, pp. 215-220.
3. Csi 2, 2, 5; SBOp 3:414; CF 37:52.
4. Csi 5, 3, 5; SBOp 3:470; CF 37:143.
5. Csi 5, 3, 5; SBOp 3:470; CF 37:144.
6. SC 22, 2; SBOp 1:130; CF 7:15.
7. See Burch, pp. 28-33, and Gilson, pp. 19-37.
8. Csi 5, 2, 4; SBOp 3:469; CF 37:142-43.
9. Csi 1, 7, 8; SBOp 3:403-404; CF 37:38.
10. Csi 1, 8, 10; SBOp 3:405; CF 37:39-40.
11. Dil 5, 14; SBOp 3:130; CF 13:106-107.
12. Dil 4, 13; SBOp 3:129-30; CF 13:106. See Dil 3, 9-10; SBOp 3:126; CF 13:101-102.
13. Par 7; SBOp 6/2:297; CSt 22:47. I judge at least three of these—readings, meditations, and contemplations—to mean at least roughly the same. 'Reading' is discussed below, pp. 75-77. I agree with Berlière (against Pourrat) that Bernard makes no sharp distinction between meditation and prayer; Bernard does not advocate modern methods of mental prayer. See Ursmer Berlière, *L'ascèse bénédictine des origines à la fin du XIIe siècle*, Collection 'Pax', I (Paris: Desclée De Brouwer, P. Lethielleux, 1927) p. 196.
14. Csi 2, 3, 6; SBOp 3:414; CF 37:52.
15. Csi 2, 4, 7; SBOp 3:415; CF 37:54.
16. Hum 15, 43; SBOp 3:49; CF 13:71.
17. See Hum 14, 42; SBOp 3:49; CF 13:70.
18. SC 42, 6; SBOp 2:37; CF 7:214.
19. Csi 2, 9, 18; SBOp 3:425; CF 37:70.
20. Adv 3, 7; SBOp 4:181; Luddy 1:30.
21. Csi 2, 3, 6; SBOp 3:414; CF 37:52.
22. Hum 10, 28; SBOp 3:38; CF 13:57.
23. V Nat 3, 8; SBOp 4:217; Luddy 1:337.
24. V Nat 3, 8; SBOp 4:217; Luddy 1:337.
25. V Nat 3, 8; SBOp 4:217; Luddy 1:337-38.
26. SC 36, 6; SBOp 2:7; CF 7:179.
27. SC 36, 6; SBOp 2:7-8; CF 7:179.
28. See above, p. 28.
29. Csi 5, 14, 32; SBOp 3:493; CF 37:178-79.
30. SC 62, 5; SBOp 2:158; CF 31:156.
31. See above, p. 68.
32. SC 62, 6; SBOp 2:159; CF 31:157.
33. SC 62, 4; SBOp 2:157; CF 31:154.
34. SC 62, 4; SBOp 2:157; CF 31:154.
35. SC 62, 1; SBOp 2:154-55; CF 31:150.
36. SC 62, 2; SBOp 2:155; CF 31:151.
37. SC 62, 2; SBOp 2:155; CF 31:152.
38. SC 62, 3; SBOp 2:156; CF 31:152.
39. SC 11, 7; SBOp 1:58; CF 4:74.
40. SC 11, 7-8; SBOp 1:59; CF 4:75.
41. SC 11, 3; SBOp 1:56; CF 4:71-72.

42. SC 25, 9; SBOp 1:168; CF 7:57.
43. SC 43, 2-3; SBOp 2:42; CF 7:221.
44. SC 43, 4; SBOp 2:43; CF 7:222-23.
45. SC 45, 4; SBOp 2:52; CF 7:235.
46. SC 61, 7; SBOp 2:153; CF 31:147.
47. SC 62, 7; SBOp 2:159; CF 31:158.
48. Of course, Bernard's admonitions to meditation on the life of Christ are not confined to his *Sermons on the Song of Songs*. A few of the many such admonitions in his other works are: Adv 4, 1 (SBOp 4:220; Luddy 1:32); I Nov 1, 2 (SBOp 5:305; Luddy 2:344-45); Div 29, 4 (SBOp 6/1:212-13); and Dil 3, 7-8 (SBOp 3:125-26; CF 13:100).
49. Par 6; SBOp 6/2:292; CSt 21:104-105.
50. See above, pp. 69-71.
51. RB 48.
52. SC 7, 5; SBOp 1:34; CF 4:41-42.
53. See OS 1, 5; SBOp 5:330; Luddy 3:335-36. The proper pace of meditative reading is indicated by Bernard's progress in commenting on the *Song of Songs*. The eighty-six *Sermons*, composed over a period of some eighteen years, are a commentary which extends only to chapter 3, verse 1, of the text. There are only ninety-one lines in the Vulgate text which constitute the source for Bernard's reflections.
54. See SC 22, 2; SBOp 1:130; CF 7:15.
55. SC 67, 7; SBOp 2:192-93; CF 40:11.
56. SC 7, 6; SBOp 1:34; CF 4:43.
57. SC 73, 1-2; SBOp 2:234; CF 40:75-76.
58. SC 51, 2; SBOp 2:84; CF 31:40.
59. SC 1, 9; SBOp 1:7; CF 4:5.

B. Self-control

Bernard believes that one can gain the time necessary for meditation on reality, on truth, only through an ordering of one's life that involves self-control, self-restraint, self-discipline.[1] Ordering one's life promotes proper ordering of ones' intellect toward truth. For Bernard, this ordering is the proper meaning of piety: 'What is piety, you ask. To take time for consideration.'[2]

Taking time for meditation is essential to making progress on the path to perfection:

> I do not intend to discuss the virtues here, but I have said this much to encourage you to set aside time for the consideration which leads to the discovery of these virtues and others like them. To give no time during your life to such pious and beneficial leisure, is this not to lose your life?[3]

Leisure is the precondition for the reflection which leads to wisdom:

> ... The faithful soul sighs deeply for his [Christ's] presence, rests peacefully when thinking of him, and must glory in the degradation of the cross [Ga 6:14] until she is capable of contemplating the glory of God's revealed face [2 Co 3:18]. Thus Christ's bride and dove [Sg 5:1-2] pauses for a little while and rests amid her inheritance after receiving by lot silver-tinted wings [Ps 67:14], the candor of innocence and purity, from the memory of your abundant sweetness [Ps 144:7], Lord Jesus. And she hopes to be filled with gladness at the sight of your face [Ps 15:11], where even her back will glitter like gold [Ps 67:14], when she is introduced with joy into the splendor of the saints [Ps 109:3]. There she will be enlightened by rays of wisdom.[4]

That leisure can be bought only by taking time from other activities, worthwhile as they may be in themselves:

> Now show me a soul which the bridegroom, the Word, is accustomed to visit often, whom friendship has made bold, who hungers for what she has once tasted, whom contempt of all things has given leisure, and without hesitation I shall assign her the voice and the name of the bride. . . .[5]

Taking time demands effort; it requires self-control: 'The wisdom of a scribe requires leisure', says Solomon [Si 38:25]. Therefore the leisure of wisdom is exertion, and the more leisure wisdom has, the harder she works in her own way.[6]

Thus Bernard proclaims the paradox that leisure (*otium*) requires effort (*negotium*) and that leisure results in renewed effort in gaining wisdom. Self-control results in a mind oriented toward reality:

> ...One [book, *Ecclesiastes*,] uproots pernicious habits of mind and body with the hoe of self-control. The other [*Proverbs*], by the use of enlightened reason, quickly perceives a delusive tinge in all that the world holds glorious, truly distinguishing between it and deeper truth.[7]

The necessity of self-control, the need to order one's time and mind toward truth is the reason people enter monasteries and embrace a life of obedience. The structured life of the monastic *horarium* facilitates meditation and makes the acquisition of humility easier. As Jean Leclercq remarks, Bernard

> ...felt that the common life of the monastery offered privileged conditions for the accomplishment of this progressive liberation from all egoism. Humility, fraternal compassion, and prayer lead the monk gradually from an experience of his own truth—which is his wretchedness—to the contemplation of God's truth, which is love, and God's mercy which has been revealed in Christ.[8]

The self-regulated life is thus supported by the regular life of a community—or, rather, of a monastic family. And the condition of this self-ordering is free submission to the structure of the monastic family through obedience to the father or mother of that family, the abbot or abbess. Having resolved to turn his steps toward Reality, the aspirant seeks to 'submit himself to a superior in all obedience for the love of God.'[9] The authority of that superior flows from his own self-knowledge; the abbot is one '...whose power rests in humility.'[10] The abbot is to exercise his authority to educe self-knowledge in the monk. That eduction comes, in part, through correction:

> Anyone who strives forward toward the spiritual heights must have a lowly opinion of himself. Because, when he is raised above himself, he may lose his grip on him-

self unless, through true humility, he has a firm hold on himself. It is only when humility warrants it that great graces can be obtained. Hence, the one to be enriched by them is first humbled by correction so that by his humility he may merit them. And so, when you see you are being humbled, look on it as a sign of a sure guarantee that grace is on its way [Ps 85:17]. Just as the heart is puffed up with pride before its destruction, so it is humbled before being honored [Pr 16:18]. You read in the Scripture of these two modes of acting, how the Lord resists the proud and gives his grace to the humble [Jm 4:6]. Did he not decide to reward his servant Job with generous blessings after the outstanding victory in which his patience was put to the severest test? He was prepared for blessings by the many searching trials that humbled him [Jb 1:8; 2:3].[11]

It is clear from the example of Job, a married man living in the world, that Bernard does not restrict God's loving correction to those who have embraced the monastic life. Yet he knows that the monastery provides an environment especially conducive to the meditative life which leads to self-knowledge. Thomas, the provost of Beverley, apparently pledged himself to the monastic life, and Bernard encourages him with these words:

But do you, dearest son, if you would prepare the ear of your heart to hear the voice of God, sweeter than honey and the honey-comb, fly exterior cares, so that with your spiritual sense free and unimpeded, you can say with Samuel: 'Speak, Lord, for your servant hears' [1 K 3:10]. This voice is a not heard in the market place; nor does it sound in public. A secret counsel demands a secret hearing.[12]

Yet it is clear that Bernard believes that the ultimate abbot, Father, is God himself. And this means that the advantages of correction are open to all:

Our Physician does not always treat our moral sores with ointment. . . .Saint Paul's pride was kept down by a sting of the flesh, but he was lifted up by his many revelations [2 Co 12:7]. Zechariah was punished by dumbness for his unbelief [Lk 1:20], but the angel's prophecy did not fail [Lk 1:57ff.]. The saints go forward, whether in honor or dishonor [2 Co 6:8]. If they are ever led to think too much of themselves by their gifts and fall into the human weakness of vanity, they will be quickly reminded of what they really are.[13]

God provides all not only with the stings of correction, but also the ointment of consolation:

> Learn from me by means of these words to expect a twofold help from above in the course of your spiritual life: correction and consolation. One controls the exterior, the other works within. The first curbs arrogance; the latter strengthens the faint-hearted. The first makes a man discreet, the latter devout. The first imbues us with fear of God; the latter tempers that fear with the joy of salvation....[14]

If God's loving concern is expressed through consolation as well as correction, it is important for Bernard that one not seek an escape from reality in false consolations:

> The proud always seek what is pleasant and try to avoid what is troublesome. In the words of Scripture: 'Where there is gladness, there is the heart of the fool' [Qo 7:5]....He is saddened every time he sees the goodness of others, impatient with humblings. He finds an escape in false consolations. His eyes are closed to anything that shows his vileness or the excellence of others, wide open to what flatters himself. He is largely saved now from his moody exaltations and depression; he has retired into a happy cloud-land....He is careful not to remember anything he has done which could hurt his self-esteem. But all his good points will be remembered, added up, and, if need be, touched up by his imagination....[15]

No, facing up to reality, the reality of oneself and of one's relationship to God and to the world, requires a genuine self-discipline.

That self-restraint requires in turn a constant attention to the corrections which God makes available. These corrections are humbling and can lead to humility if accepted with the right spirit:

> Do you see that humility makes us righteous? I say humility and not humiliation. How many are humiliated who are not humble. There are some who meet humbling experiences with rancor, some with patience, some

again with cheerfulness. The first kind are culpable, the
second are innocent, the last just. Innocence is indeed
a part of justice, but only the humble possess it perfectly. He is truly humble who can say: 'It was good
for me that you humbled me' [Ps 118:71]. The man
who endures it unwillingly cannot say this, still less the
man who murmurs.... Even if only one of them
deserves anger, neither merits grace, because it is not
the humiliated but the humble to whom God gives grace
[Jm 4:6]. But he is humble who turns humbling experiences into humility....[16]

It is not external events which determine one's progress in perfection, but one's reaction to those events:

You may take it as a general rule that everyone who
humbles himself will be exalted [Lk 14:11]. It is significant that not every kind of humility is to be exalted, but only that which the will embraces. That will
must be free of compulsion or sadness [2 Co 9:7]. Nor,
on the contrary, must everyone who is exalted be humiliated, but only he who exalts himself, who pursues
a course of vain display. Therefore it is not he who is
humbled who will be exalted, but he who voluntarily
humbles himself. Exaltation is deserved by this attitude
of will. Even suppose that the humbling occasion is sup-
plied by another—by means of insults, damages, or
sufferings—the victim who determines to accept all
these for God's sake, with a quiet, joyful conscience,
cannot properly be said to be humbled by anyone but
himself.[17]

A quiet, joyful, humble conscience is the product of obedience
to the corrections and consolations offered by God.

Silence is another important element of self-discipline, for it provides one time for the meditation necessary to humility. Bernard
writes:

And if I may appropriate the words of the Apostle, 'It
is good that we are here' [Mk 17:4] sweetly to contemplate in silence what no discourse could ever adequately
explain.[18]

Silence is not only necessary for meditation, it also removes an
occasion for pride, thus serving humility twice. Bernard writes of
the loquacious man's speech:

The talk takes a lighter turn. He is more in his element here and becomes really eloquent. If you hear him, you will say that his mouth has become a fountain of wit, a river of smart talk. He can set the most grave and serious audience laughing heartily. To say it briefly, when words are many, boasting is not lacking [see Pr 10:19].[19]

Bernard does not mean to condemn speech, but he is sure that idle chatter can be a waste of time better spent:

...A light word which slips out in a place or time of silence, or uncontrolled laughter which is more a reflex than a reasoned act, although they may be symptoms of a careless or dissipated soul, are none the less easily forgiven, since they are faults rather than sins. But what if one were to give rein to idle words deliberately and knowingly?... The Judge himself has warned us of those idle words for every one of which he will then demand an account [see Mt 12:36]. Woe unto us! How shall we be able to justify our idleness?... Indeed, who does not know how a single word of detraction can outweigh innumerable idle words in guilt and punishment?[20]

Silence is not an end but a means. Taciturnity is no virtue: 'If a word is uttered for some particular reason it cannot be classified as idle.'[21] But a soul intent on self-realization in God needs quiet; 'Otherwise how could she be still enough to know that he is God [Ps 45:11]?'[22]

Humility is the product not of external events, but of internal dispositions. Thus, reliance on external disciplinary exercises can be self-defeating if not done with the proper motivation toward truth. Bernard paints a picture both sad and amusing of the monk who engages in disciplinary practices without proper intent:

When a man has been bragging that he is better than others, he would feel ashamed of himself if he did not live up to his boast and show how much better than others he is.... He does not so much want to be better as to be seen to be better. He can then say: 'I am not like the rest of men' [Lk 18:11].[23]

This pharisaical stance leads him to acts which compound his self-deception:

> He is more pleased with himself fasting for one day
> when others are feasting than about fasting seven days
> with all the rest. He prefers some petty private devo-
> tion to the whole night office of psalms. While he is
> at dinner he casts his eyes around the tables, and, if
> he sees anyone eating less than himself, he is morti-
> fied at being outdone and promptly and cruelly deprives
> himself of even the necessary food. He would rather
> starve his body than his pride.[24]

Self-denial is not necessarily self-discipline. Bernard's satire grows broader and more biting:

> If he sees anyone more thin, more pallid than himself,
> he despises himself. He is never at rest. He wonders
> what others think about the appearance of his face, and,
> as he cannot see it, he must only guess whether it is
> rosy or wan by looking at his hands and arms, poking
> at his ribs and feeling his shoulders and thighs to see
> how skinny or fleshy they are.[25]

Singularity is a sign of pride:

> He is very exact about his own particular doings and
> slack about the common exercises. He will stay awake
> in bed and sleep in choir. After sleeping through the
> night office while the others were singing psalms, he
> stays to pray alone in the oratory while they are resting
> in the cloister. He makes sure those sitting outside know
> he is there, modestly hidden in his corner, by clearing
> his throat and coughing, by groaning and sighing.[26]

Though Bernard's picture may be overdrawn, the lesson is clear. True discipline is not self-selected or self-willed or competitive. Self-discipline is a means to the end of humility; if made an end instead of a means, it becomes a means to self-delusion, to pride.

Yet, properly motivated, self-control is an essential part of the path to perfection of the intellect. By submitting to direction in obedience, and attending humbly to the good counsel which is imparted through it, one is led to understanding and wisdom:

> Once perfectly circumcised and cauterized by the sword
> of discipline, I crossed the fiery torrent by fighting
> against my vices. And soon, thanks to the help of obe-
> dience and counsel, I was ready to be formed in virtue.
> After this I was able to receive understanding from the

commandments of God. So that I could understand for myself the ways I trod, I was found worthy to receive the light of understanding. Then I came to wisdom which is, as she herself says, 'a tree of life to all who lay hold of her' [Pr 3:18]....[27]

The humbling corrections one receives in loving obedience are means to one's perfection in self-knowledge, the humility which is itself an essential step toward the goal of happiness. Not without rhetorical exaggeration, Bernard writes:

> Now some will laugh at me as a fool; others will mock me as ignorant; still others will be indignant at my presumption. Do you not think this will be of some small profit to me, since humility, to which humiliation leads, is the foundation of the whole spiritual edifice?[28]

1. I have quite deliberately avoided 'asceticism' because this word has connotations—at least in English—which are foreign to, even antithetical to, Bernard's meaning. Roget's *Thesaurus* lists the following synonyms for 'asceticism': puritanism, sabbatarianism, cynicism, austerity, total abstinence, nephalism, Yoga, mortification, maceration, sackcloth and ashes, flagellation, penance, fasting, and martyrdom. See C. O. Sylvester Mawson (ed.), *Roget's University Thesaurus* (New York: Barnes and Noble Books, 1981) p. 424, no. 955. I am indebted to my student, Paul Edwin Lockey, for this reference.
2. Csi 1, 7, 8; SBOp 3:403; CF 37:37.
3. Csi 1, 8, 11; SBOp 3:407; CF 37:42.
4. Dil 4, 12; SBOp 3:129; CF 13:104-105.
5. SC 74, 3; SBOp 3:241; CF 40:87.
6. SC 85, 8; SBOp 2:312; CF 40:203.
7. SC 1, 2; SBOp 1:3-4; CF 4:2.
8. Leclercq, *Bernard of Clairvaux and the Cistercian Spirit*, p. 78.
9. RB 7:34, quoted by Bernard in Hum 19, 49; SBOp 3:53; CF 13:76. See also Par 3, 3-4; SBOp 6/2:276; CSt 18:287-88.
10. SC 23, 8; SBOp 1:144; CF 7:32.
11. SC 34, 1; SBOp 1:246; CF 7:160-61.
12. Ep 107, 13; SBOp 7:275-76; James, p. 164. See also Par 6; SBOp 6/2:289; CSt 21:103.
13. Hum 10, 37; SBOp 3:45; CF 13:65. See also Conv 17, 30; SBOp 4:106-107; CF 25:66-68.
14. SC 21, 10; SBOp 1:128; CF 7:11.
15. Hum 12, 40; SBOp 3:46-47; CF 13:67-68.
16. SC 34, 3; SBOp 1:247; CF 7:162.
17. SC 34, 4; SBOp 1:247-48; CF 7:163.
18. Miss 2, 17; SBOp 4:35; CF 18:31.
19. Hum 13, 41; SBOp 3:48; CF 13:69-70. See also Csi 2, 13, 22; SBOp 3:430; CF 37:76.
20. Pre 8, 18; SBOp 3:265-66; CF 1:118.
21. Pre 8, 18: SBOp 3:266; CF 1:118.
22. SC 27, 10; SBOp 1:189; CF 7:83.
23. Hum 14, 42; SBOp 3:48-49; CF 13:70.
24. Hum 14, 42; SBOp 3:49; CF 13:70.
25. Hum 14, 42; SBOp 3:49; CF 13:70-71.
26. Hum 14, 42; SBOp 3:49; CF 13:71. See also Hum 18, 46-47; SBOp 3:51-52; CF 13:73-75.
27. Par 7; SBOp 6/2:300; CSt 22:50-51.
28. Ep 87, 11; SBOp 7:230; James, p. 134.

III. LOVE: THE PERFECTION OF THE WILL

A. Empathy: The Link Between Humility and Love

The truly humble know themselves and thus know what human beings are. According to Bernard, one who is truly aware of one's own human condition will also know and have empathy for that of others:

> We must look for truth in ourselves, in our neighbors, in itself. We look for truth in ourselves when we judge ourselves [1 Co 11:31], in our neighbors when we have empathy with their sufferings [1 Co 12:26], in itself when we contemplate it with a clean heart [Mt 5:8]. It is important to observe the order of these degrees as well as their number. First let Truth himself teach you that you should seek it in your neighbors before seeking it in his own nature. You will then see easily why you must seek it in yourself before you seek it in your neighbors. For in the list of beatitudes which he distinguished in his sermon, he placed the merciful before the pure in heart [Mt 5:7-8]. The merciful quickly grasp truth in their neighbors, extending their own feelings to them and conforming themselves to them through love, so that they feel their joys and troubles as their own. They are weak with the weak; they burn with the offended [2 Co 11:29]. They 'rejoice with those who rejoice and weep with those who weep' [Rm 12:15].[1]

To see the truth in others, to have empathy for them, it is necessary that one have experienced one's own limitations:

> A man who does not live in harmony with his brothers, who mocks those who weep, who sneers at those who are glad, has no empathy for them because their feelings do not affect him. He can never really see the truth in others. The proverb fits him well: the healthy man feels not the sick man's pains, nor the well-fed man the pangs of the hungry. Fellow-sufferers readily feel compassion for the sick and the hungry. For just as pure truth is seen only by the pure of heart, so also a brother's miseries are truly experienced only by one who has misery in his own heart. You will never have real mercy

for the failings of another until you know and realize that you have the same failings in your soul....²

The truly humble know the truth about themselves; they know they are weak. The weakness of others, therefore, prompts in them a reaction not of harsh anger but of gentle compassion:

> If a man, conscious of his own sins, refuses to be angry when he sees a fellow man committing an offense, but instead approaches him with a love and empathy that comfort him like the sweetest balsam, here is something the source of which we know, about which you have already heard [Nb 13:24]—but perhaps without grasping its significance. What I said is that, when a man reflects on his own conduct, he ought to feel impelled to be gentle with all [2 Tm 2:24]. Following the wise counsel of Saint Paul, he must learn to love those who are caught in habits of sin [Ga 6:1], not forgetting that he himself is open to temptation.³

The empathy that results from humility leads to love:

> Is it not in this very thing that love of neighbor is rooted, as the commandment reveals: 'You must love your neighbor as yourself [Lk 10:27; Lv 19:18]'? For it is in intimate human relationships like this that fraternal love finds its origins. The natural inbred pleasure with which a man esteems himself is the nourishing soil that gives it growth and strength. Then, influenced by grace from above, it yields the fruits of loving concern, so that a man will not think of denying to a fellow man, who shares the same nature, the good he naturally desires for himself. When the opportunity presents itself, let him freely and spontaneously do as the occasion demands, urged on by his humane instinct. When human nature has not been perverted by sin, it possesses this choice—and the pleasant balsam that induces compassionate tenderness and not an angry severity toward sinners.⁴

Once again, Bernard insists that people's naturally good inclinations, themselves gifts of God, are complemented and fulfilled by grace, God's further gift. Grace perfects nature in the production of the empathy which flows from humility and leads to love.

One should not only 'weep with those who weep' over their weakness, one should also 'rejoice with those who rejoice' in their accomplishments:

> Measuring ourselves against ourselves [2 Co 10:12], we feel, some of us, from the experience of our own imperfection, how rare a virtue it is not to envy the virtue of another, not to mention rejoicing in it, not to mention that one should be all the happier with oneself the more one considers oneself surpassed in virtue.[5]

Bernard compares this dual virtue of weeping and rejoicing to the two breasts of the bride of Christ:

> But we must now return to the subject of the bride's breasts and see how the milk of one differs in kind from that of the other. Joyful empathy yields the milk of encouragement, compassion that of consolation. And as often as the spiritual mother receives the kiss, so often does she feel each kind [of milk] flowing richly from heaven into her loving heart. And you may see her nourishing her little ones with the milk of these full breasts, from one the milk of consolation, from the other that of encouragement, according to the need of each.[6]

Bernard offers concrete instances of the loving response of the bride to the needs of others:

> For example, if she should notice that one of those whom she begot by preaching the Good News [1 Co 4:15] is assailed by temptation, that he becomes emotionally disturbed, is reduced to sadness and timidity and therefore no longer capable of enduring the force of temptation, will she not console him, caress him, weep with him, comfort him, and bring forward every possible example of God's love in order to raise him from his desolate state? If, on the contrary, she discovers that he is eager, active, progressing, her joy abounds. She plies him with encouraging advice, fans the fire of his zeal, imparts the ways of perseverance, and inspires him to ever higher ideals. She becomes all things to all, mirrors in herself the emotions of all, and so shows herself to be a mother to those who fail no less than to those who succeed.[7]

The humble, then, '... look beyond their own needs to the needs of their neighbors, and, from the things they have themselves endured, they learn compassion.....'⁸ That compassion results in concrete actions which serve their neighbors; 'this compassion is profitable to many, because persons of a noble mind will feel ashamed to sadden one whom they perceive to be anxiously concerned for their welfare.'⁹

Bernard offers many models of empathy. A negative model is the Pharisee of Luke's *Gospel*:

> You remember the words he spoke 'in his excess': 'I give you thanks, O God, that I am not like the rest of men' [Lk 18:11]. He had admiration for himself alone, for others only insults.... The Pharisee damned all, excepting only himself—and deceiving only himself.¹⁰

A happy contrast is the example of Bernard's dear friend, Malachy, the archbishop of Armagh. Of Malachy, Bernard writes:

> Who was as sympathetic as he in sharing the sorrows of others, or so prompt in offering help, or so free in correction? For he was full of zeal, but he knew how to keep it within bounds. With the weak he was weak [1 Co 9:22], yet powerful among the strong.... No matter what the affliction of which someone complained to him, he considered it his own....¹¹

Malachy's model of compassion was also Bernard's supreme model, Jesus:

> Our Savior has given us the example. He willed to suffer that he might know compassion [Heb 2:17]. To learn mercy he shared our misery. It is written: 'He learned obedience from the things he suffered' [Heb 5:8]; and he learned mercy in the same way. I do not mean that he did not know how to be merciful before; his mercy is from eternity to eternity [Ps 102:17]. But what in his divine nature he knows from all eternity, he learned by experience in time.¹²

The process of growth in knowledge open to each human person is the very process which Jesus himself experienced. And each person should imitate him too in learning the compassion which flows from knowledge:

> And when the Lord, 'bearing his own cross went forth' [Jn 9:17] to be crucified, and when not yet 'all the tribes of the earth mourned' [Mt 24:30] but only a few Jewish women, 'turning to them he said: "Daughters of Jerusalem, weep not for me but for yourselves and your

children" ' [Lk 23:28]. Observe carefully the order he recommends: first 'weep for yourselves', then 'weep for your children'. Look well first to yourself, brother, so you may know how to be compassionate with your neighbor....[13]

Empathy is possible only to someone who is truly humble. Empathy is the bridge between the perfection of the intellect in humility and the perfection of the will in love:

In this life all kinds of fish are caught in love's net, where now it conforms to all [1 Co 9:19], drawing into itself the adversity and prosperity of all.[14]

But, what is this love of which Bernard makes a net for the capture of all?

1. Hum 3, 6; SBOp 3:20; CF 13:34-35.
2. Hum 3, 6; SBOp 3:21; CF 13:35. See also Hum 5, 16; SBOp 3:28; CF 13:44.
3. SC 44, 4; SBOp 2:46; CF 7:227. See also Hum 4, 13-14; SBOp 3:26; CF 13:41-42.
4. SC 44, 4; SBOp 2:46-47; CF 7:227-28.
5. SC 49, 7; SBOp 2:77; CF 31:27.
6. SC 10, 2; SBOp 1:49; CF 4:61-62. See also SC 43, 2; SBOp 2:42; CF 7:221.
7. SC 10, 2; SBOp 1:49; CF 4:62.
8. Hum 5, 18; SBOp 3:30; CF 13:46.
9. Pasc 2, 4; SBOp 5:97; Luddy 2:191.
10. Hum 5, 17; SBOp 3:29; CF 13:45.
11. S Mal 2-3; SBOp 6/1: 51-52; CF 10:108-109.
12. Hum 3, 6; SBOp 3:21; CF 13:35.
13. Pasc 2, 4; SBOp 5:97; Luddy 2:190.
14. Dil 15, 40; SBOp 3:154; CF 13:132.

B. The Meaning of Love

'Love' is a word with almost as many meanings as uses, with almost as many meanings as users of the word. Bernard's understanding of the word—or, rather, words (*dilectio, caritas, amor, cupiditas*)[1]—is revealed by examining the process of loving and the proper objects of love as Bernard sees them.

Love is an activity of the will for Bernard, and as such it is the supreme natural activity of a natural gift: 'Among all the natural endowments of man love holds first place, especially when it is directed toward God, who is the source from which it comes.'[2] Love is a properly ordered will, ordered toward that which the will should desire, toward the good, toward that which will benefit self:

> Desire is set in right order by the arrival of love, which moves one to reject evil altogether and prefer what is better to what is good. It desires the good only for the sake of that which is better.[3]

The lover is made free and spontaneous by his or her love:

> Love pertains to the will; it is not a transaction. It cannot acquire or be acquired by a pact. Moving us freely, it makes us spontaneous. True love is content with itself; it has its reward, the object of its love. Whatever you seem to love because of something else, you do not really love; you really love the end pursued and not that by which it is pursued. Paul does not evangelize in order to eat; he eats in order to evangelize—he loves the gospel and not the food [1 Co 9:18]. True love deserves its reward, it does not merely seek it.[4]

In love, in the proper ordering of the will, one attains freedom from the numbing constraints of fear:

> Sons are not obliged to obey a law of fear, and they cannot exist without that of liberty. Do you wish to know why there is no law for those who are good? It is written: 'But you have not received the spirit of servitude in fear' [Rm 8:15]. Do you wish to hear that they are not without the law of love? 'But you have received the spirit of the adoption of sons' [Rm 8:15]. Yet listen to the just man affirming of himself [1 Co 9:20-21] that he is not under the law, yet he is not lawless.... It

is not right, therefore, to say 'The just have no law' or 'The just are without a law', but that 'Laws are not made for those who are good', meaning they are not imposed on them unwillingly but, inspired by goodness, they are given freely to those who accept.[5]

The law of love demands that one desire that which will perfect one. Bernard contrasts the freedom born of the proper orientation of the will with the burden of a will misdirected:

Each one wants to make his own law when he prefers his own will to the common, eternal law. He seeks to imitate his Creator in a perverse way, so that, as God is his own law for himself and depends on himself alone, so man wants to govern himself and make his own will his law. This heavy and unbearable yoke weighs on all Adam's sons [Si 40:1; Ac 15:10], alas, making our necks curve and bend down so that our life seems to draw near hell [Ps 87:4].... It is proper to God's eternally just law that he who does not want to accept its sweet rule shall be the slave of his own will as a penance. He who casts away the easy yoke and light burden [Mt 11:30] of love will have to bear unwillingly the unbearable burden of his own will.[6]

Here Bernard shows the connection between humility, love, and freedom. Anyone who would be God, who sees oneself as the master of one's world, deceives oneself: he or she is not God. When one acts on this misinformation one chooses incorrectly; one does not truly love. One's will is as misdirected as is one's intellect. A misdirected will is not truly free, because it remains burdened by deceit. Love is the condition of freedom.

And the freedom which results from a properly directed will is also a gift. To the natural gift of free choice,[7] God adds the power of choosing correctly by his gift of his Spirit:

Then the Holy Spirit lovingly visited the second power, the will. He found it rotten with the infection of the flesh,[8] but already judged by reason. Gently he cleansed it, made it burn with affection, made it merciful until, like a skin made pliable with oil, it would spread abroad the heavenly oil of love, even to its enemies. The union of the Holy Spirit with the human will gives birth to love.[9]

The person who chooses to love freely and in concert with the guidance of the Spirit is happy simply because he or she loves:
> Love is sufficient for itself. It gives pleasure to itself and for its own sake. It is its own merit and own reward. Love needs no cause beyond itself; nor does it demand fruits. It is its own purpose. I love because I love; I love that I may love. Love is the great reality, and, if it returns to its own beginning and goes back to its own origin, seeking its source again, it will always draw afresh from it, and thereby flow freely. Love is the only motion of the soul, of its senses and affections, in which the creature can respond to his Creator, even if not as an equal, and repay his favor in some similar way....Now you see how different love is. For when God loves, he desires nothing but to be loved, for he knows that those who love him are blessed in their very love.[10]

The truly happy person is a lover.

That person is not merely a knower. The perfection of the intellect is necessary to happiness; one must know the good to choose it. Love demands response: human happiness lies in the perfection of the will in love. One must not merely know reality; one must seize it:[11]

> We must strive 'to seize, with all the saints, the length and the breadth, the heights and the depth' [Eph 3:18]. Paul said 'seize' and not 'know'. We must not limit our search to the areas of reason; we must desire its fruit with all our power. The fruit does not lie in knowledge, but in the act of seizing. As another Apostle says elsewhere: 'It is a sin to know the good and not do it' [Jm 4:17]. And it is Paul again, in another of his writings, who offers this counsel: 'Act like runners in the stadium. Run to seize the prize of the race' [1 Co 9:24]....We know all these things. Do we believe we have thereby seized them? Not by disputation are these matters understood, but by holiness....[12]

For Bernard, this is the way of the saints, those who have attained happiness, who have seized reality. They do not merely know about reality, they understand it because they have seized it in love:

> If it were impossible to understand [reality], the Apostle would not have said that 'we must seize, with all

the saints' [Eph 3:18]. Consequently, the saints understand. Do you wish to know how? If you are a saint, you have already understood and therefore have nothing more to learn. If you are not a saint, you must become one so that your experience will teach you. It is a saintly disposition of the heart which makes a saint. This includes two sentiments: holy fear of the Lord and holy love. The soul which has penetrated all this is equipped, so to speak, with two arms which allow her to seize, embrace, clasp, and retain. She too can cry out: 'I have seized him, and I will not let him go' [Sg 3:4].[13]

For Bernard, the conclusion is obvious:
Love, then, with fidelity and patience, and you will seize the length. Widen your love to include your enemies, and you will possess the breadth.[14]

There are different kinds and degrees of love, Bernard believes. His enumeration of these kinds and degrees are many and varied. This, I think, is not the result of confusion or inconsistency, but rather the richness of the subject and the insight of the enumerator. In his eighty-third sermon on the *Song of Songs*, Bernard contrasts filial with marital love:

Love is a great reality. But there are degrees to it; that of the bride is the highest. Children love their father, but they think of their inheritance. And, as long as they have any fear of losing it, they honor more than love the one from whom they expect to inherit. I suspect the love which seems founded on some hope of gain. It is weak; for, if the hope is removed, it may be extinguished or at least diminished. It is not pure, as it desires some return.[15]

Bernard is not deprecating filial love,[16] but urging pure love:
Pure love has no self-interest. Pure love does not gain strength through expectation; nor is it weakened by distrust. This is the love of the bride—with all that means. Love is the being and hope of a bride. She is full of it, and the bridegroom is content with it.... The love of a bridegroom—or, rather, of the Bridegroom who is love—asks only the exchange of love and trust. Let the beloved love in return. How can the bride—and the

bride of Love—do other than love? How can Love not be loved?[17]

Bernard uses other figures, other degrees and kinds, to illuminate his subject, love. In his twentieth sermon on the *Song of Songs*, he describes three degrees of proper love: carnal, rational, and spiritual—all of them good and opposed to sensual love. In this scheme, carnal love is the first step in overcoming sensual love:

> For there is no love of Christ without the Holy Spirit, even if this love is in the flesh and without its fullness. The measure of such love is this: its sweetness seizes the whole heart and draws it completely from the love of all flesh and every sensual pleasure. Really, this is what it means to love with one's whole heart. If I prefer to the humanity of my Lord someone joined to me by ties of blood, or some sensual pleasure, this would obviously prove that I do not love with my whole heart, since it is divided between its own interests and the love of the one who, as a man, taught me both by his word and example.[18]

Love for Christ's humanity is important as a first step because it fulfills the human being's natural attraction to the physical. Bernard makes bold to claim this as a reason for the Incarnation:

> I think this is the principal reason why the invisible God willed to be seen in the flesh and to converse with men as a man. He wished to recapture the affections of carnal men unable to love in any other way by first drawing them to the salutary love of his own humanity, then gradually raise them to a spiritual love.[19]

Between carnal and spiritual love lies the domain of rational love. Bernard compares carnal and rational love:

> Of course this devotion to the humanity of Christ is a gift, a great gift of the Spirit. I have called it carnal in comparison to that love which does not know the Word as flesh so much as the Word as wisdom, as justice, truth, holiness, loyalty, strength, and whatever else may be said in this manner.... Take as an example two men. One of them feels a share in Christ's sufferings, is affected and easily moved at the thought of all he suffered; he is nourished and strengthened by the sweetness of this devotion to good and honest and

worthy actions. The other is always aflame with zeal for justice, eager for truth and for wisdom. His life, his habits are saintly, ashamed of boasting, avoiding criticism, never knowing envy, hating pride. He not only flees all human glory but shrinks from it and avoids it; every stain of impurity, both in body and soul, he loathes and eradicates. He spurns every evil as if naturally; he embraces what is good.[20]

Love is the perfection of the will. But the perfection of the will involves the perfection of the affective soul, the feelings, in carnal love[21] just as it brings to fruition the rational faculty's perfection, humility:

Carnal love is worthwhile since through it sensual love is excluded and the world is condemned and conquered. It becomes better when it is rational, perfect when spiritual.... If, with the help of the Spirit, the soul attains such strength that she remains steadfast no matter what the effort or difficulty, if the fear of death itself cannot make her act unjustly, but even then she loves with her whole strength, then this is spiritual love. I think the name is very fitting for this special love because of the special fullness of the spirit in which it excels.[22]

Love fulfills the lover; this fulfillment is the gift of God, the indwelling of the Holy Spirit.

Bernard describes progress in love in still another way in his *On the Necessity of Loving God*. Here he compares the love of the slave, of the hireling, and of the son:

A man can acknowledge that the Lord is powerful, that the Lord is good to him, that the Lord is simply good. The first is the love of the slave who fears for himself; the second is that of the hireling who thinks only of himself; the third is that of the son who respects his father.[23]

Love has so many facets and dimensions that Bernard is quite comfortable in using descriptions which differ—and even seem to contradict. But the teaching behind all of them is the same: love is the perfection of the will, free to choose the good.

And that choice perfects one because by it one becomes united with the fundamental order of the universe, the law of love:

Love is called the law of the Lord both because he lives by it and because nobody possesses it except as a gift from him. It does not seem absurd for me to say God lives by a law, because that law is nothing else than love.... Such is the eternal law which creates and governs the universe. All things were made according to this law in weight, measure, and number [Ws 11:21], and nothing is left without a law. Even the Law itself is not without a law, which nevertheless is nothing other than itself. Even if it does not create itself, it governs itself all the same.[24]

Still more fundamentally, Bernard is sure that, in loving, one participates in the very being of God. For love is the principle of unity in the Trinity. Indeed, God is Love:

What else maintains that supreme and unutterable unity in the highest and most blessed Trinity if not love? Hence it is a law, the law of the Lord, that love which brings together the Trinity in the bond of peace [Eph 4:3]. All the same, let no one think I hold love to be a quality or a kind of accident in God. Otherwise I would be saying, and be it far from me, that there is something in God which is not God. Love is the divine substance. I am saying nothing new or unusual, just what Saint John says: 'God is love' [1 Jn 4:8].[25]

1. See Casey, *Athirst for God*, pp. 88-94.
2. SC 7, 2; SBOp 1:31; CF 4:39.
3. Dil 14, 38; SBOp 3:152; CF 13:130.
4. Dil 7, 17; SBOp 3:133-34; CF 13:110.
5. Dil 14, 37; SBOp 3:151; CF 13:129.
6. Dil 13, 36; SBOp 3:150; CF 13:128.
7. See above, pp. 9-11.
8. 'Flesh' does not mean the body here, but rather a misdirected will. See above, pp. 24-25.
9. Hum 7, 21; SBOp 3:32; CF 13:49.
10. SC 83, 4; SBOp 2:300-301; CF 40:184.
11. I have translated Bernard's word *comprehendere* as 'seize'. In this I am following Leclercq. See *Bernard of Clairvaux and the Cistercian Spirit*, p. 152.
12. Csi 5, 13 and 14, 27 and 30; SBOp 3:490-91 and 492; CF 37:175 and 177.
13. Csi 5, 14, 30; SBOp 3:492; CF 37:177.
14. Csi 5, 14, 30; SBOp 3:492; CF 37:177-78.
15. SC 83, 5; SBOp 2:301; CF 40:184-85.
16. See below, p. 100.
17. SC 83, 5; SBOp 2:301; CF 40:185.
18. SC 20, 7; SBOp 1:119; CF 4:153.
19. SC 20, 6; SBOp 1:118; CF 4:152.
20. SC 20, 8; SBOp 1:120; CF 4:154.
21. See above, p. 99.
22. SC 20, 9; SBOp 1:120-21; CF 4:154-55.
23. Dil 12, 34; SBOp 3:148; CF 13:126.
24. Dil 12, 35; SBOp 3:149-50; CF 13:127.
25. Dil 12, 35; SBOp 3:149; CF 13:127.

C. The Objects of Love

Because God is love, then it is clear that God must be both the source and the object of love. But it is also clear that Bernard would have human beings direct their love toward other goods. His lists of these goods are many and varied. In his fiftieth sermon on the *Song of Songs*, Bernard tells his listeners that they should love God, themselves, and others—and also that they should love the world around them with an ordered, a properly-directed love:

> Give me a man who loves God, before all things and with his whole being, who loves self and neighbor in proportion to their love for God, who loves the enemy as one who perhaps some day will love, who loves his physical parents very deeply because of the natural bond, his spiritual guides more generously because of grace. In like manner let him deal too with the other things of God with an ordered love, disregarding the earth, esteeming heaven, using this world as if not using it [1 Co 7:31], and discriminating between things used and those enjoyed with an intimate savoring of his mind. Let him pay but passing attention to things that pass as existing need demands. Let him embrace eternal things with an eternal desire. Give me such a man, I repeat, and I shall boldly proclaim him wise, because he appreciates things for what they really are, because he can truthfully and confidently boast and say: 'He set love in order for me' [Sg 2:4].[1]

One should love what is, then, with a love appropriate to the object of love. All of reality is good because created by God, and thus must be loved. This includes not only God, angels, and one's fellow human beings, but also those virtues which perfect one:

> For the love by which one loves spiritually, whether its object is God or an angel or another soul, is truly and properly an attribute of the soul alone. Of this kind also is the love of justice [Ps 44:8], truth, goodness, wisdom, and the other virtues.[2]

Love of Self

Bernard is '. . . convinced that no degree of the love that leads to salvation may be preferred to that suggested by the Wise Man:

"Have pity on your own soul, pleasing God [Si 30:24]."[3] This love of self is rooted in knowledge of oneself. One should embrace the reality of oneself:

> The bride's humility, like nard, spreads abroad its fragrance, the warmth of its love, the vigor of its fervor, the inspiring power of its good name. The bride's humility is freely embraced; it is fruitful, and it is forever.[4]

Properly ordered love means that one can never forget oneself even in one's loving concern for others. Bernard writes of his friend Malachy:

> He did not pay so much attention to others that he left himself out of consideration so as to disregard himself in caring for all the rest. He was careful of himself, guarding himself well. In a word, he was so entirely his own and so entirely everyone's that it would seem his love could not keep him or impede him in any way from care for others, nor his concern for himself from the good of all.[5]

A properly ordered love of self is a humble love, a love which is informed by knowledge that one is lovable because of the love which God has shown one:

> Then you will experience as well your own true self, since you perceive that you possess nothing at all for which you love yourself except insofar as you belong to God.[6]

Love for Others

This experience of one's true self in love enables one to experience others in love:

> As for your neighbor whom you are obliged to love as yourself [Mt 19:19], if you are to experience him as he is, you will actually experience him only as you do yourself, for he is what you are. You, who do not love yourself except for your love for God, consequently love as yourself all those who similarly love him. But you who love God cannot love as yourself a human enemy, for he is nothing in that he does not love God [1 Jn 4:20]. Yet you will love him so that he may love.... The love that is open does not permit the refusal of

some feeling, however small, to any man, even to one's greatest enemy.[7]

This seemingly equivocal attitude toward one's enemies is clarified elsewhere. In his twelfth sermon on the *Song of Songs*, Bernard informs his hearers:

> You too, if you are to become deeply compassionate [Col 3:12], must behave generously and kindly not only to parents and relatives or to those from whom you have received or hope to receive a good turn— after all, non-Christians do as much [Mt 5:47]. But, following Paul's advice, you must make an effort to do good to all [Ga 6:10]. Inspired by this God-oriented purpose, you will never refuse an act of love, whether spiritual or corporal, to an enemy, or withdraw it once offered.[8]

Again Bernard offers Malachy as a model:

> What great things we have heard and known [Ps 78:3] of the zeal of the man and the vengeance of his enemies when he was sweet and mild and full of mercy to all [Ps 86:5] who suffered need. He lived as though he were the one father of all. He cuddled them all, and he protected them under the shelter of his wings [Ps 61:4], as a hen gathers her chicks [Mt 23:37]. He did not distinguish sex, age, condition, or person. He left no one out, embracing everyone in his merciful heart.[9]

Malachy loved everyone because, in the light of God's love, everyone is lovable. He cared for them in love, doing what he could to promote their good, their well being, their happiness. This love is a moral imperative; one must love all. As Bernard puts it:

> I maintain that true and sincere love proceeds from a pure heart, a good conscience, and unfeigned faith [1 Tm 1:5]. It makes us care for our neighbor's good as much as for our own. For he who cares for his own good alone or more than for his neighbor's, shows that he does not love that good purely, that he loves it for his own advantage and not for the good itself.[10]

Since the good of all being lies in God, one must love one's neighbor in God. Just as one must love oneself in reference to the ultimate good, so must one love one's neighbor in the same way:

> In order to love one's neighbor with perfect justice [Mk 12:30-31], one must have regard to God. In other

words, how can one love one's neighbor with purity if one does not love him in God? But it is impossible to love in God unless one loves God. It is necessary, therefore, to love God first; then one can love one's neighbor in God.[11]

Love for one's neighbor requires more than the desire for his or her well-being. Bernard teaches that one must also do all one can to bring about the neighbor's well-being:

'You shall love your neighbor as yourself' [Mt 22:39].

It is just indeed that he who shares the same nature should not be deprived of the same benefits, especially that which is grafted in that nature. Should a man feel overburdened at satisfying not only his brethren's just needs but also their pleasures, let him restrain his own if he does not wish to be a transgressor. He can be as indulgent as he likes for himself, providing his neighbor has the same rights.... Then your love will be sober and just if you do not refuse your neighbor that which he needs....[12]

True love of neighbor will never be injurious to the lover; God will care for her or him: 'Without being asked, he promises to give what is necessary to him who withholds from himself what he does not need and loves his neighbor.'[13] In loving one's neighbor, one increases one's capacity for love of God and thus for happiness:

The capacity of any man's soul is judged by the amount of love he possesses. Hence he who loves much is great; he who loves a little is small; he who has not love is nothing. As Paul said: 'If I have not love, I am nothing' [1 Co 13:2].[14]

Bernard finds it easy to measure one's capacity for love; it lies in one's growth in love for others:

If a man begins to acquire some love, if he tries at least to love those who love him [Lk 6:32], and salutes the brethren and others who salute him [Mt 5:47], I may no longer describe him as nothing because some love must be present in the give and take of social life [Ph 4:15].... But if his love expands and continues to advance until it outgrows these narrow, servile confines and finds itself in open ranges where love is freely given in full liberty of spirit, when from the generous bounty of his good will he strives to reach out to all his neighbors, loving each as himself [Mt 19:19], surely one may no longer ask: 'What more are you doing than the others?' Indeed he has made himself vast. His heart is filled with a love that embraces everyone, even those to whom he is not tied by the inseparable bonds of family relationship. His is a love not allured by any hope of personal gain, that possesses nothing it is obliged to restore, that bears no burden of debt whatever, apart from that of which it is said: 'Owe no man anything, except to love one another' [Rm 13:8].[15]

The perfection of the will in loving others can reach such heights that Love himself will enter the soul of the lover:

Progressing further still, you may endeavor to take the kingdom of love by force [Mt 11:12], until by this holy warfare you succeed in possessing it even to its farthest bounds. Instead of shutting off your affections from your enemies [1 Jn 3:17], you will do good to those who hate you, you will pray for those who slander you [Mt 5:44], you will strive to be peaceful even with those who hate peace [Ps 119:7]. Then the width, height, and beauty of your soul will be the width, height, and beauty of heaven itself. And you will realize how true it is that he has 'stretched out the heavens like a curtain' [Ps 103:2]. In this heaven, the width, height, and depth of which compel our wonder, he who is supreme and immense and glorious is not only pleased to dwell, but to wander far and wide on its pathways.[16]

Friendship

The path to perfection is graced by a particularly intense form of love of another. And that is friendship.[17] Friendship is the perfection of the human, and therefore good, need to give and receive intimate affection:

It is but human and necessary that we respond to our friends with feeling: that we be happy in their company, disappointed in their absence. Social intercourse, especially between friends, cannot be purposeless. The reluctance to part and the yearning for each other when

separated indicate how meaningful their mutual love must be when they are together.[18]
Friendship requires mutual love and affection. Bernard felt this experience most deeply in his intimate association with Gerard, who was his brother by blood and his brother-monk at Clairvaux. When Gerard died, Bernard wrote this moving description of the mutuality of their friendship:

> Gerard is the reason for my weeping, my brother by blood, but closer by an intimate spiritual bond, the one who shared all my plans. My soul cleaved to his. We were of one mind, and it was this, not our blood-relationship, that joined us as one. That he was my blood-brother certainly mattered; but our spiritual affinity, our similar outlooks and harmony of temperaments, drew us closer still.[19]

Friendship is thus a union of intellect, will, and feelings—of the entire soul. Gerard's proximity made his friendship with Bernard physical as well. Friendship, then, involves the whole human being; it is totally human. And this made Gerard's death all the more devastating:

> I have made public the depth of my affliction; I make no attempt to deny it [Jn 1:20]. Will you say then that this is carnal? That it is human, yes, since I am a man. If this does not satisfy you, then I am carnal. Yes, I am carnal, sold under sin [Rm 7:14], destined to die, subject to penalties and sufferings. I am certainly not insensitive to pain; to think I shall die, that those who are mine will die, fills me with dread. And Gerard was mine—so utterly mine. Was he not mine who was a brother to me by blood, a son by religious profession, a father by his solicitude, my comrade on the spiritual highway, my bosom friend in love? And it is he who has gone from me. I feel it; the wound is deep.[20]

Gerard was not Bernard's only friend. And in writing to various other friends Bernard says much about the nature of friendship. To Peter the Venerable, abbot of Cluny, he writes of the necessity for equality between friends: 'For a long time now my soul has been firmly united to yours, and the equality of love has made equals of unequal persons.'[21] Friends must be frank and open with each other; in another letter to Peter, Bernard writes:

> I have only said this to be quite open with you and not keep anything back from you. For this true friendship demands. Because love believes all things [1 Co 13:7], I have put away all my misgivings and am glad that you have warmed to an old friendship and recalled a wounded friend.[22]

Bernard rejoices that his friendship with Peter is so open that it results in good-humored banter:

> I welcomed your letter with open hands. I have read it and re-read it greedily and gladly, and the more often I read it the better pleased I am. I must say I enjoy your fun. It is both pleasantly light-hearted and seriously grave. I do not know how you are able to be both light-hearted and grave, so that your fun has nothing about it of frivolity, and your dignity loses nothing by your light-heartedness. You are able to keep your dignity so well in the midst of your fun that those words of the holy man might be applied to you: 'If I laughed at them, they did not believe [Jb 29:24] me.'[23]

Humor is human, and friendship gives one an opportunity to perfect that human capacity.

The effects of friendship are many:

> At times when I least expected it, at the word or even the sight of a good and holy man, at the memory of a dead or absent friend, he [God] set his winds blowing and the waters flowing [Ps 147:18], and my tears were my food day and night [Ps 41:4]. How can I explain this? Only by ascribing it to the odor from the oil that anointed the friend in question. For me there was no anointing, the experience came by another's mediation.... Many of you too, I believe, have had similar experiences, and have them still. In what light then should we view them? I hold that through them our pride is shown up, our humility guarded, brotherly love fostered, and good desires aroused. One and the same food is medicine for the sick and nourishment for the convalescent; it gives strength to the weak and pleasure to the strong. One and the same food cures sickness, preserves health, builds up the body, titillates the palate.[24]

The visit of a friend brings joy to the friend visited. Bernard describes welcoming his friend Malachy to Clairvaux:

> Malachy was received as the true Orient from on high [Lk 1:78] visiting us, although he arrived from the west. Oh, what great brightness did that radiant sun add to our bright valley [Clairvaux]! What a joyous feast dawned for us at his coming! That day which the Lord gave us, how we rejoiced and were glad in it [Ps 118:24]. How I came running with a leap and a bound, shaking and weak as I was. How happily I rushed to kiss him! With what happy arms I embraced [Gn 29:13] the gift sent me from heaven!²⁵

Bernard had found the same delight in the companionship of his brother, Gerard:

> Our companionship was equally enjoyable to both because our dispositions were so alike.... All that was pleasant we rejoiced to share.... Both of us were so happy in each other's company, sharing the same experiences, talking together about them....²⁶

But as joyous as the physical proximity of a friend is, friendship overcomes the barriers of distance as well. Eskil, the archbishop of Lund, lived at the far end of Bernard's world. Still, Bernard was able to maintain an epistolary friendship with him:

> Your letter and greetings, or rather, your expressions of affection, were most welcome because of the special love you and I have for each other.... I believe I owe you, and you me, all the favor and affection that absent friends can bestow on one another.²⁷

Closer to home, but still apart, lived Ermengarde, formerly countess of Britanny. She too was Bernard's dear friend:

> I wish I could find words to express what I feel for you! If you could but read in my heart how great an affection for you the finger of God has there inscribed, then you would surely see how no tongue could express and no pen describe what the spirit of God has been able to inscribe there. Absent from you in body, I am always present to you in spirit.... You see how you have me always with you; for my part, I confess, I am never without you and never leave you.²⁸

For Bernard, the intimacies of friendship could be extended not only to those distant but to those of the opposite sex as well.

Bernard believed that it was the Spirit himself who had filled his heart with deep affection for this woman.

Because God is the ultimate source of friendship, God too will reward the faithful friend. He writes to Eskil:

> And if I cannot repay you [for your affection], I have an immortal one, the Lord, who will repay for me [Ps 137:8]. I speak of the Lord in whom and for whom you love me with such devotion and bind me to you with such affection.[29]

Love of God

If God will reward friendship, it is also clear to Bernard one's best friend is God:

> Notice then, the utter happiness of hearing the God of heaven say: 'in our land' [Sg 2:12]. 'Listen, all inhabitants of the earth, all peoples' [Ps 48:3], 'the Lord has done great things for us' [Ps 125:3]. He has done much for the earth, much for the bride, whom he has been pleased to take to himself from the earth. 'In our land', he says. This is clearly not the language of domination but of fellowship and intimate friendship.[30]

But God is not only friend, he is lover. Christ's love is that of the Bridegroom for the bride:

> He speaks as Bridegroom, not as Lord. Think of it! He is the Creator, and he makes himself one of us. It is love that speaks [in the *Song*] and knows no lordship. This is a song of love, in fact, and meant to be sung only by lovers, not by others. God loves too, though not through a gift distinct from himself. He is himself the source of loving, and therefore his love is all the more vehement. For he does not possess love; he is love. And those whom he loves he calls friends, not servants [Jn 15:15]. The master has become the friend, for he would not have called his disciples friends if it were not true.[31]

Friendship is between equals, and the Son has made himself man's equal in becoming man:

> Love neither looks up to nor looks down on anyone. It regards as equal all who love each other truly, bringing together in itself the lofty and the lowly. It makes

them not simply equal but one. Perhaps to now you have thought God should be an exception to this law of love, but anyone who is united to the Lord becomes one spirit with him [1 Co 6:17]. Why wonder at this? He has become like one of us [Gn 3:22]. But I have said too little: not 'like one of us', but 'one of us'. It is not enough for him to be on a par with men; he is a man.[32]

God has proved his love in the Son's incarnation and in his passion and death. And he is consequently deserving of one's love:

God certainly deserves much from us since he gave himself [Ga 1:4] to us when we deserved it least.... It is written: 'While we were still his enemies, he reconciled us to himself' [Rm 5:10]. Thus God loved freely— even his enemies. How much did he love? Saint John answers that 'God so loved the world that he gave his only-begotten Son' [Jn 3:16]. Saint Paul adds: 'He did not spare his only Son, but delivered him up for us' [Rm 8:32]. The Son also said of himself: 'No one has greater love than he who lays down his life for his friends' [Jn 15:13]. Thus the righteous one deserved to be loved by the wicked, the highest and omnipotent by the weak.[33]

For Bernard, the conclusion is obvious:

Hence, when seeking why God should be loved, if one asks what right he has to be loved, the answer is that the main reason for loving him is that 'He loved us first' [1 Jn 4:9-10].[34]

But this is merely a clarification of Bernard's basic teaching on the necessity for loving God: '... I can see no other reason for loving him than himself.'[35]

God is Love and should be loved. Because he is infinite, the response should be total: 'As for [the question] how he is to be loved, there is to be no limit to that love.'[36] One's love should know no limits, since everything one is, has, or does is the product of God's creation or re-creation:

The fact that man was made out of nothing, gratuitously and in this dignity, renders clearer the debt of love and proves the divine exaction more just.... If I owe all for having been created, what can I add for having been re-created, and in this way? It was less easy to re-create me than to create me.... He who made me by a single word, in remaking me had to speak many words, work miracles, suffer hardships—and not only hardships but unjust treatment. 'What shall I give to the Lord for all he has given me [Ps 115:12]?' In the first work he gave me myself; in his second work he gave me himself. When he gave me himself, he gave me back myself. Given, and re-given, I owe myself twice over.[37]

Bernard asks the obvious question: 'What can I give to God in return for himself? Even if I could give him myself a thousand times, what am I to God [see Jb 9:3]?'[38] Bernard's answer is that one should love God with all one's heart. However inadequate a response this is, it is all that is expected:

> Rightly, then, does the bride renounce all other affections and devote herself to love alone, for it is in returning love that she has the power to respond to love. Although she may pour out her whole self in love, what is that compared to the inexhaustible fountain of his love? The stream of love does not flow equally from her who loves and from him who is love, the soul and the Word, the bride and the Bridegroom, the creature and the Creator—any more than a thirsty man can be compared to a fountain. Will the bride's vow perish, then, because of this? Will the desire of her heart, her burning love, her affirmation of confidence, fail in their purpose because she does not have the strength to keep pace with a giant, or rival honey in sweetness, the lamb in gentleness, the lily in whiteness? Because she cannot equal the brightness of the sun and the love of him who is Love [1 Jn 4:16]? No. Although the creature loves less, being a lesser being, yet if she loves with her whole heart [Mt 22:37] nothing is lacking, for she has given all.[39]

If one will direct one's will to God, then one will experience God in proportion to the intensity of one's love:

> But you, if you love the Lord your God with your whole heart, whole mind, whole strength [Mk 12:30] and, leaping with ardent feeling beyond that love of love with which active love is satisfied and having received the Spirit in fullness, are wholly aflame with that divine love to which the former is a step, then God is truly ex-

perienced, although not as he truly is—a thing impossible for any creature—but rather in relation to your power to enjoy.[40]

God should be loved for his own sake. He should be loved truthfully, purely, with justice, freely. 'This is the third degree of love...'[41] in which one no longer seeks one's own benefit in one's love for oneself or for God.[42] If one continues in this love for God, one's quest will be successful; there is no fear of failure in Bernard's mind:

> The psalmist says: 'Seek his face always' [Ps 104:4].
> Nor, I think, will the soul cease to seek him even when she has found him. It is not with steps of the feet that God is sought, but with the heart's desire. And, when the soul happily finds him, her desire is not quenched but kindled. Does the consummation of joy bring about the consuming of desire? Rather it is oil poured on the flames. So it is. Joy will be fulfilled [Ps 15:11], but there will be no end to desire and, therefore, no end to the search. Think, if you can, of this eagerness to see God as not caused by his absence, for he is always present. And think of the desire for God as without fear of failure, for grace is abundantly present.[43]

God must be the object of one's loving desire and longing. That desire will be fulfilled; one will be happy in the measure that one loves.

Notes: *The Objects of Love* 115

1. SC 50, 8; SBOp 2:82-83; CF 31:36-37.
2. SC 75, 9; SBOp 2:252; CF 40:105.
3. SC 18, 3; SBOp 1:104; CF 4:135.
4. SC 42, 9; SBOp 2:39; CF 7:217.
5. S Mal 3; SBOp 6/1:52; CF 10:109.
6. SC 50, 6; SBOp 2:82; CF 31:35.
7. SC 50, 7; SBOp 2:82; CF 31:36.
8. SC 12, 7; SBOp 1:64; CF 4:82-83.
9. S Mal 3; SBOp 6/1:52; CF 10:109.
10. Dil 12, 34; SBOp 3:148; CF 13:125.
11. Dil 8, 25; SBOp 3:139; CF 13:117.
12. Dil 8, 23; SBOp 3:138-39; CF 13:115-16.
13. Dil 8, 24; SBOp 3:139; CF 13:116.
14. SC 27, 10; SBOp 1:189; CF 7:83. See also Ep 85, 3; SBOp 7:221-22; James, p. 126.
15. SC 27, 10-11; SBOp 1:189-90; CF 7:83-84.
16. SC 27, 11; SBOp 1:190; CF 7:84.
17. For an excellent discussion of Bernard and friendship, see Brian Patrick McGuire, 'Was Bernard a Friend?' in E. Rozanne Elder (ed.), *Goad and Nail: Studies in Medieval Cistercian History*, X, CS 84 (Kalamazoo, Michigan: Cistercian Publications, 1985) pp. 201-227. See also McGuire's *Friendship & Community: The Monastic Experience 350-1250*, CS 95 (Kalamazoo, Michigan: Cistercian Publications Inc., 1988) pp. 252-57.
18. SC 26, 10; SBOp 1:178; CF 7:69.
19. SC 26, 8-9; SBOp 1:177; CF 7:68.
20. SC 26, 9; SBOp 1:177; CF 7:69.
21. Ep 387; SBOp 8:355; James, p. 378.
22. Ep 228, 1; SBOp 8:98-99; James, p. 375.
23. Ep 228, 2; SBOp 8:99; James, p. 375.
24. SC 14, 6; SBOp 1:80; CF 4:102-103.
25. V Mal 31, 70; SBOp 3:374; CF 10:88.
26. SC 26, 4; SBOp 1:172; CF 7:62.
27. Ep 390, 1; SBOp 8:358; James, p. 493.
28. Ep 116; SBOp 7:296; James, p. 181. See also Leclercq, *Bernard of Clairvaux and the Cistercian Spirit*, pp. 44-45.
29. Ep 390, 1; SBOp 8:358; James, p. 493.
30. SC 59, 1; SBOp 2:135-36; CF 31:120-21.
31. SC 59, 1; SBOp 2:136; CF 31:121.
32. SC 59, 2; SBOp 2:136; CF 31:121.
33. Dil 1, 1; SBOp 3:120-21; CF 13:94.
34. Dil 1, 1; SBOp 3:120; CF 13:94.
35. Dil 1, 1; SBOp 3:120; CF 13:93.
36. Dil 1, 1; SBOp 3:119; CF 13:93.
37. Dil 5, 15; SBOp 3:131-32; CF 13:108.
38. Dil 5, 15; SBOp 3:132; CF 13:108.
39. SC 83, 6; SBOp 2:302; CF 40:185-86.
40. SC 50, 6; SBOp 2:81-82; CF 31:35.
41. Dil 9, 26; SBOp 3:141; CF 13:119.
42. See Dil 8-9, 23-26; SBOp 3:138-41; CF 13:115-19.
43. SC 84, 1; SBOp 2:303; CF 40:188-89.

D. The Nature of Love

What of the relationship between these objects of love? Where does love begin? Bernard's answers seem equivocal. Love begins with empathy, love for others.[1] Yet one cannot have empathy until one knows and loves oneself.[2] But one cannot truly love oneself except in God.[3] In the end, I think, the question is inappropriate. For Bernard, all loves are part of one love which is the proper ordering of the will toward the good. Bernard sometimes asserts, depending on the rhetorical flow of his argument, that one must begin with one love or another. Bernard is concerned not so much with which object the lover begins as with the lover's proper motivation:

> Because we are flesh and blood born of the desire of the flesh, our desire or love must begin in the flesh. And it will then, if properly directed, progress under grace by stages until it is fulfilled in the spirit.... At first man loves himself for his own sake. He is flesh and is able only to know himself. But when he sees that he cannot subsist of himself, then he begins by faith to seek and love God as necessary for himself. And so in the second stage he loves God, not yet for God's sake but for his own sake. However when, on account of his own necessity, he begins to meditate, read, pray, and obey, he becomes accustomed little by little to know God and consequently to delight in him. When he has tasted and found how sweet is the Lord, he passes to the third stage in which he loves God for God's sake and not for his own.[4]

Proper motivation, right intention, proper ordering of the will, expressed in action, is love. Bernard's message is clear: one must love to be complete, whole, happy.

E. The Fruits of Love

Happiness is the ultimate goal and realization of love. But there is other desirable fruit to be plucked on the path to perfection. Bernard's parable of the King's son tells of some of love's happy effects on the soul:

> When the King heard of the danger his son was in, he turned to Love, his royal consort, and said: 'Whom shall we send? Who will go for us?' She replied: 'Here I am. Send me' [Is 6:8]. And the King said: 'Your conquest shall be victorious. You shall set him free.' The whole heavenly court accompanied Love, the Queen of Heaven, as she went out from the face of the Lord. When they made their way down into the camp, all who were inside were enlivened by the joy and strength of her presence. Turbulence subsided, and upheaval came to rest. Light returned to these unhappy people, and boldness came back to those who were cowed. Hope, who was on the point of running away, returned, and Fortitude, who was almost overcome, revived. Wisdom's whole army became firm once more.[5]

Love brings freedom,[6] joy and peace, strength and fortitude, hope and wisdom. 'What else is the love of God but progress in wisdom.'[7]

Fire is an image of love. This fire of love burns out vice and makes meditation glow:

> The fire of holy desire ought to precede God's coming to every soul whom he will visit, to burn up the rust of bad habits and so prepare a place for the Lord. The soul will know that the Lord is near [Ps 33:19] when she perceives herself aflame with that fire. Then she can say as the Prophet did: 'He has sent a fire from on high down to my bones, and he enlightened me' [Lm 1:13]; and again: 'My heart became hot within me, and in my meditation fire burst forth' [1 Th 5:17].[8]

This fire is a flame which heals and transforms rather than destroys:

> The fire that is God does indeed devour, but it does not debase. It burns pleasantly, devastates felicitously. It is a coal of desolating fire [Ps 119:4], but a fire that rages against vices only to produce a healing unction in the soul. Recognize, therefore, that the Lord is

> present both in the power that transforms you and in
> the love which sets you aglow. The Lord's right hand
> has shown its power [Ps 117:16]. But understand that
> this change from the Lord's right hand [Ps 76:11] takes
> place only in fervor of spirit and genuine love [2 Co
> 6:6]. Then you will be a man who can say: 'My heart
> became hot within me; as I mused the fire burned' [Ps
> 38:4].[9]

The fire of love, having purified one's will, also illuminates one's intellect:

> Furthermore, when this fire has consumed every stain
> of sin and the rust of evil habits, when the conscience
> has been cleansed and pacified, there follows an im-
> mediate and unaccustomed expansion of the mind, an
> infusion of light which illuminates the intellect so that
> it can understand Scripture and comprehend the mys-
> teries.... All this undoubtedly means that his eye be-
> holds you, nurturing your uprightness as a light and your
> integrity as the noonday. As Isaiah says: 'Your light shall
> break forth as the dawn' [Is 58:8].[10]

Progress in the spiritual life is not a series of steps, from the perfection of the intellect in humility to the perfection of the will in love. The spiritual journey is a spiral progression: love leads to knowledge as knowledge leads to love.

F. The Way of Love

Spiritual progress is growth in maturity. Growth in love expands the soul, so that she becomes broad enough for the Lord to enter, high enough to be measured with the stature of the Lord:

> The soul must grow and expand so that she may be roomy enough for God. Her width is her love, if we accept what the Apostle says: 'Widen your hearts in love' [2 Co 6:13]. The soul, being a spirit, does not admit of a material expansion, but grace bestows gifts on her that nature is not equipped to bestow. Her growth and expansion must be understood in a spiritual sense; it is her virtue which increases, not her substance. Even her glory is increased. And finally she grows and advances toward 'mature adulthood, to the measure of the stature of Christ's fullness' [Eph 4:13]. Eventually she becomes 'a holy temple in the Lord' [Eph 2:21].[11]

Growth in love is a gift of God. That growth makes union with God possible.

The model for that growth is Christ himself:

> Consider the love of Christ as revealed in his passion. As he himself declares: 'Greater love than this no man has, that he lay down his life for his friends' [Jn 15:13].[12]

Christ's life exhibited love's true characteristics, characteristics which one must cultivate:

> His love was sweet and wise and strong. I call it sweet because he took on a human body, wise because he avoided sin, strong because he endured death. Even though he took a body, his love was never sensual, but always in the wisdom of the Spirit. 'A spirit before our face is Christ the Lord' [Lm 4:20], jealous of us, but with the jealousy of God [2 Co 11:2] not man, and certainly not like that of the first man, Adam, for Eve. So those whom he sought in a body, he loved in spirit and redeemed in power. How sweet it is to see as man the Creator of humanity. While he carefully protected nature from sin, he forcefully drove death from that nature as well. In taking a body he stooped to me, in avoiding sin he took counsel with himself, in accepting death he satisfied the Father. A dear friend, a wise

counselor, a strong helper.... Christian, learn from Christ how you ought to love Christ. Learn a love that is tender, wise, and strong. Love with tenderness, not with passion, wisdom not foolishness, and strength, lest you become weary and turn away from the love of the Lord.[13]

Under the impulse of God's grace, the lover grows in imitation of Christ's love. That love, Bernard teaches, will make one free. And that freedom will lead to happiness.

1. See above, pp. 90-92.
2. See above, pp. 89-90.
3. See above, p. 103.
4. Ep 11, 8; SBOp 7:58; James, p. 46.
5. Par 1, 6; SBOp 6/2:266; CSt 18:22.
6. See above, pp. 95-94.
7. Ep 107, 5; SBOp 7:271; James, p. 161.
8. SC 31, 4; SBOp 1:221-22; CF 7:127.
9. SC 57, 7; SBOp 2:123-24; CF 31:102.
10. SC 57, 8; SBOp 2:124; CF 31:102-103.
11. SC 27, 10; SBOp 1:189; CF 7:83.
12. V Nat 4, 7; SBOp 4:224; Luddy 1:350.
13. SC 20, 3-4; SBOp 1:115-16; CF 4:148-49.

IV. THE LIFE OF LOVE

Meditation and self-control are the human being's responsibility in the perfection of the intellect which is humility. The perfection of the will in love requires an exercise of the human power of free choice, a freedom not lost in the Fall.[1] One's happiness is contingent on one's proper use of this power.[2]

One is happy to the extent that one loves, and so the process by which one becomes a lover is crucial. Thus, Bernard's spiritual teaching is largely concerned with the life which promotes one's perfection in love.

A. Conversion: The Turning of the Will

The first step in the perfection of the will is its turning toward its proper end, the good. This conversion requires humility, a recognition that one is oriented toward evil, toward that which has brought, does and will bring about unhappiness. One must recognize one's own self-destructive orientation and behavior; this comes about 'When the sinner comes to know his state, when he sees himself as contrasted with what he should be....'[3] As Bernard puts it, when people see themselves in the light of truth

> ...they are brought face to face with themselves and blush at what they see. Their present state is no pleasure to them. They aspire to something better and, at the same time, realize how little they can rely on themselves to achieve it.[4]

The proper consequence of this realization is sorrow:

> Humility has its own contribution to the banquet [offered by God] and graces the dish with the bread of sorrow [Ps 126:2] and the wine of compunction [Ps 59:5]. Truth offers these first to beginners, saying: 'Rise up after you have been seated, you who eat the bread of sorrow' [Ps 126:2].[5]

Sorrowful repentance will in turn elicit forgiveness, and forgiveness will lead to a spiritual awakening. Consciousness of sin, of the disordered state of one's life, begins this process:

> All you who are conscious of sin, do not regard as unworthy and despicable that position in which the holy sinner laid down her sins and put on the garment of holiness.... You may ask what skill enabled her to

accomplish this change or on what grounds did she merit it? I can tell you in a few words. She wept bitterly [Lk 22:62]; she sighed deeply from her heart; she sobbed with a repentance that shook her very being—until the evil that inflamed her passions was cleansed away.[6]

This cleansing is accomplished by God, who, as a gift, heals the soul and prepares her for the life of love:

> The heavenly physician came speedily to her aid, for 'his word runs swiftly' [Ps 147:15]. Perhaps you think the Word of God is not a medicine? It surely is, a medicine strong and pungent, testing the mind and the heart [Ps 7:10]. 'The Word of God is something alive and active. It cuts like any double-edged sword, but more finely. It can slip through the place where the soul is divided from the spirit or the joints from the marrow. It can judge secret thoughts' [Heb 4:12].[7]

One's participation in this healing process will result in an awakening which will alert the soul to the path she is to follow:

> It is up to you, wretched sinner, to humble yourself as this happy penitent did, so that you may be rid of your wretchedness [Lk 7:37 ff.]. Prostrate yourself on the ground, take hold of his [Christ's] feet, soothe them with kisses, sprinkle them with your tears, and so wash not them but yourself. Thus you will become one of the 'flock of shorn ewes as they come up from the washing' [Sg 4:2]. Even then you may not dare to lift up a face suffused with shame and grief until you hear the sentence: 'Your sins are forgiven' [Lk 7:48], to be followed by the summons: 'Awake, awake, captive daughter of Sion; awake, shake off the dust' [Is 52:1-2].[8]

Conversion of life, then, is the first step on the path to perfection.[9]

One's motives for reorienting one's will toward the good may be many, but all of them can be useful. Shame is surely one motive:

> But as well as being my Father, he has overwhelmed me with favors, countless favors that repeatedly bear witness against me [Jb 10:17]: the daily nourishment of my body, the prolonged gift of time, and, above all, the blood of his beloved Son that cries out to him from the earth [Gn 4:10]. I blush for my ingratitude. To add to my confusion I stand convicted of returning evil for good and hatred for love [Ps 108:5].[10]

But shame should not be devastating. Bernard's shame is matched by his confidence in God's loving kindness:

> But I need fear my benefactor no more than I need fear my Father. For he is a genuine benefactor who showers down his gifts abundantly and never reproaches [Jm 1:5]. There is no reproach on account of the gifts because they are gifts, and his favors were bestowed on me, not sold. And finally, these gifts are irrevocable [Rm 11:29].[11]

However, the increasing recognition of God's loving kindness leads Bernard to shame and grief at his unworthy response:

> But the more I appreciate his kindness, the more compelled I am to recognize my unworthiness. Be ashamed and grieve, O my soul, for, though it becomes him not to utter reproaches nor revoke his gifts, it is entirely unbecoming for us to remain ungrateful and forgetful.[12]

Fear too can play a role in one's conversion: 'If shame proves slow in accomplishing what it ought, let fear be summoned to aid us.'[13] Bernard believes the world is ordered in justice; to defy that order must result in fearful consequences:

> Consider how dreadful it is, how terrifying, to have despised your Creator, the Maker of all things, to have offended so majestic a Lord. Majesty and sovereignty inspire fear, especially the majesty and sovereignty of God. If human laws impose the death penalty on one guilty of treason against the head of the state, what will be fate of those who spurn God's omnipotence?[14]

A proper response to the justice which orders the universe will result in one's justification:

> Over them the sun rises, not the sun which is seen to shine every day on the good and bad alike, since only to those who are called is the prophetic promise made: 'For you that fear my name the sun of justice shall rise' [Ml 4:2]. While the sons of unbelief stay out in the darkness, the sons of light go out from the power of darkness into this new light, providing they can truthfully say to God: 'We partake with all who fear you' [Ps 118:63]. Do you see how fear must go first that justification may follow?[15]

Fear can have salutary effects, then, but fear can also be dangerous—especially to those new to conversion:

All of us who have been converted to the Lord have felt and still feel the truth of what Scripture says: 'My son, if you come forward to serve the Lord, stand in fear and prepare your soul for temptation' [Si 2:1]. Our common experience tells us that it is fear which disturbs us at the beginning of our conversion, fear of that dismaying picture we form for ourselves of the strict life and unwonted austerities we are about to embrace. This is called a nocturnal fear [Sg 3:8; Ps 90:5], either because adversity is usually represented in Scripture by darkness or because the reward for which we are prepared to suffer adversity is not yet revealed to us. For if we could see the dawn of that day in the light of which we should perceive the rewards as well as the trials, our desire of the rewards would entirely obliterate fear. In the clear light it would be apparent that 'the sufferings we now endure bear no comparison with the splendor, as yet unrevealed, which awaits us' [Rm 8:18].... Beginners on the way to God, therefore, must in particular watch and pray against this first temptation [Mt 26:41] or they will be overcome by timidity of spirit as by a storm [Ps 54:9] and unfortunately recoil from the good work they have begun.[16]

Fear can be a good beginning. But its effectiveness is limited, and fear can be debilitating if it does not soon turn into love. Bernard uses the wedding feast at Cana as the vehicle for his instruction on this point:

And not without good reason is 'water' interpreted as 'fear', for as water quenches fire, so fear quenches libidinous desires. And as water washes away stains on the body, so does fear remove stains on the soul.... But water dulls us and fear afflicts us. Let us hasten, therefore, to him who changes fear and affliction into love....[17]

Love is also a powerful motive for conversion: 'Love converts souls because it makes them act willingly.'[18] Just as humility, realistic self-appraisal, can bring about the shame which leads to conversion, so too can love. The soul '... is confident that she is loved because she feels that she loves; because she sees that she is loved, she is ashamed not to love in return.'[19] Love is the will's desire for the good; it is the inspiration which allows one to hope for

success in the beginnings of one's conversion. Bernard expresses this allegorically in his parable of the King's son:
> Hope replied: 'Do not be afraid. He who helps us is kind; he who fights on our side is all-powerful. There are more for us than for them [2 K 6:16]. Moreover, I have brought a horse for you which your father sent, a horse named Desire. Astride this horse and with my guidance you will advance, safe from all of them.'[20]

One who wills conversion receives the power to convert as a gift of God. Indeed, the very desire is a gift from God; it is a result of 'prevenient grace':[21]
> Listen to me who was a fugitive and a wanderer: 'I have gone astray as a sheep that was lost. O seek your servant' [Ps 118:176]. O man, do you wish to return? But if it is a matter of the will, why do you ask for help? Why do you beg elsewhere for what you have within you in abundance? Clearly because one wills it but cannot do it.... If a soul desires to return and asks to be sought, I should not say that she was entirely dishonored and abandoned. Whence does she obtain this desire? If I am not mistaken, it is the result of the soul already being sought and visited. And that seeking has not been fruitless, because it has activated the will without which there would be no return.[22]

One who seeks God has already found him—or, rather, has already been found by him:
> O Lord, you are so good to the soul who seeks you [Lm 3:25], what must you be to the one who finds you? More wonderful still, no one can seek you unless he has already found you. You wish to be found that you may be sought for, and sought for to be found.[23]

Both conversion and perseverance in that conversion are the gifts of God: 'He who gave me the grace to repent must also give me the power to persevere.... Of myself I can achieve neither repentance nor perseverance....'[24]

Fear of the consequences of choosing evil and confidence that God will bestow the power to turn toward good should inspire one to love:
> But of one thing you must careful: that you do not neglect [kissing] either of these feet [of Christ]. If, for instance, you feel deep sorrow for your sins along with

fear of judgment, you have pressed your lips on the imprint of truth and of judgment. But if you temper that fear and sorrow with the thought of God's goodness and the hope of obtaining his pardon, you will also realize that you have embraced the foot of his mercy. It is clearly inexpedient to kiss one without the other. A man who thinks only of judgment will fall into the pit of despair; another who deceitfully flatters God's mercy gives birth to a pernicious security.[25]

Presumption may be an error, but confidence is most appropriate. God does call one to conversion;[26] he does want one to be converted and live.[27] God tirelessly awaits the sinner and promptly bestows on the penitent his forgiveness:

These two breasts [of the Bridegroom] are two proofs of his native kindness: his patience in awaiting the sinner and his welcoming mercy for the penitent. This twofold sweetness of inward joy overflows from the heart of the Lord Jesus in the form of tireless expectancy and prompt forgiveness. And be assured that this is no figment of mine. You yourselves have read of his patience: 'Are you abusing his abundant goodness, patience, and toleration, not realizing that this goodness of God is meant to lead you to repentance [Rm 2:4]?' To this very end he postpones his punishment of the obstinately disobedient, awaiting a favorable moment to bestow on them the grace of repentance and forgiveness. He does not wish the death of the wicked man, but that he turn back and live [Ezk 33:11]. And now let us see an example of the second breast, which I have called promptness to forgive. Of this you have read: 'At whatever hour the sinner will repent, his sin will be forgiven him' [see Ezk 33:12-19; Is 30:15]. Or again: 'Let the wicked man abandon his way, the evil man his thoughts. Let him turn back to the Lord who will take pity on him, to our God who is rich in forgiving' [Is 55:7]. David beautifully described both breasts in a few words: 'Slow to anger, most loving' [Ps 102:8].[28]

Bernard's confidence in the successful outcome of the conversion process is based on his recognition of the goodness of God. But conversion is not only the beginning of a vertical relationship between man and God. Like all other forms of love, it has a horizontal, social dimension:

> In the affection of our hearts and the perfection of our conversion, let us return devout thanks to the almighty and merciful God that he has willed that we, unworthy servants utterly without merits of our own, are at least never without someone else's prayers.[29]

Bernard believes that genuine conversion leads to confession, the expression of a deep human need: 'The heartfelt desire to admit one's guilt brings a man down in lowliness before God, as it were, to his feet. . . .'[30] That need is really a reflection of proper love of self, for confession is a means of purging the disorder in one's will: 'It is a great perversity not to have mercy on yourself and to reject the only remedy of confessing your sins.'[31]

Proper confession requires a desire for an ordered will; that desire is itself a proper ordering of the will in love. It is, again, a love which begins with oneself:

> The first step for the man extricating himself from the depths of misery is the mercy [Lk 1:79] which makes him merciful to the son of his mother [Is 49:15], to be merciful to his soul [Si 30:24], and thereby be pleasing to God. In this way he emulates the great works of divine pity, being moved to tears with him who was pierced for him, somehow dying for his own salvation, and sparing himself no longer. This first act of pity sustains the man returning to his own heart [Is 46:8] and enables him to enter the secret places of his being.[32]

Out of true love for self, the newly-converted expresses the need for confession:

> It now remains for him to link up with the royal road [Nb 21:22] and go forward to truth, to join confession of the lips to contrition of heart, as I have so often urged you to do. 'For man believes with his heart and so is justified, and he confesses with his lips and so is saved' [Rm 10:10]. Turning back to his heart [Ps 85:8], he must become little in his own eyes. As Truth himself has said: 'Unless you turn back and become as little children, you will not enter the kingdom of heaven' [Mt 18:3]. May he not hide what he knows only too well, or he will be reduced to nothing [Ps 73:21]. May he

not be ashamed to bring into the light of truth what he
cannot see in secret without being moved to pity. In
this way a man enters the ways of mercy and truth, the
ways of the Lord, the ways of life [Ps 16:11]. And the
fruit of these ways is the salvation of the wayfarer.[33]

Confession, then, is the product of proper self-love.

But self-knowledge, humility, is also necessary to a confession which sets the wayfarer on the path to perfection. Confession must proceed '...from a loving, guileless, and trusting heart. These conditions will be fulfilled if he confesses all that pricks his conscience with humility, sincerity, and trust.'[34]

Again, Bernard is confident in the results:

You must confess your sins in the spirit of faith, so that
you may confess them with the hope that has no doubt
of pardon....[35]

Bernard's confidence in the efficacy of confession is based on his reading of Scripture:

...God will not despise a humble and contrite heart
[Ps 50:19]. One is even exhorted to do this: confess
your iniquities that you may be made righteous [Is
43:26].[36]

Bernard's fortieth sermon *De diversis* summarizes his teaching on confession:

The first path and the first step in this way is undoubtedly self-knowledge. From heaven has come the familiar saying: 'Know yourself, mortal.'...Now self-knowledge embraces three things: that a man be aware of what he has done, what he has deserved, and what he has lost.... The second step in the way of confession is repentance. It is closely connected with the first, for to know oneself it is necessary to be repentant, and to be repentant it is necessary to know oneself.... The third step is sorrow.... If you are not moved at the thought of having offended your Creator, or by the fear of his almighty power, at least be ashamed of your ingratitude in despising so great a benefactor who has loaded you with so many and such precious gifts.[37]

These first three steps of confession are also a summary of the process of conversion of which confession is the culmination. That confession '...must be true, candid, and personal.'[38]

Bernard is clearly aware that the process of conversion is beset with trials and difficulties:
> Daily experience teaches us that those who are bent on conversion find themselves goaded more sharply by the lust of the flesh [1 Jn 2:16]. Those who have come out of Egypt, determined to flee from Pharaoh [Ex 2:15], are driven back to work harder at making mortar and brick [Ex 1:14].[39]

But Bernard's confidence remains firm and secure: 'The Psalmist says about our conversion: "He will not forget his holy ones; they will be kept safe forever" [Ps 36:28].'[40] This confident knowledge should inspire one to real holiness, to the vision of God which is happiness:
> Repentant sinners, therefore, who wish to attain to that holiness essential for the vision of God [Heb 12:14], should listen to your admonition: 'Be holy for I am holy' [Lv 19:2]. Let them pay attention to your ways, for you are just in all your ways and holy in all your doings [Ps 144:17]. Finally, how many are inspired to run by the sweet odor of your redemption! When you are lifted up from the earth you draw all things to yourself [Jn 12:32].[41]

Conversion, then, is the first step on the path to the perfection of the will; it is the first turning of that will toward its proper object, the good. In Bernard's eighteenth sermon on the *Song of Songs*, he describes this step:
> Therefore, when the Spirit draws near to a soul that says: 'My wounds grow foul and fester because of my foolishness' [Ps 37:6], what is the first thing he should do? Before all else he must amputate the ulcerous tumor that has grown on the wound and prevents its healing. This ulcer, caused by inveterate bad habits, must be sliced away by the scalpel of piercing sorrow. The pain will be bitter, but it can be alleviated with the ointment of devotion, which is nothing other than the joy born of the hope of pardon. This in turn springs from the power of self-control, from victory over sin.[42]

Bernard then goes on in a concatenation of metaphors to outline the further steps on the path of love:
> Soon the victor is pouring out words of thanks: 'You have loosed my bonds; I will offer you the thanksgiving

sacrifice' [Ps 115:16f.]. He then applies the medicine of penance, a poultice of fastings, vigils, prayers, and the other tasks that penitents perform. And as he toils he must be fed with the food of good works that he may not falter. We are not left in doubt about what the necessary food is: 'My food', said Christ, 'is to do the will of my Father' [Jn 4:34]. Hence works motivated by love, that are a sure source of strength, should accompany the performance of penances. For instance it is said: 'Alms is a most effective offering for all those who give it in the presence of the Most High' [Tb 4:12]. Food causes thirst; therefore one must drink. So let the food of good works be moistened with the beverage of prayer, that a work well done may rest quietly in the stomach of conscience and give pleasure to God.[43]

This is Bernard's program for the life of love, and I shall describe it in some detail in the pages that follow. But I shall follow this outline only roughly, since Bernard's lists and steps are suited to the rhetorical needs of the sermon or treatise at hand rather than being based on a systematic standard. This is quite clear in the eighteenth sermon on the *Song of Songs* I have quoted. Almost immediately after the list of steps quoted above, he gives another list, substantially the same, but differing in detail:

> We need, first of all, compunction of heart, then fervor of spirit; thirdly, the labor of penance; fourthly, works of love; fifthly, zeal for prayer....[44]

Then Bernard extends the list; the pilgrim on the path to perfection needs to cultivate,

> ...sixthly, leisure for contemplation; and seventhly, love in all its fullness. All these are the work of one and the same Spirit [1 Co 12:11]....[45]

Perfection in love, like perfection in humility, is a gift. Once more we must examine grace as well.

1. See above, pp. 21-22.
2. See above, p. 11.
3. Pierre Pourrat, *Christian Spirituality in the Middle Ages*, trans. S. P. Jacques (Westminster, Maryland: The Newman Press, 1953) p. 27.
4. Hum 5, 18; SBOp 3:29; CF 13:45. See above, pp. 55-56, where I have quoted this passage more extensively.
5. Hum 2, 4; SBOp 3:19; CF 13:32.
6. SC 3, 2; SBOp 1:15; CF 4:17.
7. SC 3, 2; SBOp 1:15; CF 4:17.
8. SC 3, 2; SBOp 1:15; CF 4:17-18.
9. SC 4, 1; SBOp 1:18; CF 4:21.
10. SC 16, 5; SBOp 1:92; CF 4:118. Conversion does not necessarily mean entering a monastery, as has been understood so often. See my 'The Intellectual Life According to Saint Bernard', Cîteaux 25 (1974) 249-56.
11. SC 16, 5; SBOp 1:92; CF 4:118.
12. SC 16, 5; SBOp 1:92; CF 4:118.
13. SC 16, 6; SBOp 1:92; CF 4:118.
14. SC 16, 7; SBOp 1:93; CF 4:119.
15. Ep 107, 4; SBOp 7:270; James, p. 160.
16. SC 33, 11; SBOp 1:241-42; CF 7:154-55.
17. Div 121; SBOp 6/1:398.
18. Dil 12, 34; SBOp 3:149; CF 13:126.
19. Ep 107, 7; SBOp 7:272; James, p. 162.
20. Par 1, 3; SBOp 6/2:263; CSt 18:19-20.
21. SC 84, 4; SBOp 2:305; CF 40:191.
22. SC 84, 3; SBOp 2:304; CF 40:190.
23. Dil 7, 22; SBOp 3:137-38; CF 13:114-15.
24. SC 3, 3; SBOp 1:16; CF 4:18.
25. SC 6, 8; SBOp 1:30; CF 4:36-37.
26. Ep 107, 4; SBOp 7:270; James, p. 160.
27. Ep 107, 7; SBOp 7:272; James, p. 162.
28. SC 9, 5; SBOp 1:45; CF 4:57. An interesting study of maternal imagery for God in twelfth-century Cistercian spirituality is found in chapter 4, pp. 110-69, of Caroline Walker Bynum's *Jesus As Mother: Studies in the Spirituality of the High Middle Ages* (Berkeley, Los Angeles, London: University of California Press, 1982).
29. Mal 8; SBOp 5:423; CF 10:104.
30. SC 4, 4; SBOp 1:20; CF 4:23. See also Sent 3, 98; SBOp 6/2:162.
31. Tpl 8, 15; SBOp 3:227; CF 19:150-51.
32. QH 11, 9; SBOp 4:454-55; CF 25:209.
33. QH 11, 9; SBOp 4:455; CF 25:209-210.
34. SC 16, 8; SBOp 1:94; CF 4:120.
35. SC 16, 12; SBOp 1:96; CF 4:123.
36. SC 56, 7; SBOp 2:118; CF 31:93.
37. Div 40, 3-5; SBOp 6/1:236-39; Luddy 3:446-47, 451.
38. Div 40, 6; SBOp 6/1:239; Luddy 3:453.
39. Conv 11, 22; SBOp 4:95; CF 25:57. See also SC 33, 13; SBOp 1:243; CF 7:156.
40. Dil 5, 14; SBOp 3:130-31; CF 13:107.
41. SC 22, 8; SBOp 1:134; CF 7:20-21.
42. SC 18, 5; SBOp 1:106; CF 4:137.

43. SC 18, 5; SBOp 1:106-107; CF 4:137.
44. SC 18, 6; SBOp 1:108; CF 4:138-39.
45. SC 18, 6; SBOp 1:108; CF 4:139.

B. Self-discipline: The Recovery of Self-possession

Self-control, self-restraint, self-discipline provide the pilgrim soul with the time she needs to progress toward the perfection of the intellect in humility.[1] That self-discipline is an exercise of the will which also promotes its orientation toward the good in love. An intellect which recognizes reality and a will oriented toward the good of the really real are necessary complements and essential components of the happy person. Self-discipline promotes both:

> ...If you persevere [in self-discipline], your 'sorrow will be turned to joy' [Jn 16:20]. For then your intellect will be enlightened and your will renewed. Rather, your will will be re-created, so that what before appeared difficult, impossible indeed, you will accomplish now with greatest pleasure and eagerness.[2]

Regulation of the will is the goal of self-discipline:

> But since there is no way to the kingdom of God without the first fruits of the kingdom, and since the man who does not yet rule his own members cannot hope for the heavenly kingdom, the [divine] voice goes on to say: 'Blessed are the meek, for they shall inherit the earth' [Mt 5:5]. Put more clearly, this means: 'Tame the savage movements of your will and take pains to tame this cruel beast.'[3]

But the goal of this regulation is not to break the will but rather to restore its freedom:

> You are all tied up; endeavor to untie what you cannot break outright. [Your will] is your Eve. Never will you be able to do her violence or overcome her.[4]

The freedom that will allow one's perfection requires the will to be oriented toward that perfection, not toward activities that will distract it from its goal:

> What can I say of her who can provide avenues spacious enough for the God of majesty to walk in! She certainly cannot afford to be entangled in law-suits or by worldly cares. She cannot be enslaved by gluttony and sensual pleasures, by the lust of the eyes, the ambition to rule, or by pride in the possession of power. If she is to become heaven, the dwelling-place of God, it is first of all essential that she be empty of all these defects.[5]

Emptying oneself of desires not directed toward one's true destiny is a hard task which requires assiduous effort. But the effort will bring the maturity of freedom:
> 'We have a wisdom to offer those who have reached maturity' [1 Co 2:6], in whose company, I feel assured, you are to be found, unless in vain you have prolonged your study of divine teaching, mortified your senses, and meditated day and night on God's law [Ps 1:2].[6]

That maturity in freedom will make one whole, consistent, and stable:
> There is a moral unity by which the man of virtue strives to be free of instability and inconsistency and be always one with himself.[7]

In obtaining the self-control which leads to maturity and freedom, one must follow the example of the man who was completely one with himself:
> ... The soul says [to Christ]: 'Draw me after you' [Sg 1:3].... Because she says 'after you', she seems to appeal for the grace to follow the example of his way of life, to emulate his virtue, to hold fast to a rule of life similar to his and achieve some measure of his self-control. This is a work for which she needs all the help possible in order to deny herself, take up her cross, and follow Christ [Mt 16:24].[8]

What are the practices which constitute Christ's 'rule of life'? Bernard gives a manifold and varied response. In his second sermon for the first Sunday after Epiphany, these practices are symbolized by the six water jars of the wedding feast at Cana:
> My brothers, it seems to me that by the six water jars we should understand the six observances instituted by the holy fathers for purifying the hearts of those who confess their sins.... The first of these spiritual water jars is the practice of continence by which we wash away the stains from our past sensual indulgence. The second is fasting, for we employ abstinence from food as a means of cleansing what gluttony has defiled. By sloth also and by idleness, which is the enemy of the soul [RB 48], we have contracted much defilement, eating our bread not, as the Lord has commanded, in the sweat of our own brow [Gn 3:19], but in the sweat of our

neighbor's. We have, therefore, a third water jar placed before us, manual labor, by which we can wash ourselves clean from the stains of sloth.[9]
This cleansing process does not deny the validity of sense-experience, of eating, or of leisure.[10] The desire for these goods must be regulated toward its proper end. The same is true of the practices symbolized by the remaining three water jars:

We have committed many sins through sleepiness and other works of the night and darkness. Hence there is another water jar set before us, the observance of regular vigils whereby we rise in the night to confess the Lord and redeem the many nights we have spent in evil. Concerning the tongue, who does not know how much defilement we have contracted from it through idle and untruthful words, through detraction and flattery, through malicious and boastful speech? A fifth water jar is plainly needed to cleanse us from this, and we have it in the observance of silence, which is the guardian and support of our spiritual life and strength. The sixth water jar is regular discipline, by which we no longer live according to our own will but in dependence on the will of another, in order to purify ourselves from the effects of our past license.[11]

Bernard is well aware that the regulation of the will, its orientation toward its proper ends, requires considerable effort:

These water jars are stony in their hardness, but we have no choice but to wash in them.... It is not merely to indicate their hardness that they are described as stony, but also, and more particularly, to signify their durability. For, unless they continue firm and stable, they cannot purify us.[12]

Self-control leads one from humility to love:

Our place is at the bottom, is humility. Our place is voluntary poverty, obedience, and joy in the Holy Spirit. Our place is under a master, under an abbot, under a rule, under discipline. Our place is to cultivate silence and exert ourselves in fasts, vigils, prayers, manual labor. And, above all, our place is to keep that 'more excellent way' [1 Co 12:31] which is the way of love.[13]

The beginning occurs in the intellect: '... By means of true self-knowledge you have learned to fear God, to humble yourself, to shed tears, to distribute alms, and participate in other works of love.'[14] One's will is then set right by self-discipline; the righteous person has '. . . wearied his heart with acts of penance and heaven with his petitions.'[15] Proper motivation is essential; the righteous person seeks not admiration but perfection: 'My brother, if you would follow Christ, conceal the treasure you have found. Love to be unknown.'[16]

But proper behavior is a powerful aid to proper motivation. One should never become

> . . . dissipated, indifferent, negligent; lukewarm at prayer, languid at work, always on the look-out for a laugh, inclined to say the wrong thing.[17]

One's unregulated actions lead to disorientation of the will: 'My interior was no steadier than my behavior.'[18] The soul must maintain her fervor in self-discipline; coldness of heart, laxity of the will, is destructive to progress in the path of love:

> 'Who will endure the cold [Ps 147:17]?' If this cold once penetrates the soul when (as so often happens) the soul is neglectful and the spirit asleep, and if no one (God forbid) is there to curb it, then it reaches into the soul's interior. It descends to the depths of the heart and the recesses of the mind, paralyzes the affections, obstructs the paths of counsel, unsteadies the light of judgment, fetters the spirit's freedom. And soon—as appears in bodies sick with fever—a rigor of mind takes over: vigor slackens, energies grow languid, repugnance for austerity increases, fear of poverty disquiets. The soul shrivels; grace is withdrawn. Time means boredom, reason is lulled to sleep, the spirit is quenched [1 Th 5:19], the fresh fervor wanes, a fastidious lukewarmness weighs down, brotherly love grows cold [Mt 24:12], pleasure attracts, security entraps, old habits return.[19]

Because the human being is an entity, because the body is as essential a human component as the soul,[20] physical activities, which orient the will toward the good, are essential to one's progress in perfection.

Self-discipline seems to imply that the body is an opponent of virtue,[21] and Bernard's works offer a number of examples which seem to make the body the foe of the soul. For example, he writes:

> The third bath, of the body, is the mortification of the members, the chastisement of the body. According to

these words of Paul: 'I chastise my body and force it to serve me' [1 Co 9:27].... Our flesh is a wanton animal, a brazen ass, but we must chastise it so that it will obey its mistress.[22]

'Mortification of the members' seems to imply the sort of rejection of the body which one sometimes finds in patristic writers.[23] The figure of the body as a recalcitrant ass likewise seems to denigrate the body to an inferior, even if not an evil, status. The body must be overcome, subjected:

> And then, like Abigail herself, she rose and mounted an ass, which is to say that she brought her flesh into subjection....[24]

There is no doubt Bernard taught that the impulses of the body must be disciplined. The teaching is forceful; his metaphors are equally so:

> Is this not the message that pounded in your ears from the school of Christ when it was proclaimed just now: 'He who loves his life loses it' [Jn 12:25]? He loses it, he said, either by dying as a martyr or by chastising himself as a penitent. Certainly, it is a kind of martyrdom to put to death the deeds of the body by the power of the Spirit [Rm 8:13], less horrifying indeed than that in which the limbs are severed by the sword, but more grueling because more prolonged. Do you not see how these words of my Master condemn that wisdom of the flesh [Rm 8:1] whereby a man either abandons himself to sensual indulgence or pays excessive attention to the body's health?[25]

The words 'abandon' and 'excessive' cast a different light on Bernard's teaching. The body is not to be rejected but directed toward its proper ends:

> You have heard from the Sage that true wisdom does not dissipate itself by living voluptuously; it is not found in the land of those who live in pleasure [Jb 28:13]. But the one who does find it can say: 'I loved wisdom more than health and beauty' [Ws 7:10]. If more than health or beauty, far more still than sensuality or debauchery.[26]

Bernard does not condemn the body and its pleasures; he wishes, rather, to direct the body toward the fulfillment of its natural desires. Pleasure should be sought where it can best be sought and found:

> How few there are, Lord, who wish to follow you, and yet there is not one who does not wish to reach you, because all know that at your right hand are everlasting pleasures [Ps 15:11].[27]

One's attitude toward one's body should be solicitude, for, though it contains within it the seeds of disorder, that disorder can be rectified by self-discipline:

> But, my brothers, there is another earth, if I may call it so, nearer to us than the one on which we walk. I mean the earth of our own bodies—with regard to which we have a greater and more reasonable solicitude. 'For no man ever hated his own flesh' [Eph 5:29].... Why then, O my flesh, do you any longer complain?... For if the spirit humbles you, chastises you, and brings you into subjection [1 Co 9:27], it does so undoubtedly quite as much for your own advantage and proper glory as it does for its own.[28]

The 'subjection' of the body, the 'mortification' of the flesh is a reorientation of its natural, and therefore good, impulses toward fulfillment.

Bernard does not condemn proper care for the body; he condemns the sensuality which allows the body's impulses to run riot. He condemns the fastidiousness in its care with which a disordered will wastes time and frustrates the very good sought. His satire is sometimes broad; in this case he considers the consumption of food:

> But why should a man bother to abstain from sensual pleasures if he spends so much time every day probing into the mysteries of the human constitution and devising ways of procuring variety in foods? 'Beans', he says, 'produce flatulence, cheese causes dyspepsia, milk gives me a headache, water is bad for my heart, cabbages bring on melancholy, I feel choleric after onions, fish from the pond or muddy waters do not agree with my constitution.' Are you not really saying that food to your taste is not available in all the rivers, fields, gardens, and cellars?[29]

He has the same disdain for those who spend equal time and effort in clothing the body 'from the work of worms and the skins of mice.'[30]

As Etienne Gilson has written: 'The natural necessity of loving the body is therefore always respected by St. Bernard, all that he asks is that this love be properly ordered....'[31] Bernard himself writes:

> I do not wish to say that you should hate your own flesh [Eph 5:28-29]. Love it as something given you as a helper [Gn 2:18] and a partner prepared to share in eternal happiness. What is more, the soul should so love the flesh that she not be thought to change into it and thus hear the Lord say: 'My spirit shall not abide in man, for he is flesh' [Gn 6:3]. The soul should love the flesh, but should even more tend her own animate life. Let Adam love his Eve, but he must not love her so much that he obeys her voice rather than God's [Gn 3:17].[32]

The real ass, the real beast of burden, is not the body. It is the whole person unregulated by a properly oriented will. Indeed, Bernard teaches that one ought to be a beast of burden who bears Christ and is regulated in one's journey by him:

> Meanwhile, dear ones, glorify and bear Christ in your bodies [1 Co 6:20]. He is a delightful burden, a gentle weight, a salutary load—even though sometimes he may seem to weigh heavily and even though from time to time he whacks your flanks and whips the laggard, and occasionally even curbs you with bit and bridle [Ps 32:10] and urges you successfully on. Be like a beast of burden [Ps 71:21], you who bear the Savior [Mt 21:7], but do not be just like a beast.... I think—or, rather, I know—that a likeness to beasts is recommended to man, but this consists not in being unintelligent, certainly not in imitating the beast's stupidity but rather its patience.... Who would not envy greatly that beast on whose lowly back our Savior graciously deigned to sit [Mt 21:7] in order to recommend his own inexpressible gentleness, if, while it was carrying so precious a burden, it had also understood the extraordinary honor? Be like a beast of burden, then, but not in everything. Be patient in carrying the burden, but understand the honor; wisely and lovingly ponder less your own comfort than the value of your burden.[33]

It is the will which must be brought into 'subjection'.

Self-discipline, is, then, what brings order to the will,[34] and this order results in genuine self-possession.[35] Self-discipline is the practice of virtue which makes one open to God:

> But a similar hope will gladden me if a discourse speaks of humility or patience, or of brotherly love and obedience to authority—but especially of the need to strive for holiness and peace and purity of heart, because Scripture says that 'holiness befits your house, O Lord' [Ps 92:5], that 'his place is in peace' [Ps 75:3], and that 'the pure in heart shall see God' [Mt 5:8]. Whenever I am reminded of these virtues, therefore, it will mean for me, as I said, that the Lord of virtues is about to visit my soul.[36]

The pursuit of virtue requires unceasing effort:

> But if in all these practices of devotion any of us should neglect to advance and to 'go forward from virtue to virtue' [Ps 83:8], let him know that he does not belong to the Savior's procession but is standing still or going backwards. For in the way of life not to advance is to fall back; in it 'a man never continues in the same state' [Jb 14:11]. Now our spiritual progress—as I remember I have told you often already—mainly consists in this: that we do not 'count ourselves as having won'. But 'forgetting the things that are behind and stretching forth ourselves to those that are before' [Ph 3:13], we strive unceasingly to become better and keep our imperfections constantly exposed to the eyes of divine mercy.[37]

The very striving itself becomes a happy activity for the just person who '... runs on to life with a ready heart and with the ease of good habit....'[38]

The person who perseveres in self-control will not only grow in virtue, that person will gain understanding and wisdom:

> Once perfectly circumcised and cauterized by the sword of discipline, I crossed the fiery torment by fighting against my vices. And soon, thanks to the help of obedience and counsel, I was ready to be formed in virtue. After this I was able to receive understanding from the commandments of God. So that I could understand for myself the ways I trod, I was found worthy to receive the light of understanding. Then I came to wis-

dom which is, as she herself says, 'a tree of life to all who lay hold of her' [Pr 3:18].³⁹

Just as knowledge is the fruit of humility, wisdom is the fruit of a love cultivated and watered by the virtues obtained, by God's grace, through self-discipline:

> The more virtue is exercised in its own sphere, the more illustrious it is; and the more ready it is to serve, the more approval it wins. If anyone defines wisdom as the love of virtue, I think he is not far from the truth. For where there is love there is no toil, but a taste. Perhaps *sapientia* [wisdom] is derived from *sapor* [taste], because when added to virtue, like some seasoning, it adds taste to that which by itself is tasteless and bitter. I think it would be permissible to define wisdom as the taste for goodness.... When wisdom enters, it makes the carnal sense taste flat. It purifies the understanding, cleanses and heals the palate of the heart. Thus, when the palate is clean it tastes the good; it tastes wisdom itself, and there is nothing better.⁴⁰

If wisdom is the fruit of the virtuous life of self-control, there are other consequences as well. Self-control stems from Christ and leads one back to him:

> For where now are the sinners whom Christ has, as it were, ground and pressed with the teeth of hard discipline, of mortification of the flesh and contrition of the heart [Qo 12:12], so that he might incorporate them into himself?⁴¹

Self-control makes possible the contemplation of Truth itself:

> If they persevere in the sorrow of repentance, desire for justice, and works of mercy, they will cleanse their hearts from the three impediments of ignorance, weakness, and jealousy. They will come through contemplation to the third degree of truth.⁴²

Those who '... long for the repose of contemplation... must take care to surround [their beds] with the flowers of good works, with the practice of virtue....'⁴³

1. See above, pp. 80-87.
2. Asc 3, 8; SBOp 5:136; Luddy 2:248-49.
3. Conv 7, 12; SBOp 4:86-87; CF 25:46-47.
4. Conv 7, 12; SBOp 4:87; CF 25:47.
5. SC 27, 10; SBOp 1:189; CF 7:83.
6. SC 1, 1; SBOp 1:3; CF 4:1.
7. Csi 5, 8, 18; SBOp 3:482; CF 37:163.
8. SC 21, 1-2; SBOp 1:122; CF 7:4.
9. p Epi 2, 7; SBOp 4:324; Luddy 2:50-51.
10. See above, p. 80, and below, pp. 161-162.
11. p Epi 2, 7; SBOp 4:324-25; Luddy 2:51.
12. p Epi 2, 7; SBOp 4:325; Luddy 2:51-52. See also SC 85, 7; SBOp 2:312; CF 40:203.
13. Ep 142, 1; SBOp 7:340; James, p. 220.
14. SC 37, 2; SBOp 2:10; CF 7:182. See also SC 9, 2; SBOp 1:43; CF 4:54.
15. SC 37, 2; SBOp 2:10; CF 7:182.
16. Nat 3, 2; SBOp 4:258-59; Luddy 1:400.
17. SC 6, 9; SBOp 1:30; CF 4:37.
18. SC 6, 9; SBOp 1:30; CF 4:37.
19. SC 63, 6; SBOp 2:165; CF 31:167. See also Sent 3, 89 (SBOp 6/2:12-16) and SC 30, 6 (SBOp 1:213-14; CF 30:117).
20. See above, pp. 15-16.
21. See above, pp. 4-5.
22. Sent 3, 88; SBOp 6/2:134. See also Dil 4, 11; SBOp 3:128; CF 13:103-104.
23. See above, p. 3.
24. Par 4, 2; SBOp 6/2:278; CSt 19:251.
25. SC 30, 11; SBOp 1:217; CF 7:121.
26. SC 30, 11; SBOp 1:217; CF 7:121-22.
27. SC 21, 2; SBOp 1:123; CF 7:5.
28. I Nov 2, 2; SBOp 5:307-308; Luddy 2:349-50.
29. SC 30, 11; SBOp 1:217; CF 7:122.
30. I Nov 2, 2; SBOp 5:308; Luddy 2:350.
31. Gilson, p. 231, n. 88.
32. QH 10, 3; SBOp 4:444-45; CF 25:195.
33. QH 7, 3; SBOp 4:414; CF 25:153-54. See also PP 1, 5; SBOp 5:191; Luddy 3:197.
34. See Par 5, 1; SBOp 6/2:282; CSt 20:28.
35. SC 39, 6; SBOp 2:22; CF 7:196.
36. SC 57, 5; SBOp 2:122; CF 31:100. Bernard gives many lists of virtues. His *Parables* are filled with such lists in which the virtues are personified. See Par 1, 5 (SBOp 6/2:264; CSt 18:21); 2, 7 (SBOp 6/2:273; CSt 18:199-200); 5, 2 (SBOp 6/2:283; CSt 20:28); and 6 (SBOp 6/2:287; CSt 21:100). On Bernard's lists of virtues, Michael Casey has remarked: 'It is probably wiser not to attempt to read too much into Bernard's division of the virtues, but to regard it simply as an *ad hoc* arrangement made to underline certain factors which appeared to him as important in the preservation of the theological virtues. These are not grave philosophical thoughts, profoundly pondered and precisely expressed. They are ephemeral homiletic exhortations, conditioned by whatever happened to be passing through

his mind as he composed these pieces.' Michael Casey, 'Introduction' to *The Story of the Three Daughters of the King by Bernard of Clairvaux*, CSt 20 (1985) 27.
37. Pur 2, 3; SBOp 4:340; Luddy 3:97.
38. Hum 21, 51; SBOp 3:54; CF 13:77.
39. Par 7; SBOp 6/2:300; CSt 22:50-51.
40. SC 85, 8; SBOp 2:312-13; CF 40:203-205. See also SC 85, 9; SBOp 2:313; CF 40:205.
41. SC 72, 2; SBOp 226; CF 40:64.
42. Hum 6, 19; SBOp 3:30; CF 13:46.
43. SC 46, 5; SBOp 2:58; CF 7:243-44. See also Pent 3, 6 (SBOp 5:174; Luddy 2:312-13) and Ep 107, 9 (SBOp 7:274; James, p. 163).

C. The Gift of Love

Exhortations to good works may seem to have a Pelagian ring, to sound the note that love is an acquisition. In urging one to run to keep up with Christ, in asserting that '...to apply oneself to perfection is to be perfect...,'[1] Bernard seems to say that one is the author of one's own salvation. This, of course, is not the case. As humility is a gift from God,[2] so too is love.[3]

'The love of God for us precedes our love for him, and it also follows it.'[4] But the relationship between those two loves is not merely temporal, it is causal: God is '...the efficient and final cause of our love.'[5] God is not simply the object of our love, he brings about that love:

> Christ died and so deserved our love. The Holy Spirit works on us and makes us love him. Christ has given us a reason for loving him; the Spirit has given us the power to love him. The one commends his great love to us; the other gives it. In the one we see the object of our love; by the other we have the power to love. The former provides the occasion of our love; the latter provides the love itself.[6]

Love, then, '...is the gift of the Holy Spirit.'[7]

But that gift does not obviate the need for effort at self-control which will lead one to a command over oneself:

> 'Who shall climb the hill of the Lord [Ps 23:3]?' If anyone aspires to climb to the summit of that mountain [Ex 24:17], that is, to the perfection of virtue, he will know how hard the climb is and how the attempt is bound to fail without the help of the Word.... Otherwise, unless the soul leans on him, her struggle is in vain. But she will gain force by struggling with herself and, becoming stronger, will impel all things toward reason: anger, fear, covetousness, and joy. Like a good charioteer, she will control the chariot of the mind, bringing every carnal affection into captivity [2 Co 10:5] and every sense under the control of reason in accordance with virtue. Surely all things are possible to someone who leans on him who can do all things. What confidence is there in the cry: 'I can do all things in him who strengthens me [Ph 4:13]!' Nothing shows

more clearly the almighty power of the Word than that he makes all-powerful all those who put their hope in him. For 'all things are possible to him who believes' [Mk 9:22]. If all things are possible to him, then he must be all-powerful [Mt 19:26]. Thus, if the mind does not rely on itself but is strengthened by the Word, it can gain such command over itself that no unrighteousness will have power over it [Ps 118:133]. So, I say, neither power, nor treachery, nor lure, can overthrow or hold in subjection the mind which rests on the Word and is clothed with strength from above [Lk 24:49].[8]

One becomes capable of self-control by the power of the Word. Regulating self-destructive impulses

...will be impossible unless you disagree with yourself and become your own adversary, fight against yourself without respite in a continual and hard struggle, and renounce your inveterate habits and inborn inclinations. But this is a hard thing. If you attempt it with your own strength, it will be as though you were trying to stop the raging of the torrent or trying to make the Jordan run backwards [Ps 113:3]. What can you do then? You must seek the Word, to agree with him, by his operation. Flee to him who is your adversary, that through him you may no longer be his adversary, but that he who threatens you may caress you and may transform you by his outpoured grace more effectively than by his outraged anger.[9]

Bernard illustrates this point by comparing the repentant Mary Magdalene, who acknowledged her own powerlessness, with the taunting Pharisee, who had not learned to rely on God:

Mary Magdalene ran in the fragrance of justice; many sins were forgiven her because she loved much [Jn 3:1-2]. She had ceased to be the sinner taunted by the Pharisee [Lk 7:47] and became a virtuous and holy woman. He did not realize that righteousness or holiness is a gift of God, not the fruit of man's effort, that the man 'to whom the Lord imputes no iniquity' [Ps 31:2] is not only just but blessed.[10]

One becomes righteous, holy, and just through the gift of love; indeed one attains perfection of the will by that gift:

> For, if to will what is evil is a defect of the willing faculty, then undoubtedly to will what is good marks a growth in that same faculty. To measure up to every good thing that we will, however, is its perfection. In order, then, that our willing, derived from our free choice, may be perfect, we need a two fold gift of grace: true wisdom, which means the turning of the will to good, and full power, which means its confirmation in the good.[11]

Bernard is no Pelagian; he is likewise no semi-Pelagian. All virtue, all self-control, comes immediately from the supreme Good.

The power to attain the good is a gift of God; the impetus to choose the good is likewise a gift. This is prevenient grace:[12]

> But it is the bride who speaks more directly, for she does not pretend to any merit but mentions first the kindness she has received, acknowledging that the grace of her Beloved goes before her. She does well. For 'who has first given a gift to him and been recompensed by him [Rm 11:35]?' Now hear John's reflections on this: 'In this is love', he says, 'not that we loved God, but that he first loved us' [1 Jn 4:10].... And there is an equally emphatic statement about prevenient grace: 'My God, his mercy shall go before me' [Ps 58:11], and again to the Lord [the Psalmist says]: 'Let your mercies go speedily before us, for we have been brought very low' [Ps 78:8].[13]

True love is a gift; true knowledge lies in acknowledging that gift:

> A little later the Bride...says: 'I am my Beloved's, and he is mine' [Sg 6:2]. Why this? Surely that she may show herself more full of grace [Lk 1:28] when she surrenders wholly to grace, attributing to him both the beginning and the ending. How indeed could she be full of grace if there were any part of her which did not itself spring from grace? There is no way for grace to enter if [a sense of] merit has taken residence in the soul. A full acknowledgment of grace, then, is a sign of the fullness of grace. Indeed, if the soul possesses anything of her own, to that extent must grace give place to it; whatever you impute to merit you steal from grace. I want nothing to do with the sort of merit which excludes grace.... Grace restores me to myself, freely justified

[Rm 8:21], and thus sets me free from the bondage of sin. For where the Spirit is, there is freedom [2 Co 3:17].[14]

God has given one the gift of free choice as a 'creating grace';[15] he moves the will to choose the good (prevenient grace), and he supplies the power to do the good in 'saving grace'.[16] But one can reject that grace through one's power of free choice,[17] and thus Bernard can say that virtues are possible, that merit is within one's reach.

But it is the love of God which makes one's actions meritorious:

> Seeing, then, that fulfillment takes place in relation to us—or even in us, but not by us—whereas creation happens also without us, reformation alone, occurring as it does to some extent with us on account of our voluntary consent, will be reckoned for us as merit. These merits are our fasting, watching, continence, works of mercy, and other virtuous practices, by means of which, as is evident, our inner nature is renewed every day [see 2 Co 4:16].[18]

Bernard sees an example of this in the life of his friend Malachy:

> In all these [his merits], God was blessed [Ps 66:20], who loved him so very much and adorned him, who made him great in the sight of kings [Si 45:3] and gave him the crown of glory [Si 47:7; 1 P 5:4]. That love was proved by his merits....[19]

'Virtue', Bernard insists, 'is God's gift and must be counted among his best gifts, coming down from the Father of the Word.'[20] But that does not mean that one's will and effort are not necessary; it is rather that they receive their impetus and fruition from God: '...A virtue persistently desired and repeatedly sought is ultimately obtained by God's gift....'[21] It is the indwelling of the Holy Spirit which brings forth virtue:[22]

> By fear he is aroused, by goodness he is called back, by knowledge he is instructed, by fortitude he is rescued, by counsel he is unbound, by understanding he is enlightened, and by wisdom he is brought to life.[23]

Grace is necessary to the proper exercise of free choice; Bernard says this allegorically in his fifth *Parable*:

> Free Will also, casting off his chains, hurried to meet Lady Grace, expressing the hope that he would indeed

be free, henceforth, under her rule.... So the daughters [of the king] returned and feasted and kept guard over the city. But if the Lord does not guard the city, then they who guard it watch in vain [Ps 126:1].[24]

Both faith and good works are the gifts of God, as one sees in the humble handmaiden, Mary;[25] only the proud person

...feels persuaded that all his actions give pleasure to God. He believes that he is somehow making God his debtor, often telling himself that the Lord has need of them, that is, of his good works.[26]

Even the pace of one's growth in virtue, of one's progress on the path to perfection, is a gift of God:

Thus you will see that he who is guided by the Spirit [Ga 16:25] does not always remain in the same state [Jb 14:2]. He does not always advance with the same facility. 'The course of man is not in his control' [Jn 10:23]. It depends rather on the guidance of the Spirit who sets the pace as he pleases, sometimes torpidly, sometimes blithely, teaching him to forget the past and strain ahead for what is still to come [Ph 3:13].[27]

The life of love, then, is a life given in love by God and accepted with love:

The bride knows that the initiative lies with the Bridegroom. Thus it is that she mentions his part first: 'My beloved is mine, and I am his' [Sg 2:16]. She knows, then, without any doubt, from her attributes which have their origin in God, that she who loves is herself loved. And so it is. The love of God gives birth to the love of the soul for God, his surpassing affection fills the soul with affection, and his concern evokes concern.[28]

Because of God's overwhelming love, one will progress in the way of love until one reaches one's goal, everlasting happiness in union with the Lover whom one loves:

Here surely the bride needs to be drawn, and drawn by no other than him who said: 'Without me you can do nothing' [Jn 15:5]. 'I know', she says, 'that I have no hope of joining you except by walking after you, and even in this I am helpless unless helped by you. Therefore I entreat you to draw me after you. Happy is the man whose help is from you. He prepared in his heart and in this valley of tears this going up [Ps 83:6], to attain one day to union with you in the mountains where joys abound.'[29]

1. Ep 254, 4; SBOp 8:158; James p. 410.
2. See above, p. 54.
3. See above, pp. 45-46, 48, and 96.
4. Ep 107, 8; SBOp 7:273; James, p. 162.
5. Dil 7, 22; SBOp 3:137; CF 13:114.
6. Ep 107, 8; SBOp 7:273; James, p. 162.
7. Ep 107, 9; SBOp 7:274; James, p. 163.
8. SC 85, 5; SBOp 2:310-11; CF 40:200-201.
9. SC 85, 1; SBOp 2:308; CF 40:196-97.
10. SC 22, 9; SBOp 1:135; CF 7:22.
11. Gra 4, 18-19; SBOp 3:180; CF 19:75.
12. See above, p. 30.
13. SC 67, 10; SBOp 2:194; CF 40:13.
14. SC 67, 10; SBOp 2:195; CF 40:14.
15. See above, pp. 9-101.
16. See above, p. 29.
17. See above, p. 22.
18. Gra 14, 49; SBOp 3:201; CF 19:109.
19. V Mal 66; SBOp 3:370; CF 10:84.
20. SC 85, 7; SBOp 2:311; CF 40:202-203.
21. SC 1, 9; SBOp 1:7; CF 4:6.
22. Michael Casey writes: 'Bernard insists that growth does not end with mere human achievement. If sin was abundant then its repair is superabundant. He aligns the seven stages of sin with seven stages of recovery and then allocates to each one of the gifts of the Holy Spirit.' Michael Casey, 'Introduction' to 'The Last Two Parables by Bernard of Clairvaux', CSt 22 (1987) 44.
23. Sent 3, 98; SBOp 6/2:166. See also Par 7; SBOp 6/2:300-301; CSt 22:51.
24. Par 5, 6; SBOp 6/2:285; CSt 20:31.
25. Div 52, 2; SBOp 6/1:275; Luddy 3:492.
26. Palm 3, 2; SBOp 5:53; Luddy 2:129.
27. SC 21, 4; SBOp 1:124; CF 7:7.
28. SC 69, 7; SBOp 2:206; CF 40:34.
29. SC 21, 2; SBOp 1:122-23; CF 7:4-5.

D. Obedience: The Response to Guidance

The path to the 'mountains where joys abound' is broad, but not without loving constraints and limits. Those limits are learned by listening to those who have trod the path. And this is the motive for obedience. Bernard praises his friend Oger who, although having been the head of a house of regular canons, decided to resign his post and embrace obedience to another:

> ...You had no confidence in yourself and scorned to become your own teacher, deservedly so because he becomes the disciple of a fool who sets himself up as his teacher.[1]

Bernard urges the need for a guide[2] to all who travel the way of love, the path to perfection: '...You need a preceptor and tutor, my child, who may teach you, set you on the way, and nourish you....'[3]

A loving response to a spiritual mentor experienced in the way of love, will bring healing, humility, and peace:

> Our primary task is to tame our willfulness of character by submission to discipline in the first room [of the King], where the stubborn will, worn down by the hard and prolonged schooling of experienced mentors, is humbled and healed. The natural goodness lost by pride is recovered by obedience, and they learn, as far as in them lies, to live peacefully and sociably with all who share their nature, with all men, no longer through fear of discipline but by the impulse of love.[4]

One learns proper motivation, love, in the school of obedience. This is not to reject or overcome nature, but to release the natural and good potential of the will:

> In the first [room], just as the vigorous pounding of a pestle presses and extracts the strong fragrance of spices, so the power of authority and strictness of discipline elicit and reveal the natural strength of good morals.[5]

The good educator educes what is naturally already present in the pupil, if the pupil humbly responds with loving attention.

One must be attentive to the rebuke of one's mentor, for this rebuke will heal the will and enable it to love more deeply:

> Even if 'a good man strike or rebuke me in kindness' [Ps 140:5], I shall draw a similar inference [that the Lord

is about to come], knowing that the zeal and benevolence of a good man make a pathway for him who ascends above the setting sun [Ps 67:5]. Happy that sunset when, at the reproof of a good man, his fellow man is raised up, error is thrown down, and the Lord ascends above it, treading it underfoot to crush it lest it rise again. Therefore, we must not despise the good man's rebuke which destroys sin, gives healing to the heart, and makes a path for God in the soul. No discourse which promotes devotion, virtue, or moral perfection is to be heard with indifference, because that too is a way by which God's salvation is revealed [Ps 49:23]. And if the discourse sounds sweet and agreeable, if antipathy is banished by eagerness to listen, then not only is the Bridegroom rightly believed to be on the way but to be speeding, coming in one's desire. His desire gives rise to yours, and, because you are eager to hear his word, he is hastening to enter your heart. For he first loved us, not we him [1 Jn 4:10]. Moreover, if you listen to a fiery discourse and, as a consequence, your conscience burns at the memory of your sins, remember what Scripture says of him: 'fire goes before him' [Ps 96:3], and be assured that the Lord is near.[6]

Rebuke and encouragement, by a word to an individual or in a sermon to many, should be heeded to one's profit. God speaks to one through one's mentors; if that speech is heeded and the mentors are godly, God will be perceived to come.

Freedom is the seemingly paradoxical result of heeding a mentor's exhortation or rebuke, of submitting one's will to the will of another:

> Perfect obedience knows no law. It can be held within no limits. Not content with the narrow bonds of obligation, it spreads to the fullness of love, carried by a generous will. Eager for every order in the strength of its free and ready spirit, it does not consider measure, but reaches out in boundless liberty.[7]

Bernard illustrates the development of that freedom in his *Sermon on the Seven Degrees of Obedience*:

> The first step of obedience is to obey with a good heart. . . . Every good work derives its value from the

good will with which it is done and without which no work is well done, even when what is done appears good in itself.[8]

Without proper motivation the will is constrained not free, and this principle underlies the six steps of obedience which follow. One should respond to one's spiritual guide with simplicity—not questioning the motive of one's mentor—with cheerfulness, speed, fortitude, humility, and perseverance.[9]

This obedient response to a spiritual mentor imposes great responsibility on the mentor. Bernard writes to Thomas of Beverley: 'Even now we are tied to each other by a mutual debt, I by a debt of faithful care for you and you by the debt of humble obedience to me.'[10] The mentor must assume the role of Martha in ministry:

> Martha holds the position of a mediatrix, and it is her business to obtain grace and salvation both for herself and for all committed to her care. This according to what is written: 'Let the mountains receive peace for the people and the hills justice' [Ps 72:3].[11]

Only one who loves and thus knows how to love should instruct others in love:

> With regard to the wine room [of the King], I do not think there is any other reason for its name than that the wine of earnest zeal for love's works is found there. One who has not been admitted to this room should never take charge of others. This wine should be the inspiring influence in the lives of those who bear authority, as we find in the teacher of the nations when he said: 'Who is weak and I am not weak? Who is made to fall and I am not indignant [2 Co 11:29]?'[12]

This means, of course, that not everyone is capable of serving as a spiritual guide. Even those who '. . . can spend their days uprightly and peacefully among their brothers . . .' are not thereby qualified to teach.[13] Bernard is particularly vehement in rejecting those '. . . who wish always to inspire fear. . . .'[14] Those who would serve as spiritual mentors must

> Learn that you must be mothers, not masters, to those in your care. Make an effort to arouse the response of love, not fear. And should there be an occasional need for severity, let it be paternal, not tyrannical. Show

> affection as a mother; correct like a father. Be gentle, avoid harshness, do not resort to blows, expose your breasts. Let your breasts expand with milk, not swell with passion. Why too impose your yoke [Is 47:6] on those whose burdens you ought rather to carry [Ga 6:2].... If you are spiritual, instruct in a spirit of gentleness, not forgetting you may be tempted yourselves [Ga 6:1].[15]

One who is called to be a spiritual guide must, in short, know the path to perfection:

> That soul who is more perfect is invited to watch over these, to correct, instruct, and save them—provided she is allotted this ministry not by her own ambition but by the call of God, as Aaron was [Heb 5:4]. What is this invitation but an inward impulse of love, lovingly inciting us to zeal for our brother's salvation, to zeal for the beauty of God's house [Ps 25:8], for an increase in his rewards, an increase in the fruits of his righteousness [2 Co 9:10], the praise and glory of his name [Ph 1:11]? The man charged with the spiritual guidance of others or the duty of preaching may believe with certainty—as often as he feels himself inwardly moved by genuine love of God—that the Bridegroom is present, inviting him each time to the vineyards.[16]

The loving mentor rejoices in his or her ministry, in seeing his or her charges '... making definite progress in the love of the Bridegroom and safely grounded in love':[17]

> Whenever I discover that any of you have benefitted from my admonitions, then I confess I never regret preferring the preparation of my sermons to my personal leisure and quiet. When, for example, after a sermon the angry man is found gentle, the proud man humble, the timid man brave. Or when someone who is gentle, humble, and brave has made progress in these gifts and admits he is better than before. When those who were perchance lukewarm and tired of spiritual study, benumbed and sleepy, are seen to grow eager and vigilant again through the burning words of the Lord. When those who, deserting the well of wisdom, have dug for themselves wells of self-will that cannot

hold water [Jr 2:13] and, afflicted in consequence by
every command, have been murmuring in dryness of
heart because they possessed no moisture of devotion
[Lk 8:6] —when these, I repeat, are shown through the
dew of the word and the abundant rain that God provides for those who are his [Ps 67:10], to prosper again
in works of obedience, to be prompt and devout in all
things, there is no reason for sorrow to invade my mind
because it is interrupted in its pursuit of sweet contemplation, for I shall be surrounded by these flowers and
fruits of love.[18]

This is the sort of person whom the pilgrim on the path to perfection cheerfully hears in obedience. The wise pilgrim
...responds with meekness on being corrected, sub-
mits respectfully, obeys modestly, and humbly admits
his fault.[19]

And the guide, in response, will
...minister to and serve him as a genuine lover of the
Lord, for he is one who can truly say: 'While the king
was on his couch, my nard gave forth its fragrance' [Sg
1:11].[20]

In the end, pilgrim and guide, both pupil and mentor, are obedient to their one Teacher. Bernard writes to Thomas of Beverley:
If you deem me worthy, accept me as your fellow dis-
ciple whom you have chosen as your teacher. We shall
both have one teacher in Christ....[21]

Those who would follow Christ listen to one who is already following him. They are obedient to one who '...is never so bent
on his own progress as to overlook their interest...',[22] to the soul
whose '...desire to bask in the Bridegroom's presence...' never
interferes with her realization that, as a bride, '...she was a mother,
that her duty was to suckle her babes, to provide food for her children.'[23] One may cheerfully obey a mentor whose contemplative
leisure one may interrupt without fear to receive counsel.[24] For
the Bridegroom himself knows how the bride's '...own love am-
ply prompts her maternal interest in her daughter's progress....'[25]

But the spiritual mentor is not always one single person; Bernard is convinced that loving direction is found in community as
well:[26]
We owe our brothers, with whom we live, aid and counsel, under the double title of confrère and human being.

For from them we too expect counsel to instruct our ignorance and aid to help our weakness.[27]
The proper response to that aid and counsel is obedience. This means that one should be obedient to all; one should '. . . be submissive to every human creature for God's sake [1 P 2:13]. . . .'[28] And, in this, one will be imitating the very God for whose sake one obeys:

> As the Evangelist tells us. . . : 'He was obedient to them' [Lk 2:51]. Who? God. To whom? To men. God, I repeat, to whom the angels are subject, he whom the principalities and powers obey [Col 2:15], was obedient to Mary. And not only to Mary but to Joseph too, for Mary's sake.[29]

Ultimate obedience, of course, is owed to God, because he is the ultimate source of aid and counsel:

> The soul seeks the Word, and consents to receive correction by which she may be enlightened to recognize him, strengthened to attain virtue, molded to wisdom, conformed to his likeness, made fruitful by him, and made to enjoy him in bliss.[30]

The direction, and correction, of God should be accepted with obedience because the soul knows that God's motive is always loving care:

> And to show clearly how pleasing to him she was even while correcting her—for she bore that correction becomingly and in the proper spirit—he [the Bridegroom] could not depart until he had praised the beauty of her cheeks and neck [Sg 1:9] in words that came from his heart.[31]

Obedience to a mentor, divine or human, is a rational and appropriate response to loving concern which provides aid and counsel to the person on the way which leads to the perfection of the will in love.

1. Ep 87, 7; SBOp 7:228; James, p. 133.
2. I have deliberately avoided terms like 'spiritual director' or even 'spiritual father' because 'We must avoid projecting ideas coming from other periods of history, either before or after Bernard.' Jean Leclercq, 'Spiritual Guidance and Counseling According to St. Bernard', in John R. Sommerfeldt (ed.), *Abba: Guides to Wholeness and Holiness East and West*, CS 38 (Kalamazoo, Michigan: Cistercian Publications, 1982) p. 64.
3. Div 8, 7; SBOp 6/1:116.
4. SC 23, 6; SBOp 1:142; CF 7:30.
5. SC 23, 7; SBOp 1:142; CF 7:31. See also Div 92, 2; SBOp 6/1:347.
6. SC 57, 6; SBOp 2:123; CF 31:101.
7. Pre 6, 12; SBOp 3:261-62; CF 1:114.
8. Div 41, 4; SBOp 6/1:247.
9. Div 41, 5-10; SBOp 6/1:248-52. Bernard offers the same teaching, negatively expressed, in SC 42, 2-4; SBOp 2:34-35; CF 7:211-12.
10. Ep 107, 1; SBOp 7:267; James, p. 158.
11. Asspt 3, 6; SBOp 5:243; Luddy 3:243.
12. SC 23, 7; SBOp 1:143; CF 7:31.
13. SC 23, 8; SBOp 1:143; CF 7:32.
14. SC 23, 2; SBOp 1:139-40; CF 7:27.
15. SC 23, 2; SBOp 1:140; CF 7:27.
16. SC 58, 3; SBOp 2:128-29; CF 31:109-110.
17. SC 21, 1; SBOp 1:122; CF 7:4.
18. SC 51, 3; SBOp 2:85-86; CF 31:42-43.
19. SC 42, 5; SBOp 2:36; CF 7:214.
20. SC 42, 5; SBOp 2:36; CF 7:214.
21. Ep 107, 13; SBOp 7:276; James, p. 165.
22. SC 23, 1; SBOp 1:139; CF 7:26.
23. SC 41, 5; SBOp 2:31; CF 7:208. See also SC 41, 6 (SBOp 2:32; CF 7:208) and Sept 1, 2 (SBOp 4:346; Luddy 2:58).
24. If not done rudely or irresponsibly. See SC 52, 7; SBOp 2:94; CF 31:56.
25. SC 52, 6; SBOp 2:94; CF 31:55.
26. See Jean Leclercq, 'St. Bernard and the Formative Community', CSt 14 (1979) 99-119.
27. Adv 3, 5; SBOp 4:178; Luddy 1:27.
28. SC 42, 9; SBOp 2:38; CF 7:217. See also Hum 19, 48, and 20, 50; SBOp 3:53 and 54; CF 13:75 and 76.
29. Miss 1, 7; SBOp 4:19; CF 18:11.
30. SC 85, 1; SBOp 2:307; CF 40:195-96. See also SC 52, 6; SBOp 2:94; CF 31:55-56.
31. SC 42, 1; SBOp 2:33; CF 7:210. See also SC 42, 4; SBOp 2:35; CF 7:212-13.

E. Silence

The counsel which the pilgrim should heed is ordinarily communicated orally, by conversation or sermon. Yet Bernard claims that silence is a valuable vehicle in progressing along the path of love:

> ... Like the Prophet I have determined to 'take heed of my ways that I do not sin with my tongue' [Ps 38:2], because, according to the same Prophet: 'A glib tongue shall not have its way on earth' [Ps 139:12]. According to another: 'The tongue holds the keys of life and death' [Pr 18:21]. Isaiah calls silence 'the work of justice' [Is 32:17], and Jeremiah says that 'it is good to await the salvation of the Lord in silence' [Lm 3:26].[1]

In commenting on chapter six of the *Rule*, Bernard gives a comic account of the monk who is unable to observe the admonition to silence:

> At times he simply cannot stop laughing or hide his empty-headed merriment. He is like a well-filled bladder that has been pricked and squeezed. The air, not finding a free vent, whistles out through the little hole with squeak after squeak. The precept of silence does not allow the monk to relieve himself of his vain thoughts and silly jokes. They gather pressure inside until they burst out in giggles. In embarrassment he buries his face in his hands, tightens his lips, clenches his teeth. It is no use! The laughter must explode, and, if his hand holds it in his mouth, it bursts out through his nose.[2]

What is one to make of these admonitions, the one straight-forward, the other satirical?

Bernard shows the proper relationship between silence and speech in his lament over his brother Gerard. There he affirms the value of a silence conducive to '... more prayerful absorption in divine contemplation....'[3] But he affirms the value of speech in serving the needs of others. Gerard's speech won Bernard the silence necessary for contemplation and 'more thorough preparation of teaching for [his] sons':[4]

> How often did you not free me from worldly conversation by the adroitness of your gifted words and return

me to the silence I loved? The Lord endowed him with a discernment that enabled him to speak with due propriety [Is 50:4]. And this prudence in his responses, accompanied by a certain graciousness given him from above, made him acceptable both to his fellow-monks and to people in the world. Anyone who spoke with Gerard rarely needed to see me.[5]

Speech is the vehicle for counsel; silence is a means of obtaining through reflection the wisdom which makes that counsel effective.

Bernard speaks much of silence in his seventeenth sermon *De diversis*. There he assails the use of speech in disparaging others.[6] Detraction is '... odious to God and hateful to life...'[7] because it is an assault on brotherly love. But he recognizes that speech can be useful to love: 'There is, therefore, great utility in words, and frequently most precious fruits are discovered through speech.'[8] The speech natural to humans should be directed by the will toward the good of fellow humans:

> Now, indeed, we must place a guard over our mouth and a guard of prudence on our lips, so that life-giving edification may not be damned up forever nor deadly evil be poured forth freely.[9]

F. Continence

It may seem strange that the abbot of a monastery committed to strict observance of the *Rule* of Benedict should give relatively little attention to silence. Bernard affirms the value of silence; he expends relatively little effort in explaining it. This may be simply because Bernard and his audience were so agreed on the value of silence that, in their opinion, that value required little explication. The same may be true of the virtue of continence.

As we have seen, Bernard's contribution to the understanding of man's sexuality and its role in the spiritual life is surprisingly positive. As Jean Leclercq says:

> In the first place we find that Bernard does not hesitate to make use of strong sexual imagery, which writers, secular and religious, in more sexually self-conscious periods, would not have dared to use. . . . As far as the emotions and affective attitudes or the heightened activity of a man and woman in love are concerned, he adds little to what was already to be found in the *Song of Songs*. But he comments on all the elements of this relationship with a disarming frankness and freedom which perhaps became a source of scandalized surprise to the pious in the later periods of history.[10]

Bernard's imagery for progress in spiritual life is often sexual; for him, sex is obviously a natural part of God's creation and, therefore, in itself a good thing.

But Bernard also assumes the value of continence, the regulation by the will of the legitimate sexual impulses of the body:

> But no age is stated for the turtle-dove, for her chastity is acknowledged at any age. She is content with one mate; if he is lost she does not take another, thus arguing against man's tendency to marry more than once. Now, as a remedy for incontinence this is only a minor fault; still the incontinence that demands it is a disgrace. It is shameful that reason cannot lead man to that uprightness which nature achieves in a bird.[11]

Sexual desires are legitimate; the will properly employs them in marital love. But, like all other human, natural, physical impulses— for food and drink, for example[12]—sexual desires must be regulated by the reason toward the good, the proper end of the human being.

Bernard also assumes that, for some, continence is properly expressed in sexual abstinence, that chastity—to which all are called—be expressed in celibacy:

> Where did you read that those who make themselves eunuchs for the sake of the kingdom of heaven [Mt 19:12] are praised? Where did you read that, though living in the flesh, we do not war with the flesh's weapons [2 Co 10:3]? Or that he who gives his virgin daughter in marriage does well, but he who does not give her in marriage does better still [1 Co 7:38]?[13]

Those who so regulate their sexual impulses that they ' ". . . neither marry nor are given in marriage" [Lk 20:35- 36], . . . are like the angels in heaven.'[14]

Continence is necessary for progress in love; celibacy is an advantage to some in that same pursuit. The important thing, for Bernard, is that the will be directed toward its proper end in all things, including sex. For this reason, he equates continence with temperance:

> To this [the arguments of the wise of this world] I answer first that temperance and continence imply the same thing. Secondly, scriptural usage identifies continence or cleanliness with holiness. And, finally, what else were those frequent rites of sanctification decreed by Moses but purifications consisting of abstinence from food, from drink, from sexual intercourse, and similar things [see Lv 22ff.]? But take special note of the freedom with which the Apostle attributed this meaning to the word holiness: 'What God wants is for you all to be holy so that each one of you may know how to possess his body in holiness, not giving way to selfish passion' [1 Th 4:3]; and again: 'God did not call us into uncleanness, but into holiness' [1 Th 4:7]. It is clear that he identifies holiness with temperance.[15]

Progress toward love demands that the will order all of one's inclinations toward the good. Continence is, in the end, an expression of the orientation of the will toward the good; it is an expression of love. In this sense all love must be chaste:

> Love will never be without fear, but it will be a chaste fear. Love will never be without cupidity, but it will be an ordered desire.[16]

In consequence, continence must be inspired by love or it has no value. Bernard uses a familiar, natural analogy to illustrate this:
> By the sun we could mean zeal for justice and fervent love, and by the moon continence. Without the sun there is no brightness in the moon, and without justice and love there is no merit in continence. Hence that saying of Wisdom: 'How beautiful is the chaste generation with its love' [Ws 4:1].[17]

By the same token, celibacy without the humility which engenders love is self-defeating. Bernard would have all imitate the humility of the Virgin Mary:
> You are told that she is a virgin; you are told that she is humble. If you are not able to imitate the virginity of this humble maid then imitate the humility of the virgin maid. Virginity is a praiseworthy virtue, but humility is by far the more necessary. The one is merely counseled; the other is demanded. To the first you have been invited; to the second you are obliged. Concerning the first he said: 'He who is able to receive this, let him receive it' [Mt 19:12]; of the second is said: 'Truly I said to you, unless you become like this little child, you cannot enter the kingdom of heaven' [Mt 18:3].... Even if Mary found favor by her virginity, she conceived on account of her humility. Thus there is no doubt that her virginity was found pleasing because her humility made it so.[18]

Bernard translates this teaching into practical advice on continence:
> It is better for you [Mt 5:29] not to be a virgin than to be puffed up over your virginity. Not everyone is a virgin, but there are still fewer who join humility to virginity. So if you can do no more than admire Mary's virginity, try to imitate her humility, and for you this will be enough [2 Co 12:9]. But if you are both virgin and humble, then, whoever you are, you are great.[19]

1. Ep 89, 2; SBOp 7:236; James, p. 138.
2. Hum 12, 40; SBOp 3:47; CF 13:68.
3. SC 26, 6; SBOp 1:174; CF 7:65.
4. SC 26, 6; SBOp 1:174; CF 7:65.
5. SC 26, 6; SBOp 1:174; CF 7:64.
6. See Leclercq, 'St. Bernard and the Formative Community', pp. 115-16.
7. Div 17, 4; SBOp 6/1:152.
8. Div 17, 7; SBOp 6/1:155.
9. Div 17, 7; SBOp 6/1:155.
10. Leclercq, *Monks and Love*, pp. 100-101. See also Stiegman, pp. 153-71.
11. SC 59, 7; SBOp 2:139; CF 31:126. See also Par 6; SBOp 6/2:290; CSt 21:104.
12. See below, p. 190.
13. Miss 3, 7; SBOp 4:41; CF 18:39.
14. SC 59, 8; SBOp 2:140; CF 31:127. See also Div 37, 5; SBOp 5:225. I assume Bernard thinks that since food and drink are necessary to life, their use must be regulated but not denied. Since sex is necessary to the life of the species but not the individual, its use may be legitimately denied by some for the sake of the time won for meditation and prayer. But I have not found Bernard saying this explicitly. An excellent study of Bernard's attitude toward chastity is Thomas Renna, 'Virginity and Chastity in Early Cistercian Thought', *Studia Monastica* 26 (1984) 43-54.
15. SC 22, 10; SBOp 1:136-37; CF 7:23-24.
16. Dil 14, 38; SBOp 3:152; CF 13:130. See also Dil 9, 26; SBOp 3:141; CF 13:118.
17. SC 27, 8; SBOp 1:187; CF 7:81.
18. Miss 1, 5; SBOp 4:17-18; CF 18:9-10.
19. Miss 1, 6; SBOp 4:18; CF 18:10.

G. Simplicity

The path of love should be walked in simplicity; Bernard encourages his hearers: '...I know that many of you walk in the love with which Christ has loved us [Eph 5:2] and seek him in simplicity of heart [Ws 1:1].'[1] Simplicity is a volitional virtue which should be cultivated in all aspects of life.

Bernard exhibits to his audience many ways in which simplicity may be expressed. In his *Apology to Abbot William*, for example, he recommends simplicity in clothing by criticizing the virtue's opposite:

> Nowadays monks look for clothes that are stylish and will make a good impression rather than for something serviceable which will keep out the cold. They do not choose what is cheap, as the *Rule* recommends [RB 55:7], but clothing of good quality which looks good.[2]

Clothing is necessary; it serves a practical and necessary function. Simplicity consists in rightly ordering the human will toward fulfilling that function. Bernard contrasts what he describes as contemporary practice with the simplicity of the Apostles:

> It was their practice to keep nothing as private property, for, as is written, 'distribution was made to each as he had need' [Ac 4:35]. There was no scope for childish behavior. All received only as they had need so that nothing was useless, much less novel or exotic. The text says: 'as he had need'; this means, in terms of clothing, something to cover nakedness and keep out the cold.[3]

Straightforward, honest clothing, chosen with a view to its practical utility, is a sign of simplicity. And this external simplicity is a sign of an important internal disposition:

> Any vice which shows up on the surface must have its source in the heart. A frivolous heart is known by frivolous conduct, external extravagance points to inward impoverishment, and soft clothes are a sign of a soul without firmness. The fact is that there would not be so much concern for the body if the fostering of spiritual values had not long since been neglected.[4]

Since a human person is both body and soul, what one wears on one's body should be and inevitably is an indication of one's internal disposition. Moreover, physical things are means to the proper disposition of the will.

This is as true of architecture as of clothing. Again, Bernard expresses his concern for simplicity in rejecting its opposite at Cluny:

> I shall say nothing about the soaring heights and extravagant lengths and unnecessary widths of the churches, nothing about their expensive decorations and their novel images which catch the attention of those who go in to pray and dry up their devotion.[5]

The central issue for Bernard is the purpose of the architecture in question: the stimulus to devotion. If decoration were necessary to devotion, as Bernard thought was the case in churches serving lay-folk, then it should be used.[6] Simplicity, like all other exercises of love, is a means to an end, not an end in itself.

Simplicity should be the standard in other aesthetic pursuits, in music and poetry, and in the liturgy which combines them. Bernard was once asked to compose a liturgical office in honor of Saint Victor. In response, he wrote of his efforts to Abbot Guy and the brethren of Montièramy:

> The unmistakable sense [of the words] should shine with truth, resound with justice, incite to humility, teach moderation. The words should offer light to the mind, shape to behavior, the cross to vices, devotion to the affections, discipline to the senses.[7]

What is true of poetry should also be true of music:

> If there is to be singing, the melody should be grave, not flippant or uncouth. It should be sweet but not frivolous; it should both enchant the ear and move the heart; it should lighten sad hearts and soften angry passions. And it should never obscure the sense of the words but rather enhance it. Not a little spiritual profit is lost when minds are distracted from the sense of the words by the frivolity of the melody, when more is conveyed by modulations of voice than by variations of meaning.[8]

Beauty is important and style is crucial; both should serve their proper end, conveying a true and instructive message:

> I have written two sermons on the life of the Saint—in my own words but based on the ancient accounts you sent me. I have tried to avoid obscure brevity, on the

one hand, and tedious length on the other. Regarding
the singing, I have composed a hymn, but I have kept
the sense clear at the expense of the meter.[9]

Simplicity regards the purpose of things and thus guides the will toward the true good.

Simplicity involves an honesty, a straight-forwardness, which rejects duplicity and deception:

> The simplicity of the soul remains unshaken in its fundamental being, but it is not seen because it is covered by the disguise of human deception, pretense, and hypocrisy. How incongruous is the mixture of simplicity and duplicity! How unworthy is so base an addition to so pure a foundation!... Yet the original simplicity persists in every soul along with duplicity, and the coexistence of these increases the confusion.[10]

Bernard urges the pilgrim on the path to love to overcome this confusion through a proper orientation of the will toward justice or right order.

The search for comfort, as opposed to a simple life style, is a misdirection of the will:

> This careless softness, this base and inactive search for comfort, acts as a wasting disease which so diminishes one's spiritual vigor that one becomes deathly cold, like one who is already dead.[11]

Simplicity is an orientation of the will toward right order, avoiding all that would confuse and distract one in one's quest for love and happiness:

> Be simple with your Lord, putting away not only all guile and simulation, but equally all multiplicity of occupation, so that you may converse freely with him whose voice is so sweet and face so comely [Sg 2:14].[12]

As always with Bernard, motivation is crucial. Simplicity, like self-discipline, is not an end but a means, and, if practiced for the sake of show, will become self-destructive:

> You [Cluniacs] say that we poor men, clothed in rags, dare pass judgment on the world, as he [Jerome] says, from our holes in the ground. You say we insult your glorious Order and shamelessly slander the holy men who belong to it and are more deserving of our praise. You say that from our base obscurity we dare to scoff

at the world's luminaries. This is more unbearable still. If true, then under sheep's disguise we are, not ravenous wolves, but nibbling fleas and gnawing moths.... If, I repeat, we are proud pharisees who look down on others, and even despise men better than ourselves, we can expect no advantage from a diet that is lean and unlovely, nor from the well-known cheapness and roughness of our clothes. The sweat of our daily toil, our continual fasts and vigils, and all the austerity of our way of life will do us no good if we are performing these works to be seen by men.[13]

True simplicity is an attitude toward things, not a deprivation of them:

...The rich of this world [1 Tm 6:17] must not imagine that because Christ said: 'Blessed are the poor in spirit, for theirs is the kingdom of heaven' [Mt 5:3], that the brothers of Christ possess heavenly gifts only. If the promise mentions only heavenly things, it does not follow that these alone are meant. They do possess earthly things, but with the spirit of men who possess nothing [2 Co 6:10]. In reality they possess all things, not like unhappy beggars who get what they beg for, but as masters—masters in the best sense because devoid of avarice. To the man of faith the whole world is a treasure house of riches—the whole world because all things, whether adverse or favorable, are of service to him; they all contribute to his good [Rm 8:28-29].[14]

A simple life style does not entail the privation of poverty; a simple life is one of freedom from enslavement by things:

The miser hungers like a beggar for earthly possessions; the man of faith has a lordly independence of them. The first is a beggar no matter what he owns, the latter by his independence is a true owner.[15]

The miser is not master of his money but its slave.[16] Simplicity brings freedom to the one so enslaved.[17]

One cannot be free of the need for material things; indeed, one should work hard to obtain them, for they are necessary to one's material well being. True poverty, which is simplicity, demands not that one reject things, but that one adopt and maintain a proper attitude toward them. Thus Bernard links simplicity and work in a happy union. He cuts off his first sermon on the *Song of Songs* with the admonition: 'The hour has come when both our rule and the poverty of our state demand that we go out to work.'[18] Bernard rejoices that the life style he has embraced is characterized by this unity of simplicity with work: 'Work, the hidden life, and the poverty of the monastery—these are the characteristics of monks, their titles to nobility.'[19] Manual labor, done in the spirit of simplicity, promotes one's physical and psychological health by focussing attention on essentials. It thus contributes to the well-being of one in search of happiness:

> Arouse yourself, gird your loins, put aside idleness, grasp the nettle, and do some hard work. If you do, you will find that you only need to eat what will satisfy your hunger, not what will make your mouth water. Hard exercise will restore the flavor to food that idleness has taken away. Much that you would refuse to eat when you have nothing to do you will be glad for after hard work. Idleness makes one hard to please; hard work makes one hungry. It is wonderful how work can make food taste sweet which idleness finds insipid. Vegetables, beans, roots, and bread and water may be poor fare for one living in ease, but hard work soon makes them taste delicious.[20]

Again, Bernard shows his conviction that the body's welfare is essential to the health of the whole person.

For Bernard, the life of love is characterized by the straightforward honesty which is strengthened by simplicity. Bernard expresses this idea negatively in an allegorical passage in his thirty-ninth sermon on the *Song of Songs*:

> The chariot of Sensuality also rolls along with four vices for wheels: Gluttony, Lust, Seductive Dress, and Enervation—the offspring of Sloth and Inertia. And it is drawn by two horses, Prosperous Life and Abundance of Goods. The two coachmen are Lazy Languor and False Security, for wealth is the ruin of the slothful and Scripture says that the prosperity of fools destroys them [Pr 1:32]—not because they are successful but because it gives them false security. 'When people say "there is peace and security" then sudden destruction will come upon them' [1 Th 5:3]. These coachmen have neither

> spurs nor whips nor any such instrument; instead they carry a canopy for shade and a fan to freshen the air. The canopy's name is Dissimulation, and its purpose is to provide a shade to ward off the heat of human cares. A person used to soft, effeminate ways will dissemble even when faced with necessary cares. And, rather than experience life's perplexing troubles, he will conceal himself in the thickets of dissimulation.²¹

Honesty not hypocrisy is the proper approach to life. Bernard has no patience with pretense. Simplicity is a way of honestly facing the truth:

> I believe two things are necessary for the interior eye to be truly simple: love in intention and truth in choice. If one loves the good but does not choose the true, he has the zeal of God, but not according to knowledge [see Rm 10:2]. Indeed, I fail to see how, in the judgment of truth, true simplicity can co-exist with error.... It is plain that the simplicity which is praised by the Lord presupposes two conditions: good will and prudence. A man needs not only a warm and undeceiving heart but a keen and undeceived eye as well.²²

Once more Bernard shows the intimate connection between the perfection of the intellect by knowledge and the perfection of the will in love—both of which are promoted and expressed by simplicity.

Simplicity is neither the destitution of a poverty which lacks the goods necessary for life nor the renunciation of the goods of the physical life for the sake of intellectual achievement:

> Note carefully that the Lord speaks of the 'poor in spirit' [Mt 5:3], not of the ordinary poor whose poverty is due to miserable necessity rather than to praiseworthy choice.... Yet not even all voluntary poverty 'has glory before God' [Rm 4:2]. For we read of certain philosophers who renounced all things that they might devote themselves more freely to the study of vanity.... The words, 'Blessed are the poor in spirit' [Mt 5:3], were spoken only of those who are poor from a spiritual intention....²³

Motivation is the key to simplicity as it is to all virtues. Physical goods are good; they are not to be rejected because they are physical. Simplicity demands the use of those physical goods in accordance with their true purpose, human well-being.

Physical goods are necessary to the perfection of persons. Yet, Bernard is sure, they should be used sparingly—to accomplish their purpose and not to become ends in themselves. Undue preoccupation with things is a distraction from the good life:

> It is for the same sort of reason, if I may say so, that Christ gives his soldiers [2 Tm 2:3] scant and scarce temporal supplies to guard their lower parts, the flesh. For he does not want them to be weighed down with a lot of such things, but wants them to have food and clothing [1 Tm 6:8], as the Apostle says, and to be content with that. But for the higher parts he gives spiritual gifts [Rm 1:11] in greater abundance and breadth. So you read: 'Seek first the kingdom of God and his righteousness and everything will be given you' [Mt 6:33], including the food and clothing for which he said we were not to be anxious [Mt 6:25-31]. Our Father in heaven [Mt 6:26], in his gracious kindness, gives them to us for two reasons: lest, thinking he is angry with us if he refused us these things, we should despair, or, lest excessive anxiety about them should be harmful to our spiritual exercises. Without them one cannot live or serve God [Ph 3:3]. But the scantier they are the better.[24]

Although the goods of the world are indeed goods, they are not the ultimate good which brings one happiness. Physical goods are not an end but a means to the end which is God:

> Oh, how wisely you have acted, most dearly beloved, in renouncing all that you might have possessed in this world, since by doing so you have deserved to become the special people of the world's Creator, to have him as your special possession. For he is, undoubtedly, 'the portion and inheritance' [Nb 18:20] of his own.[25]

1. SC 84, 4; SBOp 2:305; CF 40:191.
2. Apo 10, 24; SBOp 3:101; CF 1:59. See also I Nov 2, 2; SBOp 5:308; Luddy 2:349-50.
3. Apo 10, 24; SBOp 3:101; CF 1:59-60.
4. Apo 10, 26; SBOp 3:102; CF 1:61-62.
5. Apo 12, 28; SBOp 3:104; CF 1:63.
6. See Ep 243, 4; SBOp 8:132. See my article, 'The Social Theory of Bernard of Clairvaux', in *Studies in Medieval Cistercian History Presented to Jeremiah F. O'Sullivan*, CS 13 (Spencer, Massachusetts: Cistercian Publications, 1971) pp. 35-48, esp. pp. 46-47.
7. Ep 398, 2; SBOp 8:378; James, p. 502.
8. Ep 398, 2; SBOp 8:378; James, p. 502.
9. Ep 398, 3; SBOp 8:378; James, p. 502.
10. SC 82, 2-3; SBOp 2:293-94; CF 40:172-73. See *Thomas Merton on Saint Bernard*, CS 9 (Kalamazoo, Michigan: Cistercian Publications, 1980) pp. 112-20.
11. Sent 3, 98; SBOp 6/2:160-61.
12. Asspt 3, 7; SBOp 5:243; Luddy 3:244.
13. Apo 1, 1; SBOp 3:81-82; CF 1:34-35.
14. SC 21, 7; SBOp 1:126; CF 7:9.
15. SC 21, 8; SBOp 1:126; CF 7:9.
16. SC 21, 8; SBOp 1:126; CF 7:10.
17. As we have seen (above, p. 22), Bernard identifies man's true end as consummation, not consumption. See Dil 7, 19; SBOp 3:135; CF 13:112.
18. SC 1, 12; SBOp 1:8; CF 4:7. The fact that the admonition serves a rhetorical function does not, I think, reduce its force. The link between Bernard's teaching on work and the *Rule* of Benedict is explicated by Jean Leclercq, 'St. Bernard and the Rule of Benedict', in M. Basil Pennington (ed.), *Rule and Life: An Interdisciplinary Symposium*, CS 12 (Spencer, Massachusetts: Cistercian Publications, 1971) p. 163.
19. Mor 37; SBOp 7:130. See Jean Leclercq, 'The Intentions of the Founders of the Cistercian Order', in M. Basil Pennington (ed.), *The Cistercian Spirit: A Symposium in Memory of Thomas Merton*, CS 3 (Spencer, Massachusetts: Cistercian Publications, 1970) pp. 88-133, esp. pp. 111-14. See also Chrysogonus Waddell, 'Simplicity and Ordinariness: The Climate of Early Cistercian Hagiography', in John R. Sommerfeldt (ed.), *Simplicity and Ordinariness: Studies in Medieval Cistercian History*, IV, CS 61 (Kalamazoo, Michigan: Cistercian Publications, 1980) pp. 1-47; and Dennis R. Overman, *Manual Labor: The Twelfth-Century Cistercian Ideal* (unpublished M.A. thesis, Western Michigan University, 1983).
20. Ep 1, 12; SBOp 7:9-10; James, p. 8.
21. SC 39, 7; SBOp 2:22; CF 7:196-97.
22. Pre 14, 36; SBOp 3:279; CF 1:133.
23. OS 1, 8; SBOp 5:333; Luddy 3:338-39.
24. QH 5, 2; SBOp 4:402-403; CF 25:141-42.
25. Ded 1, 3; SBOp 5:372; Luddy 2:387.

H. Loving Service

Simplicity is an expression of honesty toward oneself—and also toward others. One should serve others, Bernard teaches, in a spirit of simplicity: 'The Lord loves not only a cheerful giver [Rm 12:18] but one who gives with simplicity. Simplicity too is radiance.'[1] And this radiance is characteristic of the one who cheerfully serves others:

> There is a brightness with which a man clothes himself when he shows mercy with cheerfulness [Rm 12:8]. If you look at a man whom the Psalmist describes as happy, a man who shows mercy and lends [Ps 111:8], do you not see that his joyfulness of spirit begets a radiance in his face and in his deeds [2 Co 9:7]? But the face and deeds of a man who gives reluctant and grudging service are not radiant but dark and gloomy. That is why the Lord loves a cheerful giver [2 Co 9:7]. How could he love a gloomy one? He looked favorably on Abel because of his radiant gladness, but turned away from Cain [Gn 4:4-5] because Cain's face was heavy, no doubt with sadness and envy. Consider what the color of sadness and jealousy must be like for God to turn his face away from it. There is a beautiful and sensitive description of the radiant joy which lights up kindness in the writings of the poet: 'The joyful of countenance have overcome all things.'[2]

Loving service is a source of the radiant joy which characterizes the happy person.

Love is the perfection of the will, but that will does not exist independently of the complete human person. The perfection of the human being involves the perfection of all human faculties: reason, will, feelings—and the body as well. Thus, progress of the will in love requires not only proper disposition or direction, but actions which express love. Those same actions also promote the development of love.[3] The body is therefore, necessary to progress in love:

> Now if you consider that the house [of Mary and Martha] is an earthly house, you will easily understand why it was Martha and not Mary who received the Lord into it. It was to Martha rather than to Mary that the Apostle

addressed himself when he said: 'Glorify and bear God
in your body' [1 Co 6:20]. For Mary uses her body as
a means of well-doing....[4]

Loving service requires the actions of the body, but not actions devoid of feeling: 'Love exists in action and in feeling.'[5] Yet, valuable as feelings of compassion are,[6] they must result in action to be genuinely loving:

...When the Lord said 'Love your enemies', he referred immediately afterward to actions: 'Do good to those who hate you' [Lk 6:27]. Scripture also says: 'If your enemy is hungry, feed him; if he is thirsty, give him drink' [Rm 12:20]. Here you have a question of actions, not of feelings. But listen also to the Lord's command about love of himself: 'If you love me, keep my words' [Jn 14:15]. And here too, by enjoining the observance of the commandments, he assigns us to action. It would have been superfluous for him to warn us to act if love were only a matter of feeling.[7]

Loving service is compassionate action directed toward the well-being of one's neighbor. Although Bernard insists on the primacy of one's love for God, that love must find expression in serving others:

...There is no doubt that, in the mind that loves rightly, the love of God is valued more than the love of man, among men the more perfect is esteemed more than the weaker, heaven more than earth, eternity more than the flesh. In well-regulated action, on the other hand, the opposite order frequently, or even always, prevails. For we are more strongly impelled toward and more often occupied with the welfare of our neighbor. We attend our weaker brothers with more exacting care. By human right and true necessity we concentrate more on peace on earth than on the glory of heaven [Lk 2:14]. Through worry about temporal concerns we are unable to think about eternal things.[8]

But this apparent reversal of true priorities is, in reality, the proper ordering of man's activities:

Who will doubt that in prayer man speaks with God? But how often, at the call of love, we are drawn away, torn away for the sake of those who need to speak to

> us, who need our help! How often does dutiful repose yield dutifully to the uproar of activity! How often is a book laid aside in good conscience that we may sweat at manual labor! How often for the sake of managing worldly affairs we very rightly omit even the solemn celebrations of Masses! A preposterous order, but necessity knows no law. Love in action devises its own order, beginning with the more recent in accord with the command of the householder [Mt 20:8]. It is certainly dutiful and correct, without favoritism [Ac 10:34; Jb 32:21], swayed not by worldly values but by human needs.[9]

Loving concern responds not to abstract formulations but to real, human need.

In this Bernard does not reject concern for one's own spiritual well-being, or the practices that promote it. Loving service builds on those practices and fulfills them:

> The ointment of contrition is good, of course, made up as it is from the recollection of past sins and poured on the Lord's feet, because 'You will not scorn, O God, this crushed and broken heart' [Ps 50:19]. But better by far is the ointment of devotion, distilled from the memory of God's beneficence, and worthy of being poured on Christ's head. Concerning it we have God's own witness: 'Whoever makes thanksgiving, his sacrifice honors me' [Ps 49:23]. The function of merciful love, however, is superior to both. It works for the welfare of the afflicted and is diffused through the whole Body of Christ.[10]

Indeed, for Bernard, the expenditure of energy in the service of others does not diminish one's store of love but augments it. True love is sufficient for all:

> Love never lacks what is her own, all that she needs for her own security. Not only does she have it, she abounds in it. She wants this abundance for herself so that she may share it with all. And she reserves enough for herself so that she disappoints no one. For love is perfect only when full.[11]

Love can be expended freely, for it is given from an inexhaustible source:

He [the Spirit] now employs my tongue for his purpose of instructing you, when he could certainly impart the same knowledge directly, with greater facility on his part and more pleasure for you. This mode of acting he has chosen represents an indulgence on his part, not indigence. He makes this promotion of welfare for you an occasion of merit for me; it does not mean he needs my assistance. This is a truth that every man should remember when he does good deeds, lest he give glory to himself and not to the Lord for the fruits of grace [1 Co 1:31].[12]

Loving service for others is, in the end, a way in which God gives his love to them. The minister of that love is a means through which God acts in love, and a happy consequence is the growth of love in the minister.

The realization that one's loving service is a mediation of God's love induces humility. Humility, knowledge of oneself, is necessary to the maintenance of a proper attitude toward those whom one serves:

You run no risk, therefore, no matter how much you lower yourself, no matter how much your self-esteem falls short of what you are, of what the Truth thinks of you. But the evil is great and the risk frightening if you exalt yourself even a little above what you are, if in your thoughts you consider yourself of more worth than even one person whom Truth may judge your equal or your better.... So, then, beware of comparing yourself with your betters or your inferiors, with a particular few, or with even one. For how do you know but that this one person, whom, perhaps, you regard as the vilest and most wretched of all, whose life you recoil from and spurn as more befouled and wicked, not merely than yours—for you trust you are a sober-living, just, and religious man [Tt 2:12]—but even than all other wicked men, how do you know, I say, but that, in God's sight, in time, with the aid of the right hand of the Most High [Ps 76:11], he will not surpass both you and them—if he has not already done so?[13]

Loving service should not be the product of condescension. The intellect, rightly ordered in humility, assists the will in its search

for love—as do the body and the feelings. In the spirit of humility, then, one should not only offer but accept loving service:
> The man who is anointed with it [the oil of gladness] becomes pleasant and temperate, a man without a grudge, who neither cheats nor attacks nor offends others. He does not exalt himself or promote himself at their expense [2 Co 7:2; Lk 3:14], but offers his services as generously as he willingly accepts theirs [Ph 4:15].[14]

Whatever the form loving service takes, the spirit which should inform it is loving kindness:
> There is another ointment... to which I give the name loving kindness, because the elements that go into its making are the needs of the poor, the anxieties of the oppressed, the worries of those who are sad, the sins of wrong-doers, and, finally, the manifold misfortunes of people of all classes who endure affliction, even if they are our enemies.[15]

The response to all of these human miseries, Bernard teaches, must be loving service:
> Who, in your opinion, is the good man who takes pity and lends [Ps 111:5], who is disposed to be compassionate, quick to render assistance, who believes there is more happiness in giving than in receiving [Ac 20:35], who easily forgives but is not easily angered, who will never seek to be avenged, and who will in all things take thought for his neighbor's needs as if they were his own? Whoever you may be, if your soul is thus disposed, if you are saturated with the dew of mercy, overflowing with affectionate kindness, making yourself all things to all men [1 Co 9:22] yet pricing your deeds like something discarded [Ps 30:13] in order to be ever and everywhere ready to supply to others what they need, in a word, so dead to yourself that you live only for others—if this be you, then you obviously and happily possess the third and best of all ointments, and your hands have dripped with liquid myrrh that is utterly enchanting [Sg 5:5].[16]

Bernard gives examples aplenty of the ways in which the ointment of loving kindness may be transferred to others in loving service. And, as Christ himself taught (Mt 25:40), that service to others is a way of ministering to Christ:

> Let the superior's assistants exercise hospitality toward the Savior in the manner determined by their office. Some are appointed to welcome him, others to attend him, others to minister to him in his members, this one in the sick brethren, that one in the poor, a third in the guests and strangers.[17]

Hospitality, demanded by the *Rule* of Benedict,[18] is particularly important to Bernard. For the sake of welcoming Christ in the guest, Bernard would cut short his sermons to his monks:

> Dear brothers, surely it is wonderful for us to be here [Lk 9:33], but the burden of the day calls us elsewhere. These guests, whose arrival has just been announced to us, compel me to break off a talk I enjoy very much. So I go to meet the guests, to make sure that the duty of love, of which we have been speaking, may not suffer neglect, that we may not hear it said of us: 'They do not practice what they preach' [Mt 23:3].[19]

The practice of love can seem an onerous burden at times, but the call to busy oneself in the service of others should be answered as generously as did Bernard's brother, Gerard:

> What a busy man he was! What a trustworthy friend! Though always glad to be in the company of friends, he was never prevented thereby from answering the call of love. Who ever went away from him empty-handed? The rich found enlightenment; the poor were given alms.[20]

The needs of others, not their spiritual status, should evoke a loving response in the humble person:

> So, if a brother sins [Ga 6:1], let a man of the Church, who has already received this spirit [of gentleness], come to his assistance with all gentleness, not forgetting that he himself may be tempted.[21]

Loving correction of the sinner is accomplished best by example, not by imposition of pharisaical commands:

> Actions speak louder than words. Practice what you preach, and not only will you correct me more easily, you will free yourself from no light reproach. You will not be the target if someone says: 'They bind heavy

burdens, hard to bear, and lay them on men's shoulders; but they themselves will not lift a finger to move them' [Mt 23:4]. Nor need you be afraid to hear: 'You who teach others, will you not teach yourself' [Rm 2:21].[22]

Yet, as important as loving service is, it is not not merely exercised in acts of love, but it should inform one's entire life:

And you too, if you permit us, your companions, to share in the gift you have received from above, if you are at all times courteous, friendly, agreeable, gentle, and humble, you will find men everywhere bearing witness to the perfumed influence you radiate. Everyone among you who not only patiently endures the bodily and mental weaknesses of his neighbors, but even, if permissible and possible, plies them with attention, inspires them with encouragement, helps them with advice, or, where the rules do not so permit, at least does not cease to assist them by fervent prayers—everyone, I repeat, who performs such deeds among you— gives forth a good odor among the brethren like a rare and delicate perfume. As balsam in the mouth so is such a man in the community. People will point him out and say: 'This is a man who loves his brothers and the people of Israel; this is a man who prays much for the people and for the holy city' [2 M 15:14].[23]

Since human beings live with others, since humans are social animals, love should permeate all of human life, all one's thoughts and actions:

Now, it seems to me, you that live in community live well if you live an orderly, sociable, and humble life: an orderly life with regard to yourself, a sociable life with regard to your brethren, a humble life with regard to God. You will live an orderly life if in all your actions you are solicitous to watch over your ways both in the sight of God and in the sight of your brother, preserving him from scandal and yourself from sin. You will live sociably if you strive to be amiable toward all and to love all, to show yourself kind and affable, to support not only with patience but even with gladness the infirmities, whether of body or soul, of your brethren. You will live humbly if, having done all this, you labor to extinguish the spirit of vainglory which such actions often engender and are careful never to consent to its suggestions, no matter how strongly you may feel them.[24]

Love for oneself, for others, and for God are, in the end, modes of the one love[25] which motivates all service.

The bond which should bind all to one another is love. Harmony, not fear, should be the cement which holds all social relationships together. All should strive '. . . to live in the harmony of spontaneous affection with your companions; to live agreeably with them at the prompting of the will is different from a life where the rod is the check on manners.'[26] Nothing can disturb the fabric of a social group which lives in the peace of love:

> What outside influence can upset you or make you sad if you are well disposed toward each other and live in peace like brothers? 'Who is there to harm you if you are zealous for what is right [1 P 3:13]?' Therefore, 'be ambitious for the higher gifts' [1 Co 12:31], that you may prove yourselves men of good zeal. The gift that exceeds all others, that is clearly incomparable, is love, a truth which the heavenly Bridegroom is so often at pains to impress on his new bride. At one time he says: 'By this all men will know that you are my disciples, that you have love for one another' [Jn 13:35]. At another time: 'A new commandment I give you, that you love one another' [Jn 15:12]. And again: 'This is my commandment, that you love one another' [Jn 17:22], while at the same time he prays that they may be one, as he and the Father are one [1 Co 12:31]. . . . This, therefore, is what I say: may peace be yours as the fruit of your zeal, and anything that may threaten from without will not intimidate you because it will not injure you.[27]

The consequences of loving service are not only social but also psychological. It brings a great joy, Bernard teaches, to minister to the needs of others. The sweetness of service is apparent in Bernard's description of his friend Malachy's last illness:

> Some four or five days of our festival had gone by when suddenly he came down with a fever and took to his

bed. And all of us were sick with him. The end of our mirth was sadness [Pr 14:13], more moderate perhaps because the fever seemed light for a time. You could see the brethren running about eager to give or receive. To whom was it not sweet to behold him? To whom was it not sweeter to minister to him? Both were sweet and both were salutary: to do him a service in loving kindness, and, once done, to receive back grace. Everyone was at hand. Everyone was there, solicitous with much serving [Lk 10:40], seeking medicine, applying poultices, more often urging him to eat.[28]

The ultimate model for this sort of loving service, and the ultimate check on self-centeredness, is Christ:

If you say you abide in Christ you ought to walk as he walked [1 Jn 2:6]. But if you seek your own glory [Jn 7:18], envy the successful, slander the absent, take revenge on those who injure you, this Christ did not do.[29]

In imitation of Christ, the pilgrim on the path to the perfection of love should ever increase works of loving service:

And if... the [bride's] bed bedecked with flowers is the conscience laden with good works, you must certainly see that it is by no means enough to do a good deed once or twice if the likeness is to be preserved. You must unceasingly add new ones to the old, so that by sowing bountifully you may reap bountifully [2 Co 9:6]. Otherwise the flower of good works withers where it lies, and all its brilliance and freshness are swiftly destroyed if not renewed continually by more and more acts of love.[30]

1. SC 71, 3; SBOp 2:216; CF 40:50.
2. SC 71, 3; SBOp 2:215-16; CF 40:49-50. The poet is Ovid; Bernard's source is the *Metamorphoses* 8:677-78.
3. Michael Casey puts it well: man must '... build up the habit of doing good and resisting evil through the practice of objective justice.... The practice of virtue by God's gift has a purifying effect on the heart.' Michael Casey, 'Introduction' to *The Story of the Feud Between Two Kings [Parable 2]* in CSt 18 (1983) 193.
4. Asspt 3, 1; SBOp 5:239; Luddy 3:236-37.
5. SC 50, 2; SBOp 2:79; CF 31:31.
6. SC 50, 4; SBOp 2:80; CF 31:32-33.
7. SC 50, 3; SBOp 2:79-80; CF 31:32.
8. SC 50, 5; SBOp 2:81; CF 31:34.
9. SC 50, 5; SBOp 2:81; CF 31:34-35.
10. SC 12, 10; SBOp 1:66-67; CF 4:85. See also SC 4, 1; SBOp 1:19; CF 4:22.
11. SC 18, 3; SBOp 1:105; CF 4:135.
12. SC 5, 9; SBOp 1:25; CF 4:30.
13. SC 37, 7; SBOp 2:13; CF 7:186.
14. SC 23, 6; SBOp 1:142; CF 7:30-31.
15. SC 12, 1; SBOp 1:60; CF 4:77.
16. SC 12, 1; SBOp 1:60-61; CF 4:78.
17. Asspt 3, 6; SBOp 5:243; Luddy 3:243.
18. RB 53.
19. SC 3, 6; SBOp 1:17; CF 4:20.
20. SC 26, 6; SBOp 1:174; CF 7:64. Examples of Gerard's loving service are multiplied in SC 26, 3-6; SBOp 1:171-75; CF 7:60-65. Examples of loving service by biblical characters are found in SC 12, 2-5; SBOp 1:61-63; CF 4:78-81.
21. SC 44, 2; SBOp 2:45; CF 7:226. See also SC 25, 1; SBOp 1:163; CF 7:50-51.
22. SC 59, 3; SBOp 2:137; CF 31:122-23. Bernard gives a humorous description of one who corrects others out of vanity in Hum 13, 41; SBOp 3:47-48; CF 13:68-69.
23. SC 12, 5; SBOp 1:63-64; CF 4:81-82.
24. PP 1, 4; SBOp 5:190; Luddy 3:196-97.
25. See above, p. 117.
26. SC 23, 8; SBOp 1:143; CF 7:32.
27. SC 29, 3; SBOp 1:204-205; CF 7:104-105.
28. V Mal 70; SBOp 3:374-75; CF 10:88.
29. SC 24, 8; SBOp 1:161; CF 7:48-49.
30. SC 47, 2; SBOp 2:63; CF 31:4-5.

J. Prudence, Discretion, and Temperance

Throughout Bernard's descriptions of the life of love he insists on the primacy of intention in the practice of virtue. He likewise asserts that the practices which promote love will do so only if governed by prudence, discretion, and temperance. In the pursuit of virtue the standard should be the middle way, the mean:

> Tell me, if you can, to which of these virtues [justice, temperance, and fortitude] you think we should especially attribute the mean, which is coterminous with them all in such a way that it seems proper to each? Or is the mean virtue itself? But then virtue would not be many-faceted, but all virtues would be one. On the other hand, because no virtue is possible without it, is the mean somehow the essential core of the virtues in which all are united so as to appear as one? Certainly they do not unite by sharing it, but each totally and perfectly possesses it. For example, what is as essential to justice as the mean? Otherwise, if justice fails to attain the mean in all respects, it clearly does not give to each his due as it should. Similarly, what is as essential to temperance, which is a virtue precisely because it allows nothing in excess? But I am sure you will admit that the mean is no less essential to fortitude, especially since it is this virtue which successfully rescues the mean unharmed from the onslaught of vices which try to strangle it, and establishes it as a solid foundation of goodness and seat of virtue. Therefore, to maintain the mean is justice, is temperance, is fortitude.[1]

Bernard renders these abstract principles concrete in his *Sermon on the Seven Steps of Confession* by pointing out the moral neutrality of many activities:

> Between things absolutely good and things absolutely evil there lies an intermediate class of actions which, of themselves indifferent, are called good or evil according to the circumstances in which they are done. To this intermediate class belong walking or sitting, speaking or observing silence, eating or fasting, sleeping or keeping watch. . . .[2]

These activities are neither virtuous nor vicious in themselves; what is important is the reason for which they are done, the intention with which they are done. Intention is a matter of the will. Virtue is in the will, not the action:

> What proceeds from a pure heart and a good conscience [1 Tm 1:5] is virtue, white and shining; and if it is followed by a good report it is a lily too, for it has both color and fragrance.[3]

Emphasis on intention does not imply that good works are unnecessary, that one may merely think compassionate thoughts. Virtuous acts are both virtuous and acts. Indeed, those acts demonstrate the sincerity of the intention:

> It is not from the leaves or the blossom but from the fruit that we can tell a good tree from a bad. For it is 'by their fruits that you shall know them' [Eph 5:6]. Therefore, it is by their works, not by their words, that the sons of God are distinguished from the sons of unbelief, and it is by works that you too will prove the sincerity of your desire and put mine to the test.[4]

Both intention and act are necessary to a good work.

And in determining which action is appropriate, which activity should be pursued, discretion and prudence and temperance all provide guidance. If virtue depends on the consent of the will,[5] temperance is a powerful means of directing that will:

> Neither of these [justice or fortitude] is possible unless the will, which shapes them, is brought under control so that it neither desires anything excessive nor presumptuously avoids anything necessary. This is the role of temperance.[6]

Love is the proper direction of the will; that love must be prudent.[7] Prudential love is taught the soul by her lover, Christ; he shares with the soul his own prudence:

> He would be the exemplar of her moral life, preparing the way of virtue [Ps 104:22]. He would teach her to become like himself and share with her his prudence [Is 40:14]. And, having thus given her the law of life and discipline [Si 45:6], he would inevitably be attracted by her beauty [Ps 44:12].[8]

If one is to live a balanced life of love, the will must be regulated by the intellect. This is why temperance, prudence, and discretion are indispensable:

Zeal without knowledge is insupportable [Rm 10:2]. Therefore, where zeal is enthusiastic, there discretion, that moderator of love, is especially necessary. Because zeal without knowledge always lacks efficacy, is wanting in usefulness, and all too often is harmful. And so the more eager the zeal, the more vigorous the spirit, the more generous the love, so also the greater the need for more vigilant knowledge to restrain the zeal, to temper the spirit, to moderate the love.[9]

Discretion, then, is the regulator of love. And this direction is essential to the life of virtue:

Discretion regulates every virtue; order assigns proportion and beauty, and even permanence.... Discretion, therefore, is not so much a virtue as a moderator and guide of the virtues, a director of the affections, a teacher of right living. Take it away and virtue becomes a vice, and natural affection becomes itself a force that disturbs and destroys nature.[10]

Discretion is crucial to the order of a well-regulated life, not only the life of the individual but the life of the community in which one lives:

'He set love in order in me' [Sg 2:4]. This took place when he appointed some in the Church as apostles, some prophets, others evangelists, others pastors and teachers, for the perfecting of the saints [Eph 4:11]. It is essential that one love should bind and merge all these into the unity of Christ's body, and love is entirely incapable of doing this if it is not itself regulated. For if each one is carried away by his own impulse in accord with the spirit he receives, if he applies himself indifferently to everything as he feels suggested rather than as he judges by reason—until no one is content with his assigned duty, but all simultaneously undertake to manage everything indiscriminately—there will clearly be no unity but confusion instead.[11]

In the life of the individual and of social groups both zeal and order are necessary:

Without the fervor of love the virtue of discretion is lifeless, and intense fervor goes headlong without the curb of discretion. Praiseworthy the man, then, who possesses both: the fervor that enlivens discretion, the discretion that regulates fervor.[12]

Bernard describes allegorically the necessary integration of discretion, prudence, and temperance into the life of love in his first *Parable*:

> Borne along in headlong flight [from the land of Unlikeness], they [the King's son and his entourage of virtues] escaped. But danger remained, for they were left without measure and without counsel. Because of this, Prudence, who was one of the most important officials of the palace, ran up, sent by the Father. With her was her friend Temperance. She restrained their haste. 'Slow down', she cried, 'please slow down. As Solomon says: "The man in a hurry goes off the path" [Pr 19:2]. If you keep running in this way, you will go off the path, and, if you go off the path, you will fall. If you fall, you will be giving the King's son back to his enemies, although you are trying to set him free. For if he falls, they will seize him.'[13]

Having warned the virtues to restrain their ardor, Prudence takes positive steps to direct their path:

> Saying this, Prudence restrained the ardor of the horse named Desire with the bridle of discretion and gave the reins into the control of Temperance. And when Fear, from his rear position, began to talk about the nearness and might of their enemies and the slowness of their flight, Prudence said: 'Get behind me, Satan [Mt 16:23], you are a source of stumbling. For it is the Lord who is our strength and our praise; he has become our savior' [Ex 15:2].[14]

Prudence thus reminds the entourage that man's happiness is a gift, not a result of undisciplined activity. Even Fortitude must thus be restrained:

> And lo, Fortitude, the Lord's military champion, appeared. He surged through the fields of Boldness, wielding the sword that is Joy. 'Do not be disturbed', he cried, 'there are more for us than for them' [2 K 6:16]. But Prudence, the seasoned counselor of the heavenly court, replied: 'Please be careful. As my servant Solomon says, "If at the beginning you hasten toward your inheritance,

then at the end there will be no blessing" [Pr 20:21]....'[15]

The balanced life of prudence, discretion, and temperance is not easily attained. The pilgrim longing for a balanced life of virtue is mightily assisted in the quest by the counsel offered by those who have advanced along the path of perfection, and the rational response should be to hear and obey that counsel.[16] In choosing how to live and which practices to perform for one's own benefit, one should avail oneself of the discretion of the wise:

> In all these matters [neither commanded nor forbidden], we must be submissive and obedient to the will of our superior, asking no questions for conscience's sake, for none of these things has God preordained as obligatory.... This is the kind of obedience which we, who are under a man, owe to a man. It is also a bond between God and man, for, whenever obedience is given to superiors, it is given to him who says: 'He who hears you, hears me' [Lk 10:16].[17]

Another powerful standard by which to judge the prudence of one's actions is the general practice of the community in which one lives:

> When the noonday devil sets out to tempt a man, there is no chance whatever of parrying him. He will tempt and overthrow his victim by suggesting what appears to be good by persuading him, unsuspecting and unprepared as he is, to commit evil under the guise of good.... How often, for example, does he not persuade a monk to anticipate the hour of rising and mock him as he sleeps in choir while the others pray. How often does he not suggest that fasts be prolonged until a man is so weak that he is useless for the service of God. How often, in envy of a man's fervor in community life, does he not persuade him to live as a hermit in order to achieve greater perfection, until the unhappy man finally discovers how true is that saying which he has read to no purpose: 'Woe to him who is alone, for when he falls, he has no one to pick him up' [Qo 4:10]. How often has he not inspired a man to work harder than necessary at manual labor until exhaustion makes him unfit for the other regular observances.[18]

Without the guidance of prudence the 'tender and affectionate love of the heart' may be led astray from the path to perfection:

> Tender affection may easily lead us astray unless it has prudence to guide it. It may easily become a source of danger, and then, perhaps, we shall find it difficult enough to guard against the poison in our honey. Prudence, therefore, must accompany our love....[19]

There are practical reasons why prudence must guide love. Excess in the pursuit of virtue may bring on a fatigue which would make the pilgrim prey to vice. Bernard's *Story of the King's Son Sitting on His Horse* provides an allegorical statement of this teaching:

> The young man, boastfully attempting to demonstrate his outstanding strength in battle, rushed toward him [Fornication]. And, although his horse [his body] needed no encouragement, he goaded it with the whip of fasting and the spurs of vigils. He was totally given to the chase. From the rear Prudence called 'Slow down!', and Discretion cried 'Wait!' And the whole of David's army shouted after him. He turned a deaf ear and disregarded them all. And so the poor man was swept on to his doom but knew it not.[20]

Bernard tells his audience that Pride and Vainglory encouraged the young man's indiscretion. The attempt to conquer virtue, to perfect oneself, indicates an intellect disordered by pride. This, in turn, affects the body by inducing a debilitating fatigue which renders it a ready victim to vice:

> Gluttony and Fornication claimed the horse [body] for themselves and would permit its owner to exercise no further rights over it. In fact, the horse was very weak and so tired that it sought something with which to amuse itself. While the fighting was still going on, it had given way under the knight and had, by its fall, grievously injured its rider.[21]

Bernard insists that the body is a friend to the soul and must not be overtaxed by self-discipline. He teaches that discretion is the means by which one differentiates prudent self-discipline from self-indulgence:

> This self-discipline ought to be attended by discretion, lest through excessive zeal we should carry bodily mortification so far that we injure our health and slay our friend, so to speak, in our eagerness to vanquish an enemy. Consider how much your body can bear, take

account of your physical constitution, and let your severity be kept in proportion. It is a duty to preserve our bodily health for the service of the Creator.[22]

The reason for self-control, for moderating one's desire for the things of the material world, is not that they are evil. As we have seen, they are, on the contrary, good. But in themselves they are not enough to satisfy man's desire for the ultimate good of happiness:

> Every rational being naturally desires always what satisfies more its mind and will. It is never satisfied with something which lacks the qualities it thinks it should have. A man with a beautiful wife, for example, looks at a more attractive woman with a wanton eye or heart. A well-dressed man wants more costly clothes. And a man of great wealth envies anyone richer than he. You can see men who already own many farms and possessions still busy, day after day, adding one field to another [Is 5:8], driven by an excessive passion to extend their holdings [Ex 34:24; Am 1:13]. You can see men living in homes worthy of a king and in sumptuous dwellings none the less daily adding house to house [Is 5:8], through restless curiosity building up then tearing down, changing squares into circles. What about men promoted to high honors? Do we not see them striving more and more in an insatiable ambition to go higher still?[23]

If these material goods were adequate to provide happiness, those who possess them would not find them wanting. The problem is not with the body which naturally seeks the goods of sex, clothing, food, and housing. The difficulty is in the will which seeks to find in these things ultimate satisfaction:

> There is no end to all this [striving], because no single one of these riches can be held to be highest or best. What wonder if man cannot be content with what is lower and worse, since he cannot find peace this side of what is highest and best? It is stupidity and madness to want always that which can neither satisfy nor even diminish your desire. While enjoying those riches, you strive for what is missing and are dissatisfied, longing for what you lack. Thus the restless mind, running to and fro among the pleasures of his life, is tired out but

never satisfied.... In like manner, a perverted will contends for what is best and hastens in a straight line toward that which will afford it the most satisfaction. Rather, vanity makes sport of it in these tortuous ways, and evil deceives itself [Ps 26:12].... The just man is not like that...; he prefers the royal road which turns neither to the right nor the left [Nb 20:17, 21:22].[24]

The body is good. It simply needs direction from a will oriented toward a yet higher good. And the will must be directed toward the highest good by an intellect which knows the truth.

This teaching on prudence, discretion, and temperance Bernard applies to all the practices he enjoins on the pilgrim seeking perfection in love. Moderation, not rejection, should govern one's decisions on clothing, food, and sleep. This moderation is the fruit of a discretion which recognizes that virtue is a matter of the intellect and will:

> There are people who go clad in tunics and have nothing to do with furs who, nevertheless, are lacking in humility. Surely humility in furs is better than pride in tunics.[25]

What is true of clothing is also true of food and drink: 'The devil persuades some to keep singular fasts, by which others are scandalized—not because he loves fasting but because he delights in scandal.'[26] Surely, Bernard thinks, '...those who fast so that they may be seen fasting by men' [Mt 6:16] intend '...not to please God but men' [Ga 1:10].[27] The use of wine should be moderate, not because wine is evil, but because its immoderate use makes one unfit for prayer:

> When the monk gets up from the table and the swollen veins in his temple begin to throb, all he is fit for is to go back to bed. After all, if you force a man to come to the Office of Vigils before his digestion is complete, all you will extract from him is a moan instead of a tone.[28]

The physiological need for sleep leads Bernard to tolerate a sleepy and even sleeping audience for his sermons; he closes his thirty-sixth sermon on the *Song of Songs* with these words:

> But there are other things to attend to—or should we come to an end for the sake those who are asleep down there?... Some, I can see, are yawning, and some are

asleep. And no wonder, for last night's vigils were prolonged—and excuses them. But what shall I say to those who were asleep then and now sleep again?[29] Moderation and common sense are again the rule. Those who need sleep should sleep; those who do not, should not.

As useful as is silence to the pursuit of love,[30] Bernard urges prudence in maintaining it:

> At this point we need to be warned not to give away what we have received for our own welfare, not to retain for ourselves what must be expended for others. For example, you keep for yourself what belongs to your neighbor if, along with your full endowment of interior virtues, you are also adorned with the external gifts of knowledge and eloquence, and, through fear or sloth or ill-judged humility, you smother this gift of speech that could be of help to so many in a useless and even pernicious silence. For 'the people's curse is on the man who hoards the wheat' [Pr 11:26].[31]

Love is the rule in silence and speaking. Much talk, motivated by pride, is as imprudent as inconsiderate silence:

> On the other hand, you squander and lose what is meant to be your own if, before you are totally permeated by the Holy Spirit, you rashly proceed to pour out your unfulfilled self on others....[32]

Motivation is again the key. Bernard is particularly hard on those whose speech is an endless discourse on the value of fasting, keeping vigil, and prayer, on patience and humility, but whose talk is 'all words, all bragging':[33]

> You deprive yourself of the life and salvation which you impart to another if, lacking right intention and inspired by pride [Ga 5:26], you become infected with the poison of worldly ambition that swells into a deadly ulcer and destroys you.[34]

Bernard's insistence on the necessity of prudence, discretion, and temperance is as applicable to continence as to the other practices of love. Without the right intention, even the virtue of continence avails nothing in the pursuit of a life of love:

> ...Do you not see how entirely necessary is the virtue of continence, if you are not to let sin reign in your mortal bodies [Rm 6:12]? Nevertheless, continence will

gain you no credit before God if you flaunt it for the praises of men. Consequently, there is the greatest need too for that uprightness of intention by which you will both strive to please God alone and find the strength to adhere to him.[35]

In all the virtues, Mary's response to the angel's salutation provides a model:

My brothers, the Virgin Mary is a model of fortitude in her purpose to remain unmarried, of temperance in her silence under praise, of prudence in her inquiries, of justice in her confession.[36]

The good life is characterized above all by a will which chooses to do everything in love. In all the works of love, Bernard is convinced, the guidance of prudence, discretion, and temperance are necessary. The good life is a balanced life, and the pursuit of the good life must be equally balanced:

But you, my brother, your salvation is not yet assured; your love as yet is either non-existent or so meager and reed-like that it bends with every breeze, puts its trust in every spirit [1 Jn 4:1], and is carried away by every wind of doctrine [Eph 4:14]. Or your love is so great that you transcend the limits of the commandment by loving your neighbor more than yourself [Mt 19:19]. Or, yet again, it is so unsound that, contrary to the commandment, it bows to flattery, flinches under fear, is upset by sadness, shriveled by avarice, entangled by ambition, disquieted by suspicions, tormented by insults, exhausted by anxieties, puffed up by honors, consumed by envy. If you discover this chaos in your own interior, what madness drives you to insinuate yourself into other people's business? But listen to what a prudent and vigilant love advises: 'This does not mean that to give relief to others you ought to make things difficult for yourselves; it is a matter of balance' [2 Co 8:13].[37]

Even loving service to others must be prudent. In this, as in all else, wisdom is the foundation of a balanced life of love:

The right hand [of Christ's bride] is activity. The right glove [he gives her] is divided into five sections to accommodate her five fingers. This is because every good action must be upright, voluntary, pure, discerning, and firm. It must be upright in intention, voluntary so that it is not due to fear or some coercion, pure so that it is not rendered useless by any hint of vanity, discerning so that it does not exceed due measure, and firm so that it is persevering.[38]

1. Csi 1, 8, 11; SBOp 3:406; CF 37:41-42.
2. Div 41, 3; SBOp 6/1:246-47; Luddy 3:466. Bernard uses virtually the same words in Ep 7, 4; SBOp 7:34; James, p. 28.
3. SC 71, 1; SBOp 2:215; CF 40:48-49.
4. Ep 107, 1; SBOp 7:268; James, p. 158. See also Mal 2; SBOp 6/1:51; CF 10:108.
5. See SC 85, 3; SBOp 2:309; CF 40:198.
6. Csi 1, 8, 10; SBOp 3:405; CF 37:40.
7. SC 18, 4; SBOp 1:106; CF 4:136.
8. SC 21, 3; SBOp 1:124; CF 7:6.
9. SC 49, 5; SBOp 2:75-76; CF 31:25. See Casey, 'Introduction', CSt 18 (1983) 193. If the intellect is misdirected, the will will be '...bound in iron chains and thrown into prison.' Par 5, 4; SBOp 6/2:283; CSt 20:29.
10. SC 49, 5; SBOp 2:76; CF 31:25.
11. SC 49, 5; SBOp 2:76; CF 31:25-26.
12. SC 23, 8; SBOp 1:144; CF 7:32. See also Circ 3, 11 (SBOp 4:290-91; Luddy 3:445-46) and SC 50, 5 (SBOp 2:80-81; CF 31:34-35).
13. Par 1, 3-4; SBOp 6/2:263; CSt 18:20.
14. Par 1, 4; SBOp 6/2:263; CSt 18:20.
15. Par 1, 4; SBOp 6/2:263-64; CSt 18:20. See also Par 2, 3; SBOp 6/2:269; CSt 18:196.
16. See above, pp. 152-157. The standard for such counsel must always be the promotion of love. See Pre 2, 5 (SBOp 3:257; CF 1:108-109) and 4, 9 (SBOp 3:259; CF 1:111).
17. Div 41, 3; SBOp 6/1:247; Luddy 3:467.
18. SC 33, 9-10; SBOp 1:240; CF 7:152-53.
19. Div 29, 4; SBOp 6/1:213; Luddy 3:500.
20. Par 3, 2; SBOp 6/2:274-75; CSt 18:286.
21. Par 3, 2; SBOp 6/2:275; CSt 18:286.
22. Div 40, 7; SBOp 6/1:241; Luddy 3:456. On occasion Bernard does seem to urge an attitude toward the body which contradicts this view. See Nat 3, 2; SBOp 4:259; Luddy 1:401. But the bulk of his pronouncements on the subject lead me to conclude that such negative statements are expressions of hyperbole. Bernard teaches that material benefits to the body are gifts of the Holy Spirit, surely an incentive to receive them thankfully. See Pent 3, 8; SBOp 5:175; Luddy 2:314-15.
23. Dil 7, 18; SBOp 3:134; CF 13:111.
24. Dil 7, 18 and 21; SBOp 3:134-35 and 136; CF 13:111-13.
25. Apo 6, 12; SBOp 3:92; CF 1:48.
26. Div 24, 1; SBOp 6/1:183.
27. Csi 1, 8, 10; SBOp 3:405-406; CF 37:40-41.
28. Apo 9, 21; SBOp 3:99; CF 1:57. Bernard cautions against using discretion as an excuse for consuming more than the 'little wine' allowed by Saint Paul (1 Tm 5:23) for the sake of health. See SC 30, 12; SBOp 1:218; CF 7:123. Indeed, he there urges moderation in all uses of medicine. Given the state of contemporary professional medicine, he is probably wise to prefer traditional herbal medicines to the 'nostrums' of the doctors of the time. See Ep 345, 2; SBOp 8:287-88; James, pp. 458-59.

29. SC 36, 7; SBOp 2:8; CF 7:179-80.
30. See above, pp. 157-158.
31. SC 18, 2; SBOp 1:104; CF 4:134.
32. SC 18, 2; SBOp 1:104; CF 4:134.
33. Hum 13, 41; SBOp 3:48; CF 13:69.
34. SC 18, 2; SBOp 1:104; CF 4:134.
35. SC 7, 7; SBOp 1:35; CF 4:43. See also SC 27, 8; SBOp 1:187; CF 7:81.
36. Div 52, 4; SBOp 6/1:276; Luddy 3:494.
37. SC 18, 4; SBOp 1:105; CF 4:135.
38. Par 6; SBOp 6/2:291; CSt 21:104.

K. Prayer

Perseverance in virtue is powerfully aided by prayer:
> In prayer one drinks the wine that gladdens a man's heart [Ps 103:15], the intoxicating wine of the Spirit that drowns all memory of the pleasures of the flesh. It drenches anew the arid recesses of the conscience, stimulates digestion of the meats of good works, fills the faculties of the soul with a robust faith, a solid hope, a love which is living and true. It enriches all the actions of our life.[1]

Bernard speaks of prayer as the messenger of both prudence and justice in his allegorical *Story of the Feud Between Two Kings*. Bernard has Prudence rebuking Fear

> ...for his panic. 'O Fear, your sword has lost its edge against your adversaries. Do you not know that our king is the king of strength—the Lord, the mighty, the valiant; the Lord, the valiant in war [Ps 23:8]. Therefore, let a messenger go forth who will inform him of our plight and ask for aid and request a helper.'. . . So they called Justice, their host, to them and said to him: 'Help us if you can' [Mk 9:21]. He replied: 'Be of good heart [Ac 27:25]. I have a loyal messenger who is well known to the king and to the court. His name is Prayer. He will go forth secretly at night, traversing hidden pathways known to him, and so obtain entrance to the inner courts of heaven. He will have access to the king's chamber, and there he will use his experience to bend the king's resolve with an appropriate importunity. He will make heart-rending supplication so that the king may provide the help he usually gives to those in trouble. He can go if you approve, for behold he stands ready.' And they all replied: 'Yes!'[2]

But Bernard thinks prayer is much more than an intercessory cry for assistance.

Prayer is a means of expressing a profound confidence in God's love. It is an expression of one's faith, hope, and love in and for one's loving Creator. Lazarus' sister Martha is Bernard's example of such faith:

> 'Lord', she said, 'if you had been here my brother would not have died' [Jn 11:21]. She must have had faith,

strong faith, if she believed that our Lord's presence could have saved her brother's life.... She added: 'But even now I know that whatever you ask from God he will give to you' [Jn 11:22].³

Martha is also a model of hope:

When Jesus asked where they had laid him, she answered: 'Come and see' [Jn 11:34]. Why did she stop at that? Martha, you have given us a wonderful example of faith; surely you do not begin to doubt now? When you said 'Come and see', was your hope not strong enough to add: 'and raise him up'? If you had no hope you would not have troubled the Master with a useless visit. It is rather that faith will sometimes gain what prayer hardly dares ask. As he approached the grave, you stopped him and said: 'Lord, by this time there will be an odor, for he has been now four days dead' [Jn 11:39]. Was it despair that made you say that? I think rather you were making a timid suggestion....⁴

Prayer, then, stems from faith and hope. But, Bernard believes, it is above all an expression of deep love. He addresses Martha and Mary:

O you two holy sisters, friends of Christ, if you really love your brother, why do you not ask for him the mercy of one whose power you cannot doubt, about whose love you can have no hesitation [Jn 11:3]? But their answer comes: 'We are praying, praying all the better when we voice no prayer. We trust all the more strongly when we seem to doubt. We show our faith; we show our love. And he who needs no telling knows what we desire [Ws 7:27; Mt 6:8]. We know that he can do all things; even this great unheard-of miracle is well within his power. But it is far beyond all the merits of our lowliness. It is enough for us to have brought him, to have set the stage for this great wonder, to have given love its opportunity. We would rather wait patiently on his will than ask impudently for something he may not will to give. Perhaps our modesty will supply for our unworthiness.'⁵

For Bernard, prayer is an attitude of the heart characterized by faith and hope in the love of God. Prayer is an affirmation of that love which 'waits patiently on his will'. Prayer too must be expression of a 'clean heart', of an 'uprightness of intention':

The man who lives in this state habitually will have the angels for his frequent and familiar guests, especially if they find him frequently in prayer.[6]

Prayer should have both a communal and an individual expression. For Bernard, the principle forms of communal prayer are the Mass and the Office:

> While offering up the sacrifice of praise [Ps 115:17] and fulfilling our vows from day to day [Ps 60:9], let us make every endeavor to give meaning to our observance, to fill the meaning with love, our love with joy, and our joy with solemnity. Let that solemnity be tempered with humility and our humility be buoyant with liberty. Then we shall advance toward our goal with the untrammeled passions of a purified mind. We may even find ourselves at times living beyond our normal powers through the great intensity of our affections and our spiritual joy, in jubilant encounters, in the light of God, in sweetness, in the Holy Spirit [2 Co 6:6] — all showing that we are among those envisioned by the Prophet when he said: 'Lord, they will walk in the light of your favor; they will rejoice in your name all day and exult in your righteousness' [Ps 88:16-17].[7]

Because communal prayer is so efficacious for progress in the life of love, it must be observed with loving attention:

> For this reason it makes me sad to see some of you deep in the throes of sleep during the night office, to see that, instead of showing reverence for those princely citizens of heaven [attending the communal prayer], you appear like corpses. When you are fervent, they respond with eagerness and are filled with delight in participating in your solemn offices. What I fear is that one day, repelled by our sloth, they will angrily depart.[8]

Communal prayer requires loving attention, which means that participation in that prayer must be diligent:

> So, dearest brothers, I exhort you to participate in divine praises always correctly and vigorously. Vigorously, that you may stand before God with as much zest as reverence, not sluggish, not drowsy, not yawning, not sparing your voices, not leaving words half-said or skipping them, not wheezing through the nose with an

effeminate stammering, not in a weak and broken tone, but pronouncing the words of the Holy Spirit with becoming manliness and resonance and affection. And correctly, that while you chant you ponder nothing but what you chant.⁹

Distractions should be shunned that one may profit fully from the texts over and through which one prays:

> Nor do I mean that only vain and useless thoughts are to be avoided. But, for at least that time and in that place, those thoughts also must be avoided with which office-holders must be inevitably and frequently preoccupied for the community's needs. Nor would I even recommend that you dwell on those you have freshly acquired as you sat in the cloister reading, or such as you are now gathering from the Holy Spirit during my discussions. They are wholesome, but it is not wholesome for you to ponder them in the midst of the psalms.¹⁰

Meditative reading and reflective attention to sermons are also forms of prayer. And there is a time and place for them as well. The quiet of early day is especially conducive to finding God in prayer:

> He says: 'I love those who love me, and they that seek me early shall find me' [Pr 8:17]. See how he assures you of his love, if you love him, and of his concern for you, if he sees you concerned for him. Do you keep watch? He keeps watch also. If you rise at night before the time of vigil [Lm 2:19] and hasten to anticipate the morning watch [Ps 76:5], you will find him there. He will always be waiting for you.¹¹

Solitude provides a great opportunity for meaningful prayer. That solitude is above all an internal disposition,¹² but physical isolation can be useful to one who wishes to pray:

> O holy soul, remain alone, so that you may keep yourself for him alone whom you have chosen for yourself out of all that exists.... You must withdraw, mentally rather than physically, in your intention, in your devotion, in your spirit. For Christ the Lord is a spirit before your face [Lm 4:20], and he demands solitude of the spirit more than of the body, although physical

withdrawal can be of benefit when the opportunity offers, especially in time of prayer. To do this is to follow the advice and example of the Bridegroom; when you want to pray, you should go into your room, shut the door, and then pray [Mt 6:6]. And what he said he did. He spent nights alone in prayer [Lk 6:12, 9:18].... You too must act like this [Lk 10:37, 22:41] when you wish to pray.[13]

But, for Bernard, even solitude has a social dimension. One prays in solitude but takes one's community with one and brings back the fruits of one's prayer to one's fellows:

> But even you too, if recollected in spirit; if with a mind serious and devoid of cares, you enter the house of prayer [Mt 21:13] alone and, standing in the Lord's presence at one of the altars, touch the gate of heaven with the hand of holy desire; if in the presence of the choirs of saints where your devotion penetrates—for 'the prayer of the righteous man pierces the heavens' [Si 35:21]—you bewail pitiably before them the miseries and misfortunes you endure, manifest your neediness, implore their mercy with repeated sighs and groanings too deep for words; if, I say, you do this, I have confidence in him who said 'Ask and you shall receive' [Jn 16:24], that if you continue knocking you will not go away empty [Lk 11:8]. Indeed, when you return to us full of grace and love, you will not be able, in the ardor of your spirit [Rm 12:11], to conceal the gift you have received. You will communicate it without unpopularity [Ws 7:13], and, in the grace that was given you, you will win the acceptance and even the admiration of everyone. And you can declare with truth: 'The king led me into the wine cellar' [Sg 2:3]. Only be careful that you glory not in yourself but in the Lord [1 Co 1:31].[14]

Prayer, both individual and social, clearly leads to growth in love if it is properly directed.

Bernard offers suggestions on ways to encourage oneself in prayer—and ways to direct one's prayer:

> Anyone who wishes to pray must choose not only the right place but also the right time. A time of leisure is best and most convenient; the deep silence when others

> are asleep is particularly suitable, for prayer will then be freer and purer.... You will not pray aright if, in your prayers, you seek anything but the Word; for in him are all things [Col 1:17]. In him is healing for your wounds, help in your need, restoration for your further growth. In him is all that men should ask or desire, all they need, all that will profit them. There is no reason to ask anything else of the Word, for he is all. Even if we should seem sometimes to ask for material things, providing we do so for the sake of the Word, as we should, it is not the things themselves we are asking for, but him for whose sake we ask them. Those who habitually use all things to find the Word know this.[15]

For Bernard, prayer is a direction of the will toward the ultimate good. And any physical assistance which aids in directing the prayer in that proper direction requires should be employed; this is particularly useful to the beginner on the path of love:[16]

> The soul at prayer should have before her a sacred image of the God-man, in his birth, or infancy, or as he was teaching, dying, rising, or ascending. Whatever form it takes, this image must bind the soul with the love of virtue and expel carnal vices, eliminate temptations, and quiet desires.[17]

Whatever time, place, or other means employed to enrich prayer, it is essential, Bernard believes, to put that prayer in proper context by remembering that its efficacy is a gift not an accomplishment:

> Even when we say 'In the morning my prayer will come before you' [Ps 87:14], we must remember that, without out first receiving divine inspiration, all prayer becomes lukewarm.[18]

With the realization that prayer is a gift of God, and when properly directed toward the Word, prayer confers salutary effects on the soul seeking love. Meditation properly begun with prayer yields rich fruit:

> In order to carry out this [meditative] examination, however, and before presuming to attempt it—'for the place is holy' [Ezk 42:13]—we must offer the usual prayers to consult and win the favor of that Spirit who 'searches the depths of God' [1 Co 2:10] and of the only-begotten

Son who is in the Father's bosom [Jn 1:18], Jesus Christ
our Lord, the Church's Bridegroom who is blessed for
ever [Rm 1:25].[19]

Bernard is sure that such prayerful meditation is a powerful means
of insight into reality:

> He [God] must still be sought who has not yet been
> sufficiently found and who cannot be sought too much.
> But he is perhaps more worthily sought and more easi-
> ly found by prayer than by discussion.[20]

Bernard is convinced that prayer is never fruitless.[21] It is a means
of acknowledging the power God gives to lead a good life:

> Avoid evil and do good. If you are not able to do this
> by your own power, then pray. Say with the Prophet:
> 'Put false ways far from me' [Ps 118:29].[22]

And the proper response to the grace acknowledged in prayer is
thanksgiving:

> Learn not to be tardy or sluggish in offering thanks; learn
> to offer thanks for each and every gift. Take careful note,
> Scripture advises, of what is set before you [Pr 23:1],
> so that no gift of God, be it great or middle-sized or
> small, will be deprived of due thanksgiving. We are even
> commanded to gather up the smallest fragments lest
> they be lost [Jn 6:12], which means that we are not to
> forget even the smallest benefits. Is that not surely lost
> which is given to an ingrate? Ingratitude is the soul's
> enemy, a voiding of merits, dissipation of the virtues,
> wastage of benefits. Ingratitude is a burning wind that
> dries up the source of love, the dew of mercy, the
> streams of grace.[23]

And these streams of grace not only affect the intellect and will;
they move the feelings and the body through which they feel:[24]

> While the bride is conversing about the Bridegroom,
> he suddenly appears, as I have said; he yields to her
> desire by giving her a kiss and so brings to fulfillment
> those words of the Psalm: 'You have granted him his
> heart's desire; you have not denied him what his lips
> asked' [Ps 20:3]. The filling up of her breasts is a proof
> of this. For so great is the potency of that holy kiss that
> no sooner has the bride received it, she conceives and
> her breasts swell with the fruitfulness of conception,

bearing witness, as it were, with this milky abundance. Those with an urge to frequent prayer will have experienced what I describe. Often enough, when we approach the altar to pray, our hearts are dry and lukewarm. But, if we persevere, there comes an unexpected infusion of grace, our breast expands, as it were, and our interior is filled with an over-flowing love. And if someone should press on it, then this milk of sweet fecundity would gush forth in streaming richness.[25]

In prayer, one realizes the fullness of God's gift which perfects the whole person, body and soul—intellect, will, and feelings. And that perfection flows over to others in love as well.

1. SC 18, 5; SBOp 1:107; CF 4:137.
2. Par 2, 6; SBOp 6/2:271; CSt 18:198.
3. Hum 22, 52; SBOp 3:55; CF 13:78.
4. Hum 22, 52; SBOp 3:55; CF 13:78-79.
5. Hum 22, 52; SBOp 3:55-56; CF 13:79. See also Hum 22, 53; SBOp 3:56; CF 13:79.
6. SC 7, 7; SBOp 1:35; CF 4:43.
7. SC 13, 7; SBOp 1:74; CF 4:94-95.
8. SC 7, 4; SBOp 1:33; CF 4:41.
9. SC 47, 8; SBOp 2:66; CF 31:9-10.
10. SC 47, 8; SBOp 2:66; CF 31:10.
11. SC 69, 8; SBOp 2:206-207; CF 40:35.
12. See SC 40, 5; SBOp 2:27; CF 7:202-203.
13. SC 40, 4; SBOp 2:27; CF 7:202.
14. SC 49, 3; SBOp 2:74-75; CF 31:23.
15. SC 86, 3; SBOp 2:319; CF 40:213-14.
16. See above, pp. 71-72.
17. SC 20, 6; SBOp 1:118; CF 4:152.
18. Dil 7, 22; SBOp 3:138; CF 13:115.
19. SC 29, 9; SBOp 1:209; CF 7:110-111.
20. Csi 5, 14, 32; SBOp 3:493; CF 37:179.
21. See Div 25, 6; SBOp 6/1:191-92.
22. Hum 9, 27; SBOp 3:37; CF 13:55. See also And 1, 10; SBOp 5:433; Luddy 3:50.
23. SC 51, 6; SBOp 2:87; CF 31:44-45.
24. For the connection between the feelings, a faculty of the soul, and the body, see above pp. 32-33.
25. SC 9, 7; SBOp 1:46; CF 4:58. However, Bernard insists that one should not be so attached to the possible sensible effects of prayer that one seeks them for themselves. See Circ 3, 11; SBOp 4:290-91.

L. The Happiness of Perfection

The person whose body and soul—intellect, will, and feelings—are all oriented toward their proper end, God, is a happy person. And the full possession of the virtues of love, justice, patience, simplicity, humility, holy fear, prudence, temperance, and fortitude renders that person beautiful in sight of God:

> The bride's form must be understood in a spiritual sense, her beauty as something grasped by the intellect. It is eternal because it is an image of eternity. Her gracefulness consists of love, and you have read that 'love never ends' [1 Co 13:8]. It consists of justice, for 'her justice endures forever' [Ps 111:3]. It consists of patience, and Scripture tells you: 'The patience of the poor shall not perish forever' [Ps 9:19]. What shall I say of voluntary poverty? Of humility? To the former an eternal kingdom is promised [Mt 5:3], to the latter an eternal exaltation [Lk 14:11]. To these must be added the holy fear of the Lord that endures forever and ever [Ps 18:10]. Prudence too, and temperance and fortitude and all the other virtues—what are they but pearls in the jeweled raiment of the bride, shining with unceasing radiance? I say unceasingly, because they are the basis, the very foundation of immortality. For there is no place for immortal and blissful life in the soul except by means and mediation of the virtues.[1]

In the perfection of human beings, the intellect leads the way. Bernard shows this primacy of the intellect in commenting on the passage from the *Song of Songs* (1:9): 'Your neck as jewels':

> And to my mind, for I can only say what I think, nothing seems more credible or probable than that the word neck signifies the soul's intellect. I think that you too will support this interpretation when you examine the reason for the comparison. Do you not see that the function of the neck somehow resembles that of the intellect, by which your soul receives its vital spiritual nourishment and communicates it to the inward faculties of the will and feelings? And so, when this neck of the bride, understood as the pure and simple intellect, is radiant through and through with the clear and naked

truth [Heb 4:13], it has no need of embellishment. On the contrary, it is itself a precious jewel that becomingly adorns the soul, which is why it is portrayed as resembling jewels. The truth is a jewel of great excellence, so are purity and candor, and especially the power to make a sober estimate of oneself [Rm 12:3].[2]

The perfection of the intellect in humility is fundamental to progress on the path to fulfillment, to happiness.

And that happiness also requires the perfection of the will in love:

Show me a soul who loves nothing but God and what is to be loved for God's sake, to whom to live is Christ [Ps 15:8], and of whom this has been true for a long time. Show me a soul who, in work and leisure alike, endeavors to keep God before her eyes and walks humbly with the Lord her God [Mi 6:8], who desires that her will may be one with the will of God, and who has been given the grace to do these things. Show me a soul like this, and I shall not deny that she is worthy of the Bridegroom's care, of the regard of God's majesty, of his sovereign favor, and of the attention of his governance.[3]

To such a soul the Bridegroom opens the door to happiness, for he recognizes the ardor of her love:

The bride runs; so do the maidens [attending her]. But the one to arrive first is the one whose love is the most ardent, because she runs more quickly [Jn 20:4]. On arrival she brooks no refusal or delay. The door is promptly opened to her as to one of the family, one highly esteemed, one loved with a special love, one uniquely favored.[4]

This highly favored soul is adorned with the virtues of love. And she possesses in addition the perfections of her feelings — cheerfulness and joy:

Would that I possessed an abundance of the trees that grow so thickly in the Bridegroom's garden, the Church: peace, goodness, kindness, joy in the Holy Spirit [Ga 5:22], cheerful compassion, open-hearted almsgiving [Rm 12:8], rejoicing with those that rejoice and weeping with those that weep [Rm 12:15]. Does it not seem to you that the house, the ceiling of which you perceive to be adequately and skillfully covered with these timbers, is adorned richly enough? 'Lord, I love the beauty of your house' [Ps 25:8]. I desire that you will always give me wood like this, so that I may exhibit my conscience to you as a room that is always adorned—both my conscience and my neighbor's. With this I shall be content.[5]

The bride wills her neighbor's happiness and feels her own happiness bound to that of her neighbor's. Both the will's love and the feelings' affection necessarily involve a social dimension.

In Bernard's *Story of the Three Daughters of the King*, he provides an allegorical statement of the importance of this social dimension of perfection. This passage also demonstrates the close link between the virtues of the intellect, will, and feelings. It also shows the intimate union of body and soul in human happiness:

Love's house was built on a north-south axis. She committed it to her friend Kindness and communicated all her own privileges to her. At her service she placed, first, Purity of body, and then, suitable Exercises: reading, meditation, prayer, and outpourings of spiritual feeling. And so that Misery could not find entrance into the house to disturb the happiness of the children of God, who dwell at the seventh level and there, in the house of Love, play and rejoice in the fullness of happiness, Peace was assigned to guard the gate, since 'Happy are the peacemakers' [Mt 5:9].[6]

The peace which fills the virtuous enables them to rise above the changing circumstances of life, because they do not '...pin their hopes on ephemeral well-being':[7]

You will ride above the vicissitudes of good and evil times with the poise of one sustained by values that are eternal, with that enduring, unshakable equanimity of the man of faith who thanks God in every circumstance [Ps 33:2].[8]

In the center of the banquet God provides for the virtuous is the love which makes that equanimity possible and which infuses all the virtues:

Love is the excellent food. Its place is in the middle of the dish of Solomon [Sg 3:9f.], the dish which diffuses the mingled odor of the virtues, fragrant as all the

powders of the perfumer [Sg 3:6]. It fills the hungry
and gives joy to those being filled. On this dish we find
peace and patience and longaminity [Ga 5:22] and joy
in the Holy Spirit [Rm 14:17], and every other virtue,
any other fruit of wisdom of which you can think.⁹

All the virtues, Bernard teaches, are gifts of God. If these gifts are not willfully rejected, God shall bestow on the soul the greatest gift of all, himself:

If I feel that my eyes are opened to understand the Scriptures [Lk 24:45], so that I am enlightened from above to preach the word of wisdom from the heart [l Co 12:8] or reveal the mysteries of God, or, if riches from on high are showered on me so that fruits of meditation are produced in my soul, I have no doubt that the Bridegroom is with me. For those are the gifts of the Word, and it is of his fullness that we have received these gifts [Jn 1:16]. Again, if I am filled with a feeling of humility rich with devotion whereby the love of truth I have received produces in me so urgent a hatred and contempt for vanity that I cannot be inflamed with pride [1 Co 8:1] because of knowledge or elated by frequent heavenly visitations [2 Co 12:7], then truly I am aware of fatherly activity and do not doubt the Father's presence. But if I continue as far as I can to respond to this condescension in worthy disposition and action, and the grace of God in me has not been fruitless [1 Co 15:10], then the Father will make his abode with me [Jn 14:23] to nourish me, as the Son will teach me.¹⁰

God is the source of all that makes one happy: one's being, feelings, will, justification, zeal, justice, benevolence, wisdom, virtue, consolation, knowledge, immortality, and security:

I tell you, Father Eugenius, it is God alone who can never be sought in vain [see Is 45:19], even when he cannot be found....What is God? Omnipotent will, benevolent virtue, eternal light, unchangeable reason, supreme blessedness. He creates souls to share in his life, vivifies them to give them feelings, touches them to excite their desires, enlarges them to receive his good things, justifies them that they may merit him. He inflames them with zeal, fertilizes them to bring them to fruition, leads them in justice, molds them in benevolence, directs them in wisdom, strengthens them in virtue, visits them in consolation, enlightens them with knowledge, preserves them for immortality, fills them with happiness, surrounds them with security.[11]

The God who cannot be found by human beings, finds humans and bestows on them the happiness of perfection.

The happiness of perfection, Bernard claims, is not reserved for the afterlife, but is possible in this life, in this world:

> I say more. Even among ourselves there are some who, it seems to me, have already climbed to the same height of perfection [as Saint Andrew].[12]

To be sure, the perfection of one in this life is not an absolute perfection: 'No one is perfect who does not wish to be still more perfect; the more perfect a man is, the more he reaches out to an even higher perfection.'[13] For Bernard, perfection is a process, not a conclusion: 'Unwearied effort to progress, unflagging effort to be perfect, is accounted perfection.'[14] Yet that very process produces a state of happiness:

> Happy the mind which has clothed itself in the beauty of holiness and the brightness of innocence, by which it manifests its glorious likeness, not to the world but to the Word, of whom we read that he is the brightness of eternal life [Ws 7:26], the splendor and image of the being of God [Heb 1:3].[15]

Happiness is possible, even in this world, because the soul's likeness to God, lost in the Fall, is restored by grace so that she becomes once more the image and likeness of God:

> Even among the fluctuating events and inevitable shortcomings of this giddy world you will ensure for yourself a life of durable stability, provided you are renewed and reformed according to the glorious and original plan of the eternal God. You become the likeness of him in whom there is no alteration, no shadow of change [Jm 1:7]. Even in this world you will become as he is [1 Jn 4:17], neither dismayed by adversity nor dissolute in prosperity. Living thus, this noble creature, made in the image and likeness of his Creator [Gn 1:26], indicates that he is reacquiring the dignity of that primal honor.[16]

Perfection in this life is part of a process which will end only in everlasting life. In this process are joined together the perfection of all one's faculties:

> He flies securely who combines love with understanding and zeal with knowledge. And he shall fly on forever because he flies toward everlastingness.[17]

Everlasting salvation is open to all who live a virtuous life: 'At all times and for all persons they [the virtues] bring salvation when they are kept....'[18] Although one can never be absolutely certain of salvation, Bernard teaches that the confidence of hope in God is well placed:

> We are given certain signs and manifest indications of salvation, such that, in whomever they continue, make it practically indubitable that he is one of the elect....
> Let him continue steadfast and make progress in that manner of life which is a sign of salvation and an evidence of predestination. Now, among all the indications which minister to our confidence and furnish a solid basis for hope, the most important is that of which I have already begun to speak: 'He that is of God, hears the words of God' [Jn 8:47].[19]

The person who is living the life of perfection will be granted the ultimate happiness of union with God:

> God in his righteousness made man righteous like himself, without iniquity, since 'there is no iniquity in him' [Ps 91:16]. Iniquity is a fault of the heart, not of the flesh, and so you should realize that the likeness of God is to be preserved or restored in your spirit, not in your body of dust. For 'God is a spirit' [Jn 4:24], and those who wish to preserve or attain his likeness must enter into their hearts and apply themselves spiritually to that task—until 'with unveiled face, beholding the glory of the Lord', they 'become transfigured into the same likeness, borrowing glory from that glory, as the Spirit of the Lord enables them' [2 Co 3:18].[20]

But the glory of union with God, Bernard teaches, is not entirely reserved for the life to come. The experience of God is possible in this life too, in contemplation.

Notes: Perfection

1. SC 27, 3; SBOp 1:183; CF 7:76-77.
2. SC 41, 1; SBOp 2:28-29; CF 7:204-205.
3. SC 69, 1; SBOp 2:202; CF 40:27.
4. SC 23, 1; SBOp 1:138; CF 7:25.
5. SC 46, 9; SBOp 2:61; CF 7:247.
6. Par 5, 3; SBOp 6/2:283; CSt 20:29.
7. SC 21, 6; SBOp 1:125; CF 7:8.
8. SC 21, 6; SBOp 1:125; CF 7:8.
9. Hum 2, 4; SBOp 3:19; CF 13:32.
10. SC 69, 6; SBOp 2:205-206; CF 40:33.
11. Csi 5, 11, 24; SBOp 3:486-87; CF 37:169.
12. And 1, 10; SBOp 5:433; Luddy 3:50.
13. Ep 34, 1; SBOp 7:90; James, p. 68.
14. Ep 254, 3; SBOp 8:158; James, p. 410.
15. SC 85, 11; SBOp 2:315; CF 40:208.
16. SC 21, 6; SBOp 1:125; CF 7:8.
17. I Nov 4, 2; SBOp 5:316; Luddy 2:364.
18. Pre 3, 7; SBOp 3:258; CF 1:110.
19. Sept 1, 1-2; SBOp 4:345; Luddy 2:56-57.
20. SC 24, 5; SBOp 1:157; CF 7:46.

CONTEMPLATION

I. THE BRIDEGROOM AND THE BRIDE

UNDERSTANDING THE ROLE of contemplation in the spirituality of Bernard of Clairvaux presents many difficulties. Bernard's vocabulary of contemplation is complex. What Bernard means by contemplation is not always clear. And Bernard seems to give contradictory evidence on the question whether he was indeed a contemplative.

It is clear that, for Bernard, contemplation is an experience which transcends ordinary exposition. In describing this unique relationship between God and human beings, Bernard most often uses the metaphor of the Bridegroom and bride of the *Song of Songs*:

> What is this that she says: 'He is mine, and I am his' [Sg 2:16]? We do not know what she says because we do not know what she feels [Jn 16:18]. O holy soul, what is your beloved to you? What are you to him? What is this intimate relationship, this pledge given and received?... If you will, speak to us, to our understanding; tell us clearly what you feel [Jn 10:24]. How long will you keep us in expectation? Is your secret to be for you alone [Is 24:16]?[1]

The answer Bernard puts in the mouth of the bride is rich, but deliberately arational:

> It is thus: it is the feeling not the intellect which has spoken. And it is not for the intellect to grasp. What then is the reason for these words? There is none, except that the bride is transported with delight and enraptured by the long-awaited words of the Bridegroom. And when the words ceased she could neither keep silence nor yet express what she felt.[2]

Bernard then gives a reasoned explanation for the arational expressions of the bride:

> The feelings have their own language, in which they disclose themselves even against their will. Fear has its trembling, grief its anguished groans, love its cries of delight.... Do they constitute a reasoned discourse, a deliberate utterance, a pre-meditated speech? Most certainly such expressions of feeling are not produced by the processes of the mind but by spontaneous impulses. So a strong and burning love, particularly the love of

God, does not stop to consider the order, the grammar, the flow, or the number of the words it employs when it cannot contain itself, providing it senses that it suffers no loss thereby. Sometimes it needs no words, no expression at all, being content with aspirations alone. Thus it is that the bride, aflame with holy love, doubtless seeking to quench a little the fire of the love she endures, gives no thought to her words or the manner of her speech. But, impelled by love, she does not speak clearly but bursts out with whatever comes to her lips.[3]

There is much here that is instructive. Contemplation is an 'intimate relationship' involving 'delight' and 'rapture'. It is an experience which cannot be expressed in the language of reason alone.

II. THE CONTEMPLATIVE EXPERIENCE

What is the nature of contemplation as Bernard understands it? It is above all an experience, the experience of a lover:
> Happy the man who has attained the fourth degree of love; he no longer loves even himself except for God. 'O God, your justice is like the mountains of God' [Ps 35:7]. This love is a mountain, God's towering peak. Truly indeed, it is a fat, fertile mountain [Ps 67:16]. 'Who will climb the mountain of the Lord [Ps 23:3]?' 'Who will give me the wings of a dove, that I may fly away to find rest [Ps 54:7]?' This place is made peaceful, 'a dwelling place in Sion' [Ps 75:3]. 'Alas for me, my exile has been lengthened' [Ps 119:5]. When will flesh and blood [Mt 16:17], this vessel of clay [2 Co 4:7], this earthly dwelling [Ws 9:15], understand the fact? When will this sort of affection be felt that, inebriated with divine love, the mind may forget itself and become in its own eyes a broken dish [Ps 30:13], hastening toward God and clinging to him, becoming one with him in spirit [1 Co 6:17], saying: 'My flesh and my heart have wasted away, O God of my heart, O God my share for all eternity' [Ps 72:26]. I would say that man is blessed and holy to whom it has been given to experience something like this, so rare in life, even if it be but once and for the space of a moment. To lose yourself, as if you no longer existed, to cease completely to be aware of yourself, to reduce yourself to nothing, is not a human sentiment but a divine experience [see Ph 2:7].[4]

In this experience not only the feelings are affected, but the intellect in understanding and the will in love. Contemplation may occur in this life, but it is an experience in which one transcends one's normal state and which taxes one's faculties to their utmost. The '. . . contemplative gift [is that] by which a kind and beneficent Lord shows himself to the soul with as much clarity as bodily frailty can endure.'[5]

Because of the transcendent nature of the contemplative experience, it is incommunicable, ineffable:
> Do you suppose that, were I granted that experience, I could describe to you what is beyond description? . . .

> The tongue does not teach this, grace does. It is hidden from the wise and prudent, and revealed to children [Lk 10:21].[6]

The desire to communicate the incommunicable, to express the ineffable, requires Bernard to resort to poetic language:

> In such matter the understanding is altogether unable to transcend the bonds of experience.... None but the Bridegroom himself can tell us with what infusions of spiritual delight he ravishes the soul of his beloved, with what aromas of sweetness he intoxicates her senses, with what inspiration he wondrously illuminates and refreshes her mind. Let her be as a fountain entirely his own, unshared by any stranger, untouched by unworthy lips. For she is 'a garden enclosed, a sealed fountain' [Sg 4:12]....[7]

The image which Bernard employs again and again to evoke his understanding of the contemplative experience is sexual. The love between God and the human person culminates in an intimate and rapturous union. The delights of that union are expressed in silent song:

> Only the touch of the Spirit [see 1 Jn 2:27] can inspire a song like this, and only personal experience can unfold its meaning. Let those who are versed in the mystery revel in it. Let all others burn with desire not so much to know as to attain this experience. For it is not a song that resounds abroad but the very music of the heart, not a trilling on the lips but an inward pulsing of delight, a harmony not of voices but of wills. It is a melody not heard on the streets; these notes do not sound where crowds assemble [Is 42:2]. Only the singer hears it and the one to whom he sings—the lover and the beloved. For it is above all a nuptial song telling of chaste souls in loving embrace, of their wills in sweet concord, of the mutual exchange of the hearts' affections.[8]

Sometimes Bernard's sexual imagery is more violent. He speaks of a '... spirit ravished out of itself [2 Co 5:13]....'[9] Those thus ravished are the happiest of humans:

> ...Their free will is, so to speak, buried in the depths of God's mercy. The fervor of the spirit ravishes them

to the heights of glory. In the body? Out of the body? They do not know [see 2 Co 12:3]. All they know is that they are ravished.[10]

Whether Bernard's imagery is marital union or ravishment, the result of the contemplative experience is ecstasy: '. . . The delights of contemplation lead on to that ecstatic repose that is the fruit of the kiss of his mouth.'[11] Bernard associates the images of repose, sleep, and even death with contemplative ecstasy:

> Consider, therefore, that the bride has retired to this solitude. There, overcome by the loveliness of the place, she sleeps sweetly within the arms of her Bridegroom, in ecstasy of spirit.[12]

The sleep the bride experiences in the suspension of sensory awareness Bernard likens to death, a death which at the same time is full of life:

> It is a slumber which is vital and watchful, which enlightens the heart, drives away death, and communicates eternal life. For it is a genuine sleep that does not stupify the mind but transports it. And—I say it without hesitation—it is a death. For the Apostle Paul, in praising those still living in the flesh, spoke thus: 'For you have died, and your life is hidden with Christ in God' [Col 3:3].[13]

But this death of the soul in ecstatic union with her Bridegroom is also a form of birth:

> In this kind of birth the soul leaves even its bodily senses and is separated from them, so that, in her awareness of the Word, she is not aware of herself. This happens when the mind is enraptured by the unatterable sweetness of the Word, so that it withdraws—or, rather, is transported—and escapes from itself to enjoy the Word.[14]

Birth and death, then, are both images of the soul's transcendent experience in contemplation.

Whatever image Bernard employs, he indicates that ordinary sensation ceases in contemplation—this time symbolized by Adam's sleep:

> It seems to me that this slumber of Adam resulted from the contemplation of the immutable Truth and the abyss of divine Wisdom which suspended the activities of the bodily senses.[15]

Yet the senses, suspended in contemplation, also provide images of contemplation. Bernard employs visual imagery to communicate the incommunicable:

> The glory we have seen is the glory of the Father's only-begotten [Jn 1:14]. For whatever glory has been manifested in this way is totally kind, truly paternal. This glory will not oppress me [Pr 25:27], though I lean on it with all my strength; it will rather impress itself on me. 'And we all, beholding the glory of the Lord with unveiled face, are being transformed into his likeness from one degree of glory to another. For this comes from the Lord who is the Spirit' [2 Co 3:18]. We are transformed when we are conformed....[16]

Bernard employs auditory imagery as well. In this case the contemplative experience is expressed as the conversation of lovers who are also friends:

> Just as Moses once spoke to God as friend to friend, and God answered him [Ex 33:11], so now the Word and the soul converse with mutual enjoyment, like two friends. And no wonder. The two streams of their love have but a single source from which they are sustained. Winged words, honey-sweet, fly to and fro between them, and their eyes, like heralds of holy love, betray to each other their fullness of delight. He calls her his dearest one, proclaims her beauty, and repeats that proclamation—only to win a like response from her.[17]

Contemplation, however expressed, Bernard knows as a rare and brief experience: '...Contemplation holds the beholder suspended in astonishment and ecstasy, if only for a brief moment.'[18] Bernard bemoans this rarity and brevity: 'Alas, how rare the time and how short the stay!'[19] His dismay is the result of the intense joy contemplation imparts:

> But when does this happen, and for how long? It is sweet intercourse, but lasts only a short time and is experienced so rarely![20]

III. WAS BERNARD A CONTEMPLATIVE?

Bernard laments that the contemplative experience is rare. The question is whether the experience was so rare as to be non-existent—at least for Bernard himself.[21] The question may seem absurd, given the descriptions Bernard gives of contemplative experience—descriptions which seem to shout out that they were the product of his own intimate awareness of what he describes. Yet Bernard frequently denies that he has received the gift of contemplation.

In his eighth sermon on the *Song of Songs*, Bernard seems to deny all possibility of contemplation as an experience '. . . past comprehension, beyond the experience of any mere creature. . . .'[22] But this occurs immediately following a statement that contemplation '. . . is so rare an experience and extremely difficult to understand.'[23]

In his *Steps of Humility and Pride*, Bernard is more specific:

> What business has a poor wretch like me prowling about the two higher heavens [of love and contemplation], and that not in spirit but only with a flow of empty talk? I have quite enough work for my hands and feet beneath the lowest heaven [of humility].[24]

But the tone of the whole treatise seems to indicate that Bernard is here employing a rhetorical humility. The *Steps* concludes with a statement which points clearly in this direction:

> Well, Brother Godfrey, you will perhaps complain that I have not given you just what you asked and I promised. It seems I have described the steps of pride rather than those of humility. All I can say is that I can teach only what I know. I could not very well describe the way up because I am more used to falling than to climbing.[25]

Bernard's rhetorical humility seems to be the source of still another disclaimer:

> But a soul like mine, burdened with sins, still subject to carnal passions [2 Tm 3:6], devoid of any knowledge of spiritual delights, may not presume to make such a request [for the kiss of the Bridegroom], almost totally unacquainted as it is with the joys of the supernatural life.[26]

Bernard is surely identifying with those in his audience who are taking the first steps in the path to perfection and who need his support and encouragement. Bernard continues in the same place:

However, I should like to point out to persons like this
that there is an appropriate place for them on the way
of salvation. They may not rashly aspire to the lips of
the Bridegroom, but, with me, let them prostrate themselves in fear at the feet of a most severe Lord.[27]

Bernard is ever aware of his role as teacher, a role which requires
identification with those whom he would teach:

Far from disapproving of those whose purer minds enable them to grasp more sublime truths than I can present, I warmly congratulate them. But I expect them to
allow me to provide simpler doctrine for simpler
minds.[28]

In the course of Bernard's twenty-third sermon on the *Song of
Songs*, he seems to deny once more an experience of God in contemplation:

For the moment it suffices to know that no maiden,
concubine, or even queen may gain access to the mys-
tery of that bedroom which the Bridegroom reserves
solely for her who is his dove, beautiful, perfect, and
unique [Sg 6:8]. Hence it is not for me to take umbrage
if I am not admitted there....[29]

Almost immediately, however, Bernard describes contemplation
as his own experience:

But let me tell you what I have attained, or believe I
have attained. And you should not accuse me of boasting, because I reveal it solely in the hope of helping
you.[30]

Bernard's motivation is clear. In denying or revealing his contemplative experience, he wishes to serve those who seek the same
goal as he. Bernard was indeed a contemplative.

IV. WHAT CONTEMPLATION IS NOT[31]

Contemplation is so important to Bernard's spirituality that it is important to avoid confusion about the subject. For Bernard, contemplation is not meditation, does not entail visions or dreams, and it is not the Beatific Vision of the blessed in the life he firmly believed would come.

Bernard clearly differentiates meditation or consideration from contemplation:[32]

> First of all, consider what it is I call consideration. For I do not want it to be understood as entirely synonymous with contemplation. The latter concerns more what is certainly known, while consideration pertains more to the investigation of what is unknown. Consequently, contemplation may be defined as the mind's true and sure intuition, the apprehension of truth without doubt. Consideration, on the other hand, can be defined as thought searching for truth, the mind's searching to discern truth. Nevertheless, both terms are often used interchangeably.[33]

It is precisely the interchangeability of the terms which can lead to confusion.

For example, in Bernard's long letter *On Consideration*, he sometimes uses language which could be taken as an expression of contemplative experience. In Book V, Bernard writes:

> What if the soul were totally recollected and with affections recalled from all the places they were held captive by fearing what should not be feared, loving what was unworthy, grieving vainly and more vainly rejoicing? What if she began to soar upward with total liberty, to drive on under the impulse of the spirit, and to glide along in abundance of grace? And when the soul has begun to move about the illuminated mansions and to examine carefully even the bosom of Abraham, and to look again upon the souls of martyrs under the altar [Rv 6:9] (whatever that may be) dressed in their first robes [Lk 15:22] and patiently awaiting their second, will she not say with the Prophet: 'One thing I have asked of the Lord, this I will seek, that I may dwell in the house of the Lord all the days of my life, that

I may see the will of the Lord and visit his temple' [Ps 26:4]?³⁴

Bernard continues in a still more exalted vein:

Is not the heart of God to be seen there? Is it not shown what is the good, the acceptable, the perfect will of God [Rm 12:2]—good in itself, pleasing in its effects, acceptable to those enjoying it, perfect to those who are perfect and who seek nothing beyond it? His heart of mercy lies open [Lk 1:78]; his thoughts of peace lie revealed [Jr 29:11], the riches of his salvation [Is 33:6], the mysteries of his good will, the secrets of his kindness, which are hidden from mortals and beyond the comprehension of even the elect. This, indeed, is for the good of their salvation, so they do not cease fearing before they are found suitable for loving worthily.³⁵

The language of vision is surely here, but it seems to be a vision acquired by 'driving on', by 'examining carefully,' by 'looking again'. The language is of aspiration not acquisition. And the souls described seem to be in a relatively early stage on their journey along the path to perfection, somewhere after the fear inspiring conversion and before perfection in love. Bernard, I believe, is here describing the activity of meditation, not the blissful repose of the bride in ecstatic union.³⁶

Bernard is careful to distinguish contemplation from meditation. For mediation the prerequisite is '. . . an eye that is pure and simple' [Lk 11:34].³⁷ For contemplation, the prerequisite is not human activity, but the action of God: '. . . If at times she [the soul] is even rapt toward it [God's majesty] in ecstasy, this is the finger of God deigning to raise man up. . .' [Ex 8:19; Lk 11:20].³⁸

Visions and dreams may be works of God, but they too are not what Bernard means by contemplation:

For his [the Bridegroom's] living, active word [Heb 4:12] is to me a kiss, not indeed an adhering of the lips that can sometimes belie a union of hearts, but an unreserved infusion of joys, a revealing of mysteries, a marvelous and indistinguishable mingling of the divine light with the enlightened mind, which, joined in truth to God, is one spirit with him [1 Co 6:17]. With good reason, then, I avoid any truck with visions and dreams. . . .³⁹

Bernard does not deny that God may communicate with his people through visions. But he does insist that contemplation is communication of a vastly different sort:
> Another kind of vision is that by which, in former times, the Fathers were often graciously admitted to sweet communion with God. He became present to them, though they did not see him as he is but only in the form he thought fitting to assume.... This manifestation, though not apparent to everyone, took place exteriorly and consisted of images or the spoken word. But there is another form of divine contemplation, very different from the former because it takes place interiorly, when God himself is pleased to visit the soul....[40]

In describing what contemplation is not, Bernard often offers greater insight into what he believes himself to have experienced in contemplation:
> Be careful, however, not to conclude that I see something corporeal or perceptible to the senses in this union between the Word and the soul. My opinion is that of the Apostle who said: 'He who is united to the Lord becomes one spirit with him' [1 Co 6:17]. I try to express with the most suitable words I can muster the ecstatic ascent of the purified mind to God, and the loving descent of God into the soul, submitting spiritual truths to spiritual men [1 Co 2:13].... One who is so disposed and so beloved will by no means be content either with that manifestation of the Bridegroom given to many in the world of creatures [Rm 1:20] or to the few in visions and dreams. By a special privilege she wishes to welcome him down from heaven into her inmost heart, into her deepest love. She wishes to have the one she desires present to her, not in bodily form but by inward infusion, not by appearing externally but by laying hold of her within. It is beyond question that the vision is all the more delightful the more inward it is, and not external. It is the Word who penetrates without sound, who is effective though not pronounced, who wins the affections without sounding in the ears. His face, though without form, is the source of form. It does not dazzle the eyes of the body but gladdens

the watchful heart. Its pleasure is in the gift of love and
not in the color of the lover.[41]
Contemplation, then, is an internal experience of the soul which
delights in ecstatic union with God.

Bernard sometimes uses the word contemplation to indicate yet
another sort of ecstatic union with God. And this usage can also
lead to confusion. For example, in his fourth *Sermon in Praise of
the Virgin Mother*:

> O how glorious is that kingdom where kings have assembled, have come together [Ps 48:5] to praise and glorify him who is above all [Eph 4:6], King of kings and Lord of lords [1 Tm 6:15], in brilliant contemplation of whom the righteous shine as the sun [Mt 13:43] in the kingdom of their Father.[42]

Both text and context indicate that Bernard is here speaking of
the Beatific Vision. The same is true of an appealing passage in
Bernard's *On the Necessity of Loving God*. There he speaks not of
contemplation but of a deifying experience of God. The context
shows Bernard is describing the state of the blessed in the next
life.[43]

In the Beatific Vision, Bernard believes, '...the only activity
is repose, and contemplation and affection will be the only duty.'[44]
There the blessed will be able to see God as he is.[45] Bernard writes
in his first sermon on All Saints of 'a banquet most desirable, at
which there can never be any anxiety, never any lack of relish,
because the fullness there will always be perfect and the appetite
always keen!'[46] All this sounds very much like the contemplation
bestowed on man in this life, yet the passage clearly refers to the
Beatific Vision.

The similarity of expression is based on Bernard's deep conviction that contemplation here is a foretaste in this life of the happiness of heaven:

> Contemplation then brings [to the soul's banquet] its offering, the solid bread [Heb 5:14] of wisdom made of the finest wheat [Ps 147:14] and the wine which gladdens the heart of man [Ps 103:15], to which Truth calls the perfect with the words: 'Eat, my friends, and drink; be inebriated, my dearest ones' [Sg 5:1]. Truth does not fail to make provision for the less perfect. 'Love is placed in the middle of the daughters of Jerusalem'

[Sg 3:10]. These are the ones not yet able to take solid food, so Truth gives them love's milk instead of bread, and oil instead of wine. This portion is 'in the middle', because beginners could not yet relish it, being too fearful. The perfect find it insufficient now that they have plenty of the sweet food of contemplation.... The perfect now turn from milk since they have had a glorious foretaste of the feast of glory.[47]

Contemplation is the food of the perfect in this life; here human beings may experience a foretaste of the banquet they will enjoy forever in the Beatific Vision.

1. SC 67, 3; SBOp 2:189-90; CF 40:4-6.
2. SC 67, 3; SBOp 2:190; CF 40:6.
3. SC 67, 3; SBOp 2:190; CF 40:6-7.
4. Dil 10, 27; SBOp 3:142; CF 13:119.
5. SC 4, 1; SBOp 1:19; CF 4:22.
6. SC 85, 14; SBOp 2:316; CF 40:210.
7. SC 22, 2; SBOp 1:130; CF 7:15.
8. SC 1, 11; SBOp 1:7-8; CF 4:6-7.
9. SC 41, 3; SBOp 2:30; CF 7:206-207.
10. Asc 2, 6; SBOp 5:130; Luddy 2:239. See also SC 31, 5 (SBOp 1:222; CF 7:128) and Hum 6, 19 (SBOp 3:30-31; CF 13:46-47).
11. SC 4, 4; SBOp 1:20; CF 4:23.
12. SC 52, 6; SBOp 2:93; CF 31:54.
13. SC 52, 3; SBOp 2:92; CF 31:52.
14. SC 85, 13; SBOp 2:315-16; CF 40:209.
15. Sept 2, 1; SBOp 4:350; Luddy 2:64.
16. SC 62, 5; SBOp 2:158; SC 31:156.
17. SC 45, 1; SBOp 2:50; CF 7:232.
18. Csi 5, 14, 32; SBOp 3:493; CF 37:178.
19. SC 23, 15; SBOp 1:148; CF 7:38.
20. SC 85, 13; SBOp 2:316; CF 40:209-210.
21. For a discussion of this question, see Ingeborg Brauneck, *Bernard von Clairvaux als Mystiker* (Hamburg: G. H. Nolte, 1935) pp. 29-31.
22. SC 8, 1; SBOp 1:36; CF 4:45.
23. SC 8, 1; SBOp 1:36; CF 4:45.
24. Hum 9, 24; SBOp 3:35; CF 13:53.
25. Hum 22, 57; SBOp 3:58; CF 13:82.
26. SC 3, 1; SBOp 1:14; CF 4:16.
27. SC 3, 2; SBOp 1:14; CF 4:16-17. See also SC 69, 1; SBOp 2:202; CF 40:27. See too Leclercq, *Saint Bernard mystique*, p. 137.
28. SC 22, 3; SBOp 1:130; CF 7:15.
29. SC 23, 10; SBOp 1:145; CF 7:35. See also SC 23, 9; SBOp 1:144; CF 7:33.
30. SC 23, 11; SBOp 1:145; CF 7:35.
31. For me, it is a happy coincidence that this title is the same as that used by Thomas Merton to designate chapter 2 of his *New Seeds of Contemplation* ([New York]: New Directions, [1972]). This book is about contemplation, not about Bernard of Clairvaux; hence I have not listed it in the bibliography. It is, however, a noble effort to do for the twentieth century something of what Bernard did for his age.
32. See above, p. 66, where I have given the quotation which follows.
33. Csi 2, 2, 5; SBOp 3:414; CF 37:52.
34. Csi 5, 4, 9; SBOp 3:474-75; CF 37:149-50.
35. Csi, 5, 4, 9; SBOp 3:475; CF 37:150.
36. Other examples of passages in which meditation is described in language which may lead the reader to think that contemplation is the subject are SC 31, 7 (SBOp 1:223-24; CF 7:129-31) and SC 45, 5 (SBOp 2:52-53; CF 7:235-36).
37. SC 62, 4; SBOp 2:157; CF 31:154.
38. SC 62, 4; SBOp 2:158; CF 31:155.
39. SC 2, 2; SBOp 1:9; CF 4:9.
40. SC 31, 4; SBOp 1:221; CF 7:127.

41. SC 31, 6; SBOp 1:223; CF 7:128-29.
42. Miss 4, 2; SBOp 4:48; CF 18:47.
43. Dil 10, 28-29; SBOp 3:143-44; CF 13:120-21.
44. SC 72, 2; SBOp 2:226; CF 40:64.
45. SC 31, 3; SBOp 1:221; CF 7:126. See also Div 9, 1; SBOp 6/1:118.
46. OS 1, 11; SBOp 5:336; Luddy 3:344.
47. Hum 2, 4; SBOp 3:19; CF 13:32-33.

V. THE POSSIBILITY OF CONTEMPLATION

Bernard is confident that the earthly contemplative experience, so like that of the blessed in heaven, is indeed possible in this life:

> Actually, our race is not without one who happily deserved to enjoy this gift, who experienced within herself this sweetest mystery, unless we entirely disbelieve the passage of Scripture at hand [Sg 2:7], in which the heavenly Bridegroom is plainly shown defending passionately the repose of his beloved, eager to embrace her within his arms as she sleeps, lest she be roused from her delicious slumber by annoyance or disquiet. I cannot restrain my joy that this Majesty did not disdain to bend down to our weakness in a companionship so familiar and sweet, that the supreme Godhead did not scorn to enter into wedlock with the soul in exile and reveal to her with the most ardent love how affectionate was this Bridegroom she had won. As I read on earth, I do not doubt that it is like this in heaven or that the soul will certainly experience what this passage suggests—except that here she cannot fully express what she will there be able to grasp, but cannot as yet. What do you think she will receive there, when now she is favored with an intimacy so great that she feels herself embraced by the arms of God, cherished on the breast of God, guarded by the care and zeal of God lest she be roused from her sleep until she wakes of her own accord.[1]

But it is not only the allegorical bride of the *Song of Songs* who has experienced the delights of contemplation. Bernard acknowledges that he has experienced contemplative ecstasy, not once but many times. And, in his acknowledgment, he instructs his audience about the nature of the experience:

> I wish to tell you of my experience—as I promised. Not that it is of any importance [2 Co 12:1]. But I make this disclosure only to help you, and if you derive any profit from it I shall be consoled for my foolishness. If not, my foolishness will be revealed. I admit that the Word has also come to me—I speak as a fool [2 Co 11:17]—and has come many times.[2]

Bernard is ignorant of the time, direction, and mode of the coming:

> But although he has come to me, I have never been conscious of the moment of his coming. I perceived his presence; I remembered afterward that he had been with me. Sometimes I had a presentment that he would come, but I was never conscious of his coming or his going [Ps 120:8]. And where he comes from when he visits my soul, where he goes, and by what means he enters and goes out, I admit I do not know even now. As John says: 'You do not know where he comes from or where he goes' [Jn 3:8].[3]

Bernard finds his ignorance perfectly understandable:

> There is nothing strange in this, for of him it was said: 'Your footsteps will not be known' [Ps 76:20]. The coming of the Word was not perceptible to my eyes, for he has no color; nor to my ears, for there was no sound; not yet to my nostrils, for he mingles with the mind, not the air. He has not acted on the air, but created it. His coming was not tasted by my mouth, for there was no eating or drinking; nor could he be known by the sense of touch, for he is not tangible.[4]

Bernard's senses are no help. His intellect likewise knows only that it does not know:

> How, then, did he enter? Perhaps he did not enter because he does not come from outside. He is not one of the the things which exists outside us [1 Co 5:12]. Yet he does not come from within me; for he is good [Ps 51:11], and I know there is no good in me. I have ascended to what is highest in me, and, behold, the Word is towering above that. In my curiosity I have descended to explore my lowest depths; yet I found him still deeper. If I looked outside myself, I saw him stretching beyond the farthest I could see. And if I looked within, he was yet farther within. Then I knew the truth of what I had read: 'In him we live and move and have our being' [Ac 17:28]. And blessed is the man in whom he has his being, who lives for him and is moved by him.[5]

Although Bernard does not understand when or how the Bridegroom comes and goes in visiting the bride in contemplation, he is sure that impermanence is characteristic of their union. That fact fills him with expectant desire and confident hope:

> If, then, any of us, like the holy Prophet, finds that it is good to cling close to God [Ps 72:28], and—that I may make my meaning clearer—if any of us is so filled with desire [Dn 9:23] that he wishes to depart and be with Christ [Ph 1:23], with a desire intense, a thirst ever burning, an unflagging effort, he will certainly meet the Bridegroom on whatever day he comes [1 P 5:6]. At such an hour he will find himself locked in the arms of Wisdom; he will experience how sweet is divine love as it flows into his heart. His heart's desire will be given to him [Ps 20:3] even while still a pilgrim on earth [2 Co 5:6]—though not in its fullness and only for a time, a short time.[6]

But Bernard's desire and confidence seem only increased by the impermanence of contemplative ecstasy:

> For when, after vigils and prayers and a great shower of tears, he who was sought presents himself, suddenly he is gone again, just when we think we hold him fast. But he will present himself anew to the soul who pursues him with tears. He will allow himself to be taken hold of but not detained, for suddenly he flees from our hands a second time. And if the fervent soul persists with prayers and tears, he will return each time and not defraud her of her express desire [Ps 20:3]—but only to disappear soon again and not return unless sought with all her heart. And so, even in this body, we can often enjoy the happiness of the Bridegroom's presence. But it is a happiness that is never complete because the joy of the visit is followed by the pain of his departure.[7]

The contemplative experience is indeed possible. Moreover, the happy soul who has been visited by the Bridegroom can eagerly anticipate a frequent return:

> ...Any one who has received this spiritual kiss from the mouth of Christ at least once, seeks again that intimate experience and eagerly awaits its frequent renewal.[8]

And the bride's anticipation is confident, for she knows that the Bridegroom loves her:

It is in this confidence that she says he cares for her, and she for him. And she sees nothing but herself and him. How good you are, Lord, to the soul who seeks you [Lm 3:25]. You come to meet her, you embrace her, you acknowledge yourself as her Bridegroom [Rm 9:5]—you who are the Lord, God blessed forever above all things.[9]

And this confidence is proper to all who seek God, all who have traveled the path to perfection:

We find a contemplative Mary [the sister of Martha and Lazarus] in those who, cooperating with God's grace over a long period of time, have attained to a better and happier state. By now confident of forgiveness, they no longer brood anxiously on the sad memory of their sins, but day and night they meditate on the ways of God with insatiable delight [Ps 1:2]—even at times gazing with unveiled face [2 Co 3:18], in unspeakable joy, on the splendor of the Bridegroom, being transformed into his likeness from splendor to splendor by the Spirit of the Lord.[10]

VI. READINESS FOR CONTEMPLATION

The outwardly unheard song which the bride hears and sings in contemplative union with the Bridegroom requires a highly trained ear and voice:

> Novices, the immature, those but recently converted from a worldly life, do not normally sing this song or hear it sung. Only the mind disciplined by persevering effort, only the man whose years, as it were, make him ripe for marriage—years measured not in time but in merits—is truly prepared for nuptial union with the divine partner....[11]

Only those whose intellect is ready for Truth and whose will is prepared for Love are the 'friends and lovers [to whom] God communicates his secrets'.[12] The Bridegroom's kiss of the mouth '...is the experience of only a few of the more perfect.'[13] Since perfection is a process, not a state—at least in this life[14]—the perfection Bernard describes is '...only a sort of imperfect perfection.'[15]

One who has traveled the path to this perfection, who has turned toward the Lord and devoted oneself to the practice of virtue, should be open to the gift of contemplation:

> Once you have had this twofold experience of God's benevolence in these two kisses [of repentance and virtue], you need no longer feel abashed in aspiring to a holier intimacy. Growth in grace brings expansion of confidence. You will love with a greater ardor and knock on the door with greater assurance, to gain what you perceive as still wanting to you. 'The one who knocks will always have the door opened to him' [Lk 11:10]. It is my belief that, to a person so disposed, God will not refuse that most intimate kiss of all, a mystery of supreme generosity and ineffable sweetness.[16]

One is made capable of contemplation both by one's created nature and by one's properly oriented desire:

> For the soul is made not only in the image of God [Gn 1:27] but in his likeness [Gn 5:1]. In what does this likeness consist, you ask. Take first the Image. The Word is Truth; the Word is Wisdom; the Word is Justice. These constitute the Image. The Image of what? Of Justice, of Wisdom, and of Truth. For the Image, the Word, is Justice of Justice, Wisdom of Wisdom,

Truth of Truth—just as he is Light of Light and God of God. The soul is none of these things, since she is not the Image. Yet she is capable of them and yearns for them. Perhaps that is why she is said to be made in the image. She is a noble creature in her capacity for greatness, and in her longing we see a token of her righteousness.[17]

The soul which thus longs for union with her lover seduces him: So now, when she feels the opportunity is ripe, she announces that the bridal suite has been furnished. And, pointing to the bed with her finger, she invites the beloved to rest there, as I have said. Like the disciples on the way to Emmaus, she cannot restrain the ardor of her heart [Lk 24:13- 29]. She entices him to be the guest of her soul and compels him to spend the night with her. With Peter she says: 'Lord, it is good for us to be here' [Mt 17:4].[18]

Her desire for union is clearly the result of her overwhelming love: 'I cannot rest', she said, 'unless he kisses me with the kiss of his mouth [Sg 1:1]. I thank him for the kiss of the feet; I thank him too for the kiss of the hand. But, if he truly cares for me, let him kiss me with the kiss of his mouth. There is no question of ingratitude on my part; it is simply that I am in love. The favors I have received are far more than I deserve, but they are less than I desire. It is desire that drives me, not reason. Please do not accuse me of presumption if I yield to this impulse of love. My shame indeed rebukes me, but my love is stronger still. I am well aware that he is a king who loves justice [Ps 98:4]. But headlong love does not wait for judgment, is not chastened by advice, not shackled by shame nor subdued by reason. I ask; I crave; I implore. Let him kiss me with the kiss of his mouth.'[19]

The soul's overwhelming love for her beloved is a sign of the perfection which renders her ripe for nuptial union:

The soul which has attained this degree [of perfection] now ventures to think of marriage. Why should she not, when she sees that she is like him and therefore ready for marriage? His loftiness has no terrors for her because her likeness to him associates her with him. And her declaration of love is a betrothal.... When you see a soul leaving everything [Lk 5:11] and clinging to the Word with all her will and desire, living for the Word, ruling her life by the Word, conceiving by the Word what she will bring forth by him... you know that the soul is the spouse and the bride of the Word.[20]

1. SC 52, 2; SBOp 2:91; CF 31:50-51.
2. SC 74, 5; SBOp 2:242; CF 40:89.
3. SC 74, 5; SBOp 2:242; CF 40:89-90.
4. SC 74, 5; SBOp 2:242; CF 40:90.
5. SC 74, 5; SBOp 2:242-43; CF 40:90-91. Jean Leclercq has demonstrated that many elements of SC 74, 5, were inspired by Origen. He concludes: 'As usual, however, he did not copy: he transformed his source and enriched it by his literary talent.' *Bernard of Clairvaux and the Cistercian Spirit*, p. 74.
6. SC 32, 2; SBOp 1:227; CF 7:135.
7. SC 32, 2; SBOp 1:227; CF 7:135.
8. SC 3, 1; SBOp 1:14; CF 4:16.
9. SC 69, 8; SBOp 2:207; CF 40:35. See also SC 8, 9; SBOp 1:41-42; CF 4:52.
10. SC 57, 11; SBOp 2:126; CF 31:106. See also Div 8, 1; SBOp 6/1:111.
11. SC 1, 12; SBOp 1:8; CF 4:7.
12. Div 29, 1; SBOp 6/1:210.
13. SC 4, 1; SBOp 1:18; CF 4:21.
14. See above, p. 209.
15. QH 10, 1; SBOp 4:443; CF 25:193.
16. SC 3, 5; SBOp 1:17; CF 4:19.
17. SC 80, 2; SBOp 2:277-78; CF 40:146.
18. SC 46, 1; SBOp 2:56; CF 7:241. See also SC 46, 7; SBOp 2:60; CF 7:245-46.
19. SC 9, 2; SBOp 1:43; CF 4:54. See also SC 32, 3; SBOp 1:227; CF 7:135.
20. SC 85, 12; SBOp 2:315; CF 40:208-209.

VII. THE GIFT OF CONTEMPLATION

While perfection which readies the spouse to be ravished in contemplation is the result of the growth of the intellect in knowledge and of the will in love, the contemplative experience itself is pure gift. The soul may desire her lover and prepare the couch, but he must come into her bed as a free gift of love. Bernard gives the example of Paul's rapture:

> ...As he tells us, he was rapt up to third heaven [2 Co 12:2]. Why does he use 'rapt', not 'led'? It is a lesson for me. If the great Apostle had to be transported to that place which he could not know by his own learning or ascend to even with a guide, then I, so small compared to Paul, must never presume I can climb to the third heaven by my own strength and effort. I must not presume, but on the other hand I need not be daunted by the difficulty of the journey. He whose way is pointed out to him or who is assisted, contributes something by his own efforts to unravel the problem or go step by step to the goal. He will say: 'Not I, but the grace of God working in me' [1 Co 15:10]. One who is carried up—he knows not where—by another's power, contributing not the slightest effort by his own strength to the action of his helper, has nothing of which to boast, either in whole or part. The Apostle could climb to the lowest and the middle heaven by the help and guidance given him, but to the third he had to be lifted up.[1]

Bernard insists that all is gift. Preparation for contemplation requires the gift of virtue, but the ecstatic transcendence of contemplation is a gift of a higher order:

> This ecstasy, in my opinion, is alone or principally called contemplation. Not to be gripped during life by material desires is a mark of human virtue, but to gaze without the use of bodily likenesses is the sign of angelic purity. Each, however, is a divine gift; each is a going out of oneself; each a transcending of oneself. But, in the one, one goes much farther than in the other. Happy the man who can say: 'See, I have escaped far away and have found a refuge in the wilderness' [Ps 54:8]. He was not content with going out if he could not go

far away, so that he could be at rest. You have so overleaped the pleasures of the flesh that you are no longer responsive to its concupiscence [Rm 6:12], even in the least, or gripped by its allure. You have gone far; you have placed yourself apart. But you have not yet put yourself at a distance unless you succeed in flying with purity of mind beyond the material images that press in from every side. Until that point, promise yourself no rest. You err if you expect to find before then a place of rest [Is 66:1], the quiet of solitude, unclouded light, the abode of peace. But show me the man who has attained this, and I shall promptly declare him at rest. Rightly may he say: 'Return, O my soul, to your rest, for the Lord has dwelt bountifully with you' [Ps 114:7].[2]

Both the humility which perfects the intellect and the love which perfects the will are the fruits of God's generous gifts. The gift of the Bridegroom's kiss can only be desired and requested:

And hence the bride, when seeking him whom her soul loves [Sg 3:1], quite properly does not put her trust in mere human prudence or yield to the inane conceits of human curiosity. She asks rather for a kiss; she calls on the Holy Spirit by whom she is simultaneously awarded the choice repast of knowledge and the seasoning of grace.[3]

Contemplation is not the fruit of man's striving, but the generous gift of God:

...Such is the courtesy of the Word, such the tenderness of the Father toward the well-disposed, the well-ordered soul—itself the gift of the Father and the work of the Son—that they honor with their own presence the one they have fore-ordained and prepared for themselves. And not only do they come to her, they make their dwelling-place with her [1 Co 8:1]. For it is not enough that their presence is revealed; they must also give their fullness.[4]

The gift they give the soul is no less than their own Spirit, and in him participation in the very life of the Trinity:

For her it is no mean or contemptible thing to be kissed by the kiss, for it is nothing less than the gift of the Holy Spirit. If, as is properly understood, the Father is he who kisses, the Son he who is kissed, then it cannot be wrong to see in the kiss the Holy Spirit. For he is the imperturbable peace of the Father and the Son, their unshakable bond, their undivided love, their indivisible unity.[5]

VIII. THE EFFECTS OF CONTEMPLATION

The bride who longs for her beloved seeks only his loving kiss and nothing else:
> Now one who asks for a kiss is in love. It is not for liberty that she asks, not for an award, not for an inheritance, not even for knowledge, but for a kiss.[6]

But in that kiss she receives much not requested.

She receives the gift of knowledge in contemplative union with her spouse.[7] And the knowledge she receives is on a truly cosmic scale:
> The Bridegroom, who exercises control over the whole universe, has a special place from which he decrees his laws and formulates his plans as guidelines in weight, measure, and number for all created things [Ws 11:20]. This is a remote and secret place, but not a place of repose. For, although, as far as in him lies, he arranges all things sweetly [Ws 8:1], he does indeed arrange them. And he does not allow the contemplative who perchance reaches that place to rest and be still. In a way wondrous yet delightful, he teases the awe-struck viewer until he reduces her to restlessness. Further on [Sg 5:2], the bride beautifully describes both the delight and the restlessness of this stage of contemplation when she says that though she sleeps her heart is awake.[8]

Not only are the nature of reality and the reality of nature known in contemplation, the right ordering of things, justice, is open to the contemplative gaze.[9] Bernard believes 'Justice is the vital natural food of the rational soul....'[10] In knowing justice, the contemplative knows much about God, for God is Justice itself:
> As for your justice, so great is the fragrance it diffuses that you are called not only just but even Justice itself, the Justice that makes man just.[11]

The contemplative kiss conveys a transcendent knowledge of God to the bride who receives it:
> She dares to ask for this kiss, actually for that Spirit in whom both the Father and the Son will reveal themselves to her. For it is not possible that one of these could be known without the other. That is why Christ

said: 'To have seen me is to have seen the Father' [Jn 14:9]. And John in his turn: 'No one who has the Father can deny the Son, and to acknowledge the Son is to have the Father as well' [1 Jn 2:23]. From these declarations it is clearly evident that the Father cannot be known apart from the Son, or the Son apart from the Father. Rightly, therefore, did Christ point out that one achieves supreme happiness not by knowing any one of them, but by knowing both.... [And] where there is perfect knowledge of the Father and the Son, how can there be ignorance of the goodness of both, which is the Holy Spirit?[12]

But, in the contemplative kiss, the bride receives not only knowledge of God, his creation, and its right order. She also receives wisdom, an appreciation of the proper moral order. As knowledge perfects the intellect, so does wisdom perfect the will in love:

What does it mean for the Word to come into the soul? It means that he will instruct her in wisdom [Ps 89:12]. What does it mean for the Father to come? It means that he will draw her to love of wisdom, so that she may say: 'I was a lover of her beauty' [Ws 8:2]. It is the Father's nature to love, and therefore the coming of the Father is marked by an infusion of love.[13]

This infusion of love is accompanied by awe, awe at the experience which will make the bride wise:

There is another place from which God, the just judge [Ps 7:12]... watches ceaselessly, with an attention rigorous yet hidden, over the world of fallen man.... That place is awe-inspiring [Gn 28:17] and totally devoid of quiet.... Do not be surprised that I have assigned the beginning of wisdom to this place and not to the first. For there we listen to Wisdom as a teacher in a lecture-hall, delivering an all-embracing discourse [1 Jn 2:27], here we receive it within us. There our minds are enlightened, here our wills are moved to decision. Instruction makes us learned; experience makes us wise.[14]

This profound knowledge of the moral order has important consequences:

This revelation made through the Holy Spirit not only conveys the light of knowledge but also lights the fire of love. As Saint Paul testifies: 'The love of God has been poured into our hearts by the Holy Spirit who has been given us' [Rm 5:5].... It is clear that even the knowledge of those [who knew God but did not honor him] was not perfect, because they did not love. For if their knowledge had been complete, they would not have been blind to the goodness by which he willed to be born a human being and die for their sins.[15]

The soul blessed by the kiss of her beloved is not only filled with love, but that love is directed toward continuing perfection:

You ask, then, how I knew he was present, when his ways can in no way be traced [Rm 11:33]? He is life and power [Heb 4:12], and, as soon as he enters, he awakes my slumbering soul. He stirs and soothes and pierces my heart, before this hard as stone [Si 3:27; Ezk 11:19, 36:26] and diseased. So he has begun to pluck out and destroy, to build up and plant, to water dry places and illuminate dark ones. He has begun to open what was closed and warm what was cold, to make the crooked straight and the rough places smooth [Is 40:4], so that my soul may bless the Lord and all that is within me may bless his holy name [Ps 102:1]. So when the Bridegroom, the Word, came to me, he did not make known his coming by any signs—not by sight, not by sound, not by touch.... Only by the movement of my heart, as I have told you, did I perceive his presence. And I knew the power of his might [Eph 1:13] because my faults were put to flight and my human yearnings brought into subjection. I have marveled at the depth of his wisdom [Qo 7:25] when my secret faults [Ps 18:13] have been revealed and made visible. At the very slightest amendment of my way of life I have experienced his goodness and mercy. In the renewal and re-making of the spirit of my mind [Eph 4:23], of my inmost being, I have perceived the excellence of his glorious beauty [Ps 49:2]. And when I contemplate all these things I am filled with awe and wonder at his manifold greatness.[16]

Bernard's awe and wonder derive not simply from his contemplative view of the moral order, but from the moral effects of God's goodness in his soul.

Thus, in the ecstatic embrace of the Bridegroom, the bride's intellect is filled with knowledge and her will fulfilled in love:
> For the favor of the kiss bears with it a twofold gift: the light of knowledge and the fervor of devotion. Truly, the Spirit of wisdom and knowledge [Is 11:2], like the bee bearing its burden of wax and honey, is fully equipped both to kindle the light of knowledge and infuse the delicious nectar of grace.... So let the bride, about to receive the twofold grace of this most holy kiss, set her lips in readiness—her reason for the gift of knowledge, her will for that of wisdom—so that, overflowing with joy in the fullness of this kiss, she may be privileged to hear the words: 'Your lips are moist with grace, for God has blessed you forever' [Ps 44:3].[17]

The soul, perfected in humility and love, is united to God in contemplative marriage:
> See now this perfect soul. Her two powers, reason and will, are without spot or wrinkle. Her reason is instructed by the Word of Truth [2 Co 6:7], her will inflamed by Truth's Spirit [1 Jn 4:6]. She is sprinkled with the hyssop of humility [Ps 50:9]; she is fired with the flame of love. She is cleansed from any spot by humility, smoothed of wrinkle by love [Eph 5:27]. Her reason does not shrink from the truth; her will does not strive against reason. This blessed soul the Father binds to himself as his own glorious bride.[18]

Bernard maintains that the perfection of the intellect and will are inextricably linked in the happy bride:
> Felicitous is this kiss of participation that enables us not only to know but love the Father, who is never fully known until he is perfectly loved.[19]

Indeed, Bernard insists, on the level of the infinite, in the embrace of God, knowledge and love are one:
> Only to his friends and lovers does God communicate his secrets, for to them alone was it said: 'All things whatsoever I have heard from my Father I have make known to you' [Jn 15:15]. Indeed, as the blessed Gregory teaches, love not merely merits but is itself this knowledge.[20]

But even the fulfillment of intellect and will does not exhaust the effects of contemplation. The soul's third faculty is also per-

fected in the contemplative union. The feelings too are purged of pain and filled with pleasure:
> But what of those who, at times, are caught up in the Spirit through the ecstasy of contemplation and become capable to savor something of the sweetness of heavenly bliss? Do these attain to freedom from sorrow as often as this happens to them? Yes, indeed. Even in this present life, those who with Mary have chosen the better part, which will not be taken from them [see Lk 10:42], enjoy—rarely, however, and fleetingly—freedom of pleasure. This is undeniable. For those, who possess what will never be taken away, plainly experience what is to come: happiness.[21]

'To complete your happiness [Jn 16:24]', Bernard believes, 'he will show you himself; he will fill you with gladness by letting you see his face' [Jn 14:21].[22] The Father '...invites the bride, as his daughter-in-law, to the sweet caresses of his Son....'[23]

To pleasure God will add peace:
> This is a kiss from mouth to mouth, beyond the claim of any creature. It is a kiss of love and peace—of the love which is beyond all knowledge [Eph 3:19] and that peace beyond all understanding [Ph 4:7].[24]

And to peace he will add joy:
> There is a place where God is seen in tranquil rest—where he is neither Judge nor Teacher, but Bridegroom. To me—for I do not speak for others—this is truly a bedroom to which I have sometimes gained happy entrance.... [There] God's purpose stands fast; the peace he has planned for those who fear him is without recall. Overlooking their faults and rewarding their good deeds, with a divine deftness he turns to their benefit not only the good they do but even the evil [Rm 8:28].... 'Happy the man whose fault is forgiven, whose sin is blotted out' [Ps 31:1]. When I say these words I am suddenly inspired with so great a confidence, filled with such joy, that it surpasses my fear experienced in...that place of the second vision. And I even look on myself as a member of that blessed band. Would that this moment lasted! Visit me, Lord, again and again in your saving mission. Let me rejoice in the joy of your nation [Ps 105:4-5].[25]

The joy of the bedroom is an image on which Bernard builds to express the fullness of the bride in all of her soul's faculties:
> If it should ever happen to one of you to be enraptured and hidden away in this secret place, this sanctuary of God, safe from the call and concern of the greedy senses, from the pangs of care, the guilt of sin, and the obsessive fancies of the imagination—so much more difficult to hold at bay—then on returning you may well boast and tell us: 'The King has brought me into his bedroom' [Sg 1:3].[26]

Another image of the fullness of contemplative ecstasy is intoxication:
> Holy contemplation has two forms of ecstasy: one in the intellect, the other in the will; one of enlightenment, the other of fervor; one of knowledge, the other of devotion. So too a tender affection, a heart glowing with love, the infusion of holy ardor, the vigor of a spirit filled with zeal, are obviously not acquired from any other place than the wine-cellar.[27]

Still another image Bernard employs is death. He uses this image to express once more the totality of the contemplative experience:
> It is not absurd for me to call the bride's ecstasy a death, a death which snatches away not life but life's snares, so that she can say: 'We have escaped like a bird from the snare of the fowlers' [Ps 123:7]. In this life we move about surrounded by traps. But these cause no fear when the soul is drawn out of herself by a thought both powerful and holy, provided she so separates herself and flies away from the mind that she transcends the normal manner and habit of thinking.... Why dread wantonness when there is no awareness of life? Since the soul in ecstasy is cut off from awareness of life, though not from life itself, she must necessarily be cut off from the temptations of life.... How often I long to be the victim of this death, that I may escape the snares of death [Ps 17:6], that I may not feel the deadening blandishments of a sensual life, that I may be steeled against evil desire, against the surge of cupidity, against the goads of anger and impatience, against the anguish of worry and the miseries of care. Let me die the death

of the just [Nb 23:10], that no injustice may ensnare
or wickedness seduce me. How good the death that
does not take away life but makes it better, how good
in that the body does not perish but the soul is exalted.[28]

In all of these images Bernard expresses the human longing for
union. In all of them he shows confidence in the human being's
total fulfillment.

The bride's soul is indeed full; her intellect, will, and feelings
are perfected. The bride's body, which has never lost its likeness
to its Creator, is in perfect harmony with her soul. It is she who
is totally united with God:

Who could lay claim to any clear knowledge of the nature of this token of love in which she glories, bestowed on her and repaid again by her? Who indeed, except one worthy herself of a like experience, being pure in soul and holy in body?... How few are there who can say: 'But we all, with unveiled face, beholding the glory of the Lord, are being changed into his likeness, from glory to glory, by the Spirit of the Lord' [2 Co 3:18].[29]

IX. THE OVERFLOW

What can be added to this? Perhaps only the permanence of the Beatific Vision. But the very impermanence of the contemplative experience brings with it a question. What is the activity, function, role of the bride after she has left her nuptial bed and until she returns to it? The bride, overflowing with love for her Bridegroom, is called back from her bed by the 'violent' demands of brotherly love.[30] Bernard addresses this question through the speech of the bride to her bridesmaids:

> She speaks to them this way: 'Be happy, be confident, "the King has brought me into his bedroom" [Sg 1:3]. You may view yourselves brought in too. Even though I alone seem to have been brought in, that is not for my advantage alone. Every gift I enjoy is a joy for you all. The progress I make is for you. And with you I shall divide all that I merit over your measure.'[31]

Like Paul, Bernard is compelled to share the fruits of contemplation with the world:

> Most gladly, too, I shall follow Paul, who, in the ecstasy of his delight, wept over those who had sinned and done no penance [2 Co 12:21]. He was mightier than powers and principalities [Rm 7:38] who brought down wisdom in abundance and the most hidden sense of Scripture, not from the first, not from the second, but from the third and highest heaven [2 Co 12:2].[32]

And the overflowing love which brings the bride back to the world leads her to follow the will of the Bridegroom:

> When the Bridegroom perceives, as he always does, that the bride has taken her rest for some time on his bosom, he does not hesitate to entice her out again to what seems more serviceable. It is not that she is unwilling or that he himself is doing what he had forbidden. But, if the bride is enticed [out of the bedroom] by the Bridegroom, this is because she receives from him the desire by which she is enticed: the desire for good works, the desire to bring forth fruit for the Bridegroom; for to her the Bridegroom is life and death is gain [Ph 1:21].[33]

And the invitation which the Bridegroom gives the bride is accepted with desire.

And that desire is vehement. It urges her not only to arise but to arise quickly. For we read: 'Arise, make haste, and come' [Sg 2:10]. It is no small consolation to her that she hears 'come' and not 'go', knowing from this that she is being invited rather than sent, and that the Bridegroom will be coming with her. For what will she reckon difficult with him as her companion? 'Set me beside you', she says, 'and let any man's hand fight against me' [Jb 17:3]. Or: 'Even though I walk through the valley of death's shadow, I fear no evil, for you are with me' [Ps 22:4]. She is not, therefore, aroused against her will; for it is no other than an instilled eagerness to advance in holiness.[34]

The task the Bridegroom assigns his bride is manifold: She is animated with zeal for the task allotted her and given livelier awareness of the fittingness of the time. 'My bride', he says, 'it is time to act [Ps 118:126], for the winter is past [Sg 2:11] when no one could work [Jn 9:4]. The rain too that covered the earth with floods, that precluded tillage, that either hindered the sowing of crops or destroyed what was sown—that rain, I say, has quickly vanished. 'It is over and gone; the flowers have appeared in our land' [Sg 2:11]. And this shows that the spring is here, that it is the season to work, that harvests and fruits are not far off.' Then he suggests both where and what she should do first, saying: 'The time for pruning has come' [Sg 2:12]. The bride is led out to cultivate the vines. If they are to yield more abundant fruits for the farmers, it is necessary that sterile branches be gotten rid of, that noxious ones be cut away, that superfluous ones be pruned.[35]

The bride, fresh from her bed of union with God, is sent out to work in the vineyards of the Lord. She who is filled with the fruits of contemplation—knowledge, wisdom, and joy—is sent to share her happiness with mankind.

Bernard saw himself as the bride. And he believed himself sent. These convictions had enormous consequences for the society of his time.

1. Hum 8, 22; SBOp 3:33; CF 13:50-51.
2. SC 52, 5; SBOp 2:93; CF 31:53-54.
3. SC 8, 6; SBOp 1:39; CF 4:49.
4. SC 69, 2; SBOp 2:202; CF 40:28.
5. SC 8, 2; SBOp 1:37; CF 4:46.
6. SC 7, 2; SBOp 1:32; CF 4:39.
7. See my 'The Epistemological Value of Mysticism in the Thought of Bernard of Clairvaux', in John R. Sommerfeldt (ed.), *Studies in Medieval Culture [I]* ([Kalamazoo, Michigan]: Western Michigan University, [1964]) pp. 48-58. See also my 'Bernard of Clairvaux: The Mystic and Society', in E. Rozanne Elder (ed.), *The Spirituality of Western Christendom*, CS 30 (Kalamazoo, Michigan: Cistercian Publications, Inc., 1976) pp. 72-84 and 194-96, esp. pp. 76-81.
8. SC 23, 11; SBOp 1:145-46; CF 7:35. See also OS 4, 4 (SBOp 5:358; Luddy 3:377) and Par 2, 4 (SBOp 6/2:270; CSt 18:197).
9. On at least one occasion, Bernard indicates that the vision of the contemplative is assisted by 'images of earthly things well-adapted to the divinely illumined senses.' SC 41, 3; SBOp 2:30; CF 7:207. Sometimes the contemplative's knowledge is very specific. For example, Bernard asserts that he has 'absolutely certain evidence' that many of his monks have flown straight to their heavenly reward 'once freed from the prison of our mortality.' Div 22, 2; SBOp 6/1:171; Luddy 3:543. Whether this knowledge was the result of a contemplative experience, I do not know.
10. Dil 7, 21; SBOp 3:137; CF 13:114.
11. SC 22, 8; SBOp 1:134; CF 7:20.
12. SC 8, 3-4; SBOp 1:37-38; CF 4:46-47.
13. SC 69, 2; SBOp 2:203; CF 40:28.
14. SC 23, 12-14; SBOp 1:146-47; CF 7:36-37.
15. SC 8, 5; SBOp 1:38-39; CF 4:48.
16. SC 74, 6; SBOp 2:243; CF 40:91-92.
17. SC 8, 6; SBOp 1:39-40; CF 4:49-50. See also SC 9, 3; SBOp 1:43-44; CF 4:55.
18. Hum 7, 21; SBOp 3:32; CF 13:49.
19. SC 8, 9; SBOp 1:41; CF 4:52.
20. Div 29, 1; SBOp 6/1:210; Luddy 3:496.
21. Gra 5, 15; SBOp 3:177; CF 19:71.
22. SC 41, 2; SBOp 2:30; CF 7:206.
23. SC 8, 9; SBOp 1:41-42; CF 4:52.
24. SC 8, 7; SBOp 1:40; CF 4:51.
25. SC 23, 15; SBOp 1:148-49; CF 7:38-39.
26. SC 23, 16; SBOp 1:149-50; CF 7:40.
27. SC 49, 4; SBOp 2:75; CF 31:24-25.
28. SC 52, 4; SBOp 2:92; CF 31:52-53.
29. SC 67, 8; SBOp 2:193-94; CF 40:12.
30. Dil 10, 27; SBOp 3:142; CF 13:119-20.
31. SC 23, 2; SBOp 1:139; CF 7:26.
32. PP 1, 2; SBOp 5:189; Luddy 3:195. See also SC 8, 7; SBOp 1:40; CF 4:50-51.
33. SC 58, 1; SBOp 2:127; CF 31:108.
34. SC 58, 2; SBOp 2:128; CF 31:108-109.
35. SC 58, 2; SBOp 2:128; CF 31:109.

SELECTED BIBLIOGRAPHY

I. Primary Sources

A. The Works of Bernard of Clairvaux

1. *Critical Edition*
   Jean Leclercq et al. (edd.). *Sancti Bernardi opera*. Rome: Editiones Cistercienses, 8 vols. in 9, 1957-1977.
2. Individual Works and Translations
   Apologia ad Guillelmum abbatum. Opera 3:80-108.
   Trans.: *Apology to Abbot William*. Trans. Michael Casey; intro. Jean Leclercq. The Works of Bernard of Clairvaux, I; Treatises I. Cistercian Fathers 1. Spencer, Massachusetts: Cistercian Publications, 1970, pp. 3-69.
   De consideratione ad Eugenium papam. Opera 3:393-493.
   Trans.: *Five Books on Consideration: Advice to a Pope*. Trans. John D. Anderson and Elizabeth T. Kennan. The Works of Bernard of Clairvaux 13. Cistercian Fathers 37. Kalamazoo, Michigan: Cistercian Publications, 1976.
   Epistolae. Opera 7 and 8.
   Trans.: *The Letters of St. Bernard of Clairvaux*. Trans. Bruno Scott James. London: Burns Oates, [1953].
   Letter to Abbot Guy and the Monks of Montièramey.
   Trans. Martinus Cawley. The Works of Bernard of Clairvaux, I; Treatises I. Cistercian Fathers 1. Spencer, Massachusetts: Cistercian Publications, 1970, pp. 180-82.
   Liber de diligendo Deo. Opera 3:119-54.
   Trans.: *On Loving God*. Trans. and intro. Robert Walton. The Works of Bernard of Clairvaux, V; Treatises II. Cistercian Fathers 13. Washington, D.C.: Cistercian Publications, 1974, pp. 91-132.
   Liber de gradibus humilitatis et superbiae. Opera 3:13-59.
   Trans.: *The Steps of Humility and Pride*. Trans. M. Ambrose Conway; intro. M. Basil Pennington. The Works of Bernard of Clairvaux, V; Treatises II. Cistercian Fathers 13. Washington, D.C.: Cistercian Publications, 1974, pp. 25-82.
   Liber de gratia et libero arbitrio. Opera 3:165-203.
   Trans.: *On Grace and Free Choice*. Trans. Daniel O'Donovan; intro. Bernard McGinn. The Works of Bernard of Clairvaux, VII; Treatises III. Cistercian Fathers 19. Kalamazoo, Michigan: Cistercian Publications Inc., 1977, pp. 51-111.

Liber ad milites Templi de laude novae militiae. Opera 3:213-39.
Trans.: *In Praise of the New Knighthood.* Trans. Conrad Greenia; intro. R. J. Zwi Werblowsky. The Works of Bernard of Clairvaux, VII; Treatises III. Cistercian Fathers 19. Kalamazoo, Michigan: Cistercian Publications Inc., 1977, pp. 127-67.

Liber de praecepto et dispensatione. Opera 3:254-94.
Trans.: *Monastic Obligations and Abbatial Authority: St. Bernard's Book on Precept and Dispensation.* Trans. Conrad Greenia; intro. Jean Leclercq. The Works of Bernard of Clairvaux, I; Treatises I. Cistercian Fathers 1. Spencer, Massachusetts: Cistercian Publications, 1970, pp. 103-150.

Parabolae. Opera 6/2:261-303.
Trans.: *The Parables of Saint Bernard.* Trans. Michael Casey. Cistercian Fathers 55A. Kalamazoo: Cistercian Publications, to appear in 1991.
Parable 1: 'St. Bernard of Clairvaux: The Story of the King's Son'. Trans. Michael Casey. *Cistercian Studies* 18 (1983) 16-23.
Parable 2: 'The Story of the Feud Between Two Kings'. Trans. Michael Casey. *Cistercian Studies* 18 (1983) 192-200.
Parable 3: 'The Story of the King's Son Sitting on His Horse'. Trans. Michael Casey. *Cistercian Studies* 18 (1983) 283-88.
Parable 4: 'The Story of Ecclesia Held Captive in Egypt'. Trans. Michael Casey. *Cistercian Studies* 19 (1984) 248-54.
Parable 5: 'The Story of the Three Daughters of the King'. Trans. Michael Casey. *Cistercian Studies* 20 (1985) 21-31.
Parable 6: 'The Story of the Egyptian Woman Whom the King's Son Took as His Wife'. Trans. Michael Casey. *Cistercian Studies* 21 (1986) 96-108.
Parables 7 and 8: 'The Last Two Parables by Bernard of Clairvaux'. Trans. Michael Casey. *Cistercian Studies* 22 (1987) 37-54.

Sermones per annum. Opera 4:161-492; 5; and 6/1:9-55.
Trans.: *St. Bernard's Sermons for the Seasons & Principal Festivals of the Year.* Trans. A Priest of Mount Melleray [Ailbe J. Luddy]. Reprint, Westminster, Maryland: The Carroll Press, 3 vols., 1950.
Note: a translation of some of these sermons, *Sermones in Quadragesima de psalmo 'Qui habitat'* (*Opera* 4:383-492), appears as *Lenten Sermons on the Psalm 'He Who Dwells'* in *Sermons*

on Conversion. Trans. Marie-Bernard Saïd. Cistercian Fathers 25. Kalamazoo, Michigan: Cistercian Publications, 1981, pp. 111-261. The Sermon on the Passing of Saint Malachy the Bishop (*In transitu sancti Malachiae episcopi*; *Opera* 5:417-23) and the Homily on the Anniversary of the Death of Saint Malachy (*De sancto Malachia*; *Opera* 6/1:50-55) are translated in *The Life and Death of Saint Malachy the Irishman*. Trans. Robert T. Meyer. Cistercian Fathers 10. Kalamazoo, Michigan: Cistercian Publications, 1978, pp. 95-112.

Sermones super Cantica canticorum. *Opera* 1 and 2.
Trans.: Sermons 1-20: *On the Song of Songs, I*. Trans. Kilian Walsh; intro. M. Corneille Halflants. The Works of Bernard of Clairvaux, II. Cistercian Fathers 4. Kalamazoo, Michigan: Cistercian Publications, Inc., 1981 (first printing 1971).
Sermons 21-46: *On the Song of Songs, II*. Trans. Kilian Walsh; intro. Jean Leclercq. The Works of Bernard of Clairvaux, III. Cistercian Fathers 7. Kalamazoo, Michigan: Cistercian Publications, 1976.
Sermons 47-66: *On the Song of Songs, III*. Trans. Kilian Walsh and Irene M. Edmonds; intro. Emero Stiegman. Cistercian Fathers 31. Kalamazoo, Michigan: Cistercian Publications, 1979.
Sermons 67-86: *On the Song of Songs, IV*. Trans. Irene Edmonds; intro. Jean Leclercq. Cistercian Fathers 40. Kalamazoo, Michigan: Cistercian Publications, 1980.

Sermo ad clericos de conversione. *Opera* 4:69-116.
Trans.: *On Conversion, A Sermon to Clerics*. Trans. and intro. Marie-Bernard Saïd. In *Sermons on Conversion*. Cistercian Fathers 25. Kalamazoo, Michigan: Cistercian Publications, 1981, pp. 31-79.

Sermones de diversis. *Opera* 6/1:73-406.
Note: a few of these sermons, titled *Miscellaneous Sermons*, are translated in *St. Bernard's Sermons for the Seasons & Principal Festivals of the Year*. Trans. A Priest of Mount Melleray [Ailbe J. Luddy]. Reprint, Westminster, Maryland: The Carroll Press, 3 vols., 1950, 3: 397-552.

Sermones in laudibus Virginis Matris [*Homiliae super 'Missus est' in laubibus Virginis Matris*]. *Opera* 4:13-58.
Trans.: *Four Homilies in Praise of the Virgin Mother*. Trans. Marie-Bernard Saïd and Grace Perigo; intro. Chrysogonus Waddell. In *Magnificat: Homilies in Praise of the Blessed Virgin*

Mary. Cistercian Fathers 18. Kalamazoo, Michigan: Cistercian Publications Inc., 1979, pp. 1-58.

Vita sancti Malachiae episcopi. Opera 3:307-378.
Trans.: *The Life of Saint Malachy.* Trans. Robert T. Meyer. In *The Life and Death of Saint Malachy the Irishman.* Cistercian Fathers 10. Kalamazoo, Michigan: Cistercian Publications, 1978, pp. 9-93.

B. Works by Other Authors

Augustine of Hippo. *Contra academicos.* Ed. J.-P. Migne. *Patrologia latina.* Paris: apud J.-P. Migne editorem, 1841. Vol. 32, cols. 905-958.

_____. *Epistola 166.* Al. Goldbacher (ed.). *S. Aurelii Augustini Hipponiensis episcopi epistolae,* pars III. Corpus scriptorum ecclesiasticorum latinorum, 44. Vienna: F. Tempsky; Leipzig: G. Freytag, 1904. Reprint, New York: Johnson Reprint Corporation; London: Johnson Reprint Company Ltd., [1970], pp. 545-85.

_____. *In Ioannis evangelium.* Ed. J.-P. Migne. *Patrologia latina.* Paris: apud J.-P. Migne editorem, 1841. Vol. 35, cols. 1379-1977.

_____. *De moribus ecclesiae.* Ed. J.-P. Migne. *Patrologia latina.* Paris: apud J.-P. Migne editorem, 1841. Vol. 32, cols. 1300-344.

_____. *De Trinitate.* Ed. J.-P. Migne. *Patrologia latina.* Paris: apud J.-P. Migne editorem, 1841. Vol. 42, cols. 819-1098.

Benedict of Nursia. *Regula monachorum.* Ed. Cuthbertus Butler. 3rd ed., St. Louis: B. Herder Book Co., 1935.
Trans.: *Households of God: The Rule of St. Benedict with Explanations for Monks and Lay-people Today.* Trans. David Parry. Cistercian Studies 39. Kalamazoo: Cistercian Publications, 1980.

Hugh of St. Victor. *Didascalion.* Ed. Charles Henry Buttimer. Washington, D.C.: Catholic University Press, 1939.

Thomas Aquinas. *Summa contra Gentiles.* Rome: apud Sedem Commissionis Leoninae, 1934.

II. Secondary Sources

Baeumker, Clemens. *Der Platonismus im Mittelalter.* Munich: Verlag der K. B. Akademie der Wissenschaften, 1916.

Benson, Robert L., and Giles Constable (edd.). *Renaissance and Renewal in the Twelfth Century*. Cambridge, Massachusetts: Harvard University Press, 1982.

Berlière, Ursmer. *L'ascèse bénédictine des origines à la fin du XIIe siècle*. Collection 'Pax', I. Paris: Desclée De Brouwer, P. Lethielleaux, 1927.

Bernhart, Joseph. *Die philosophische Mystik des Mittelalters von ihren antiken Ursprung bis zur Renaissance*. Geschichte der Philosophie in Einzeldarstellungen, III; Die christliche Philosophie, 14. Munich: Verlag Ernst Reinhardt, 1922.

Bouyer, Louis. *The Cistercian Heritage*. Trans. Elizabeth A. Livingstone. London: A. R. Mowbray & Co. Limited, 1958.

Braceland, Lawrence, S.J. 'Bernard and Aelred on Humility and Obedience'. In John R. Sommerfeldt (ed.), *Erudition at God's Service: Studies in Medieval Cistercian History, XI*. [Kalamazoo, Michigan]: Cistercian Publications Inc., 1987, pp. 149-59.

Brauneck, Ingeborg. *Bernhard von Clairvaux als Mystiker*. Hamburg: G. H. Nolte, 1935.

Burch, George Boswell. 'Introduction' to *The Steps of Humility by Bernard, Abbot of Clairvaux*. Cambridge, Massachusetts: Harvard University Press, 1942, pp. 3-112.

Butler, Cuthbert. *Western Mysticism: The Teaching of SS. Augustine, Gregory and Bernard on Contemplation and the Contemplative Life, with Afterthoughts*. 2nd ed., London: Arrow Books, 1960.

Bynum, Caroline Walker. *Jesus as Mother: Studies in the Spirituality of the High Middle Ages*. Berkeley, Los Angeles, London: University of California Press, 1982.

Casey, Michael. *Athirst for God: Spiritual Desire in Bernard of Clairvaux's Sermons on the Song of Songs*. Cistercian Studies 77. Kalamazoo: Cistercian Publications, 1988.

_____. 'Introduction' to 'The Last Two Parables [7 and 8] by Bernard of Clairvaux'. *Cistercian Studies* 22 (1987) 37-45.

_____. 'Introduction' to *The Story of the Feud Between Two Kings [Parable 2]*. *Cistercian Studies* 18 (1983) 192-94.

_____. 'Introduction' to *The Story of the Three Daughters of the King [Parable 5]*. *Cistercian Studies* 20 (1985) 21-27.

Déchanet, Jean-Marie. 'Les fondements et les bases de la spiritualité bernardine'. *Cîteaux in de Nederlanden* 4 (1953) 292-313.

De Ganck, Rogerius. 'Nederigheid uit waarheidsdwang en uit liefdedrang bij Bernardus'. In *Sint Bernardus van Clairvaux:*

Gedenkboek door monniken van de noord- en zuidnederlandse Cisterciënser abdijen samengesteld bij het achtste eeuwfeest van sint Bernardus' dood, 20 Augustus 1153-1953. Rotterdam: N.V. Uitgeverij De Forel, 1953, pp. 165-94.

Delfgaauw, Pacifique. 'La nature et les degrés de l'amour selon s. Bernard'. In *Saint Bernard théologien: Actes du Congrès de Dijon, 15-19 Septembre 1953.* 2nd ed., Rome: Editiones Cistercienses, 1954, pp. 234-52. [= *Analecta Sacri Ordinis Cisterciensis* 9 (1953).]

Evans, G. R. *The Mind of St. Bernard of Clairvaux.* Oxford: Clarendon Press, 1983 (reprinted with corrections, 1985).

Forest, Aimé. 'Das Erlebnis des consensus voluntatis beim heiligen Bernhard'. In Joseph Lortz (ed.), *Bernhard von Clairvaux, Mönch und Mystiker: Internationaler Bernhardkongress Mainz 1953.* Veröffentlichungen des Instituts für europäische Geschichte Mainz, 6. Wiesbaden: Franz Steiner Verlag GMBH, 1955, pp. 120-27.

Frischmut, Gertrud. *Die paulinische Konzeption in der Frömmigkeit Bernhards von Clairvaux.* Beiträge zur Förderung christlicher Theologie, 37/4. Gütersloh: C. Bertelsmann, 1933.

Gilson, Etienne. *The Mystical Theology of Saint Bernard.* Trans. A.H.C. Downes. London, New York: Sheed & Ward, 1940.

Himpens, Vedastus. 'De h. Bernardus en de bekering'. In *Sint Bernardus van Clairvaux: Gedenkboek door monniken van de noord- en zuidnederlandse Cisterciënser abdijen samengesteld bij het achtste eeuwfeest van sint Bernardus' dood, 20 Augustus 1153-1953.* Rotterdam: N.V. Uitgeverij De Forel, 1953, pp. 153-65.

Hiss, Wilhelm. *Die Anthropologie Bernhards von Clairvaux.* Quellen und Studien zur Geschichte der Philosophie, VII. Berlin: Walter de Gruyter, 1964.

Ivánka, Endre von. 'La structure de l'âme selon saint Bernard'. In *Saint Bernard théologien: Actes du Congrès de Dijon, 15-19 Septembre 1953.* 2nd ed., Rome: Editiones Cistercienses, 1954, pp. 202-208. [= *Analecta Sacri Ordinis Cisterciensis* 9 (1953).]

Leclercq, Jean. *Bernard of Clairvaux and the Cistercian Spirit.* Trans. Claire Lavoie. Cistercian Studies 16. Kalamazoo, Michigan: Cistercian Publications, 1976.

_____. 'The Intentions of the Founders of the Cistercian Order'. In M. Basil Pennington (ed.), *The Cistercian Spirit: A Symposium in Memory of Thomas Merton.* Cistercian Studies 3. Spencer, Massachusetts: Cistercian Publications, 1970, pp. 88-133.

_____. 'Monastic Life Today'. *Cistercian Studies* 15 (1980) 126-41, 239-46.

_____. *Monks and Love in Twelfth-Century France: Psycho-Historical Essays*. Oxford: at the Clarendon Press, 1979.

_____. 'St. Bernard and the Formative Community'. *Cistercian Studies* 14 (1979) 99-119.

_____. *Saint Bernard mystique*. N.p.: Desclée De Brouwer, 1948.

_____. 'St. Bernard and the Rule of St. Benedict'. In M. Basil Pennington (ed.), *Rule and Life: An Interdisciplinary Symposium*. Cistercian Studies 12. Spencer, Massachusetts: Cistercian Publications, 1971, pp. 151-68.

_____. 'Spiritual Guidance and Counseling According to St. Bernard'. In John R. Sommerfeldt (ed.), *Abba: Guides to Wholeness and Holiness East and West*. Cistercian Studies 38. Kalamazoo, Michigan: Cistercian Publications, 1982, pp. 64-87.

Linhardt, Robert. *Die Mystik des heiligen Bernhard von Clairvaux*. Munich: Verlag Natur u. Kultur, [1923].

McGinn, Bernard. 'Introduction' to *On Grace and Free Choice*. The Works of Bernard of Clairvaux, VII; Treatises III. Cistercian Fathers 19. Kalamazoo, Michigan: Cistercian Publications Inc., 1977, pp. 3-50.

_____. 'Introduction' to *Three Treatises on Man: A Cistercian Anthropology*. Cistercian Fathers 24. Kalamazoo, Michigan: Cistercian Publications, 1977, pp. 1-100.

McGuire, Brian Patrick. *Friendship & Community: The Monastic Experience 350-1250*. Cistercian Studies 95. Kalamazoo, Michigan: Cistercian Publications Inc., 1988.

_____. 'Was Bernard a Friend?' In E. Rozanne Elder (ed.), *Goad and Nail: Studies in Medieval Cistercian History, X*. Cistercian Studies 84. Kalamazoo, Michigan: Cistercian Publications, 1985, pp. 201-227.

[Merton, Thomas.] *Thomas Merton on Saint Bernard*. Cistercian Studies 9. Kalamazoo, Michigan: Cistercian Publications, 1980.

Mouroux, Jean. 'Sur les critères de l'expérience spirituelle d'après les sermons sur le Cantique des cantiques'. In *Saint Bernard théologien: Actes du Congrès de Dijon, 15-19 Septembre 1953*. 2nd ed., Rome: Editiones Cistercienses, 1954, pp. 253-67. [= *Analecta Sacri Ordinis Cisterciensis* 9 (1953).]

Overman, Dennis R. *Manual Labor: The Twelfth-Century Cistercian Ideal.* Unpublished M.A. thesis, Western Michigan University, 1983.

Pennington, M. Basil. 'Three Stages of Spiritual Growth According to St. Bernard'. In M. Basil Pennington, *The Last of the Fathers, The Cistercian Fathers of the Twelfth Century: Collected Essays.* Studies in Monasticism I. Still River, Massachusetts: St. Bede's Publications, [1983], pp. 82-93.

Pourrat, Pierre. *Christian Spirituality in the Middle Ages.* Trans. S. P. Jacques. Westminster, Maryland: The Newman Press, 1953.

Renna, Thomas. 'Virginity and Chasity in Early Cistercian Thought'. *Studia Monastica* 26 (1984) 43-54.

Ries, Joseph. *Das geistliche Leben in seinen Entwicklungsstufen nach der Lehre des hl. Bernhard.* Freiburg i. Br.: Herder, 1906.

Sommerfeldt, John R. 'Bernard of Clairvaux: The Mystic and Society'. In E. Rozanne Elder (ed.), *The Spirituality of Western Christendom.* Cistercian Studies 30. Kalamazoo, Michigan: Cistercian Publications, Inc., 1976, pp. 72-84 and 194-96.

_____. 'The Educational Theory of St. Bernard: The Role of Humility and Love'. *Benedictine Review* 20 (1965) 25-32 and 46-48.

_____. 'The Epistemological Value of Mysticism in the Thought of Bernard of Clairvaux'. In John R. Sommerfeldt (ed.), *Studies in Medieval Culture [I].* [Kalamazoo, Michigan]: Western Michigan University, [1964], pp. 48-58.

_____. 'The Intellectual Life According to Saint Bernard'. *Cîteaux: Commentarii cistercienses* 25 (1974) 249-56.

_____. 'The Social Theory of Bernard of Clairvaux'. In *Studies in Medieval Cistercian History Presented to Jeremiah F. O'Sullivan.* Cistercian Studies 13. Spencer, Massachusetts: Cistercian Publications, 1971, pp. 35-48.

Stiegman, Emero S., Jr. *The Language of Asceticism in St. Bernard of Clairvaux's* Sermones super Cantica canticorum. Unpublished doctoral dissertation, Fordham University, 1973.

Waddell, Chrysogonus. 'Simplicity and Ordinariness: The Climate of Early Cistercian Historiography'. In John R. Sommerfeldt (ed.), *Simplicity and Ordinariness: Studies in Medieval Cistercian History, IV.* Cistercian Studies 61. Kalamazoo, Michigan: Cistercian Publications, 1980, pp. 1-47.

CISTERCIAN PUBLICATIONS INC.
Kalamazoo, Michigan

TITLES LISTING

CISTERCIAN TEXTS

THE WORKS OF BERNARD OF CLAIRVAUX

Apologia to Abbot William
Five Books on Consideration: Advice to a Pope
Grace and Free Choice
Homilies in Praise of the Blessed Virgin Mary
The Life and Death of Saint Malachy the Irishman
Parables
Sermons on the Song of Songs I-IV
Steps of Humility and Pride

THE WORKS OF WILLIAM OF SAINT THIERRY

The Enigma of Faith
Exposition on the Epistle to the Romans
The Golden Epistle
The Mirror of Faith
The Nature and Dignity of Love

THE WORKS OF AELRED OF RIEVAULX

Dialogue on the Soul
The Mirror of Charity
Spiritual Friendship
Treatises I: On Jesus at the Age of Twelve, Rule for a Recluse, The Pastoral Prayer

THE WORKS OF JOHN OF FORD

Sermons on the Final Verses of the Song of Songs I-VII

THE WORKS OF GILBERT OF HOYLAND

Sermons on the Songs of Songs I, II, III
Treatises, Sermons and Epistles

OTHER EARLY CISTERCIAN WRITERS

The Letters of Adam of Perseigne I
Baldwin of Ford: Spiritual Tractates
Guerric of Igny: Liturgical Sermons I-II
Idung of Prüfening: Cistercians and Cluniacs: The Case for Cîteaux
Isaac of Stella: Sermons on the Christian Year
Serlo of Wilton & Serlo of Savigny
Stephen of Lexington: Letters from Ireland
Stephen of Sawley: Treatises

MONASTIC TEXTS

EASTERN CHRISTIAN TRADITION

Besa: The Life of Shenoute
Cyril of Scythopolis: Lives of the Monks of Palestine
Dorotheos of Gaza: Discourses
Evagrius Ponticus: Praktikos and Chapters on Prayer
The Harlots of the Desert
Iosif Volotsky: Monastic Rule
The Lives of the Desert Fathers
Menas of Nikiou: Isaac of Alexandra & St Macrobius
Pachomian Koinonia I-III
The Sayings of the Desert Fathers
Spiritual Direction in the Early Christian East (I. Hausherr)
The Syriac Fathers on Prayer and the Spiritual Life

WESTERN CHRISTIAN TRADITION

Anselm of Canterbury: Letters I-[II]
Bede: Commentary on the even Catholic Epistles
Bede: Commentary on Acts
Bede: Gospel Homilies
Gregory the Great: Forty Gospel Homilies
Guigo II the Carthusian: Ladder of Monks and Twelve Meditations
Peter of Celle: Selected Works
The Letters of Armand-Jean de Rance I-II
The Rule of the Master

CHRISTIAN SPIRITUALITY

Abba: Guides to Wholeness and Holiness East and West
Athirst for God: Spiritual Desire in Bernard of Clairvaux's Sermons on the Song of Songs (M. Casey)
Cistercian Way (A. Louf)
Fathers Talking (A. Squire)
Friendship and Community (B. McGuire)
From Cloister to Classroom
Herald of Unity: The Life of Maria Gabrielle Sagheddu (M. Driscoll)
Life of St Mary Magdalene... (D. Mycoff)
Rancé and the Trappist Legacy (A.J. Krailsheimer)
Roots of the Modern Christian Tradition
Russian Mystics (S. Bolshakoff)
Spirituality of Western Christendom
Spirituality of the Christian East (T. Spidlék)

MONASTIC STUDIES

Community and Abbot in the Rule of St Benedict I-II (Adalbert De Vogüé)
Consider Your Call: A Theology of the Monastic Life (Daniel Rees et al.)
The Finances of the Cistercian Order in the Fourteenth Century (Peter King)

Fountains Abbey and Its Benefactors
(Joan Wardrop)
The Hermit Monks of Grandmont
(Carole A. Hutchison)
In the Unity of the Holy Spirit
(Sighard Kleiner)
Monastic Practices (Charles Cummings)
The Occuptation of Celtic Sites in Ireland by
the Canons Regular of St Augustine and the
Cistercians (Geraldine Carville)
The Rule of St Benedict: A Doctrinal and
Spiritual Commentary (Adalbert de Vogüé)
The Rule of St Benedict (Br. Pinocchio)
St Hugh of Lincoln (D. H. Farmer)
Serving God First (Sighard Kleiner)

CISTERCIAN STUDIES

A Second Look at Saint Bernard (Jean Leclercq)
Bernard of Clairvaux and the Cistercian
Spirit (Jean Leclercq)
Bernard of Clairvaux: Studies Presented to
Dom Jean Leclercq
Christ the Way: The Christology of Guerric
of Igny (John Morson)
Cistercian Sign Language
The Cistercian Spirit
The Cistercians in Denmark (Brian McGuire)
Eleventh-century Background of Citeaux
(Bede K. Lackner)
The Golden Chain: Theological Anthropology of
Isaac of Stella (Bernard McGinn)
Image and Likeness: The Augustinian
Spirituality of William of St Thierry (David
N. Bell)
The Mystical Theology of St Bernard
(Étienne Gilson)
Nicholas Cotheret's Annals of Citeaux
(Louis J. Lekai)
William, Abbot of St Thierry
Women and St Bernard of Clairvaux
(Jean Leclercq)

MEDIEVAL RELIGIOUS WOMEN

Distant Echoes (Shank-Nichols)
Gertrud the Great of Helfta: Spiritual Exercises
(Gertrud J. Lewis-Jack Lewis)
Peace Weavers (Nichols-Shank)

STUDIES IN CISTERCIAN ART AND ARCHITECTURE
Meredith Parsons Lillich, editor

Studies I, II, III now available
Studies IV scheduled for 1991

THOMAS MERTON

The Climate of Monastic Prayer (T. Merton)
The Legacy of Thomas Merton (Patrick Hart)
The Message of Thomas Merton (Patrick Hart)
Solitude in the Writings of Thomas Merton
(Richard Cashen)
Thomas Merton Monk (Patrick Hart)
Thomas Merton Monk and Artist
(Victor Kramer)
Thomas Merton on St Bernard
Toward an Integrated Humanity
(M.Basil Pennington et al.)

CISTERCIAN LITURGICAL DOCUMENTS SERIES
Chrysogonus Waddell, ocso, editor

Cistercian Hymnal: Text & Commentary
(2 volumes)
Hymn Collection of the Abbey of the Paraclete
Molesme Summer-Season Breviary
(4 volumes)
Institutiones nostrae: The Paraclete Statutes
Old French Ordinary and Breviary of the
Abbey of the Paraclete: Text and
Commentary (5 volumes)

STUDIA PATRISTICA

*Papers of the 1983 Oxford Patristics Conference
Edited by Elizabeth A. Livingstone*

XVIII/1 Historica-Gnostica-Biblica
XVIII/2 Critica-Classica-Ascetica-Liturgica
XVIII/3 Second Century-Clement & Origen-
         Cappodician Fathers
XVIII/4 *available from Peeters, Leuven*

TEXTS AND STUDIES IN THE MONASTIC TRADITION

North American customers may order these books through booksellers or directly from the warehouse:

Cistercian Publications
St Joseph's Abbey
Spencer, Massachusetts 01562
(508) 885-7011

Editorial queries and advance book information should be directed to the Editorial Offices:

Cistercian Publications
Institute of Cistercian Studies
Western Michigan University
Kalamazoo, Michigan 49008
(616) 387-5090

A complete catalogue of texts in translation and studies on early, medieval, and modern monasticism is available at no cost from Cistercian Publications.